Explaining Labour's Landslide

Explaining Labour's Landslide

Robert M. Worcester
&
Roger Mortimore

First published in Great Britain 1999
by Politico's Publishing
8 Artillery Row, London, SW1P 1RZ, England

Tel. 0171 931 0090
Email politicos@artillery-row.demon.co.uk
Website http://www.politicos.co.uk

A catalogue record for this book is available from the British Library.

ISBN 1 90230 135 8

Typeset by ensystems, Saffron Walden, Essex.
Printed and bound in Great Britain by St Edmundsbury Press.
Cover design by Ad Vantage. Caricature by Evan Fotis

Contents

List of tables

List of figures and graphs

Foreword

The precedents to this book stem back 25 years ago, when after the British General Election of 28 February 1974, I felt the need to set down the real story of that election, as measured systematically and objectively through the medium of private opinion polls conducted for the Labour Party.

It had been an interesting, challenging and exciting experience, far different from the fragmented, outsider's involvement on the fringe of the 1970 election. For two years I had been an insider in the Wilson campaign, listened to by both the Leader of the Party, Harold Wilson – one of the most attentive clients I have ever had the privilege of working for – and the Party machine. The 1970 result had been a shock to everyone, more so for having been forecast on the Tuesday before Labour's defeat by their inexperienced American pollster, whose final poll before election day had come up with a two percent Tory lead.

No outsiders in the 1970 campaign knew that I was doing Labour's private polling; nobody asked, and I was under strict instruction from Percy Clarke, Labour's Head of Publicity, to keep a low profile lest it be discovered that an American, horrors, was conducting the polls for the Prime Minister. If it leaked, he had warned me, I was for the chop. By July 1972 however, my role in the 1970 election had been written about, first by John Whale in the *Sunday Times*, and then by Butler and Pinto-Duschinsky in the 1970 Nuffield book. From the work behind the scenes of Wilsonian PR advisors David Kingsley, dropped after the 1970 election, Dennis Lyons (the late Lord Lyons of Brighton) and Peter Davis (Lord Lovell-Davis), by Clarke, by Labour Party Deputy General Secretary Gwen Morgan and most of all by Harold Wilson himself, in July 1972 the National Executive Committee of the Labour Party was persuaded to provide some funding for me to carry out serious, in depth, qualitative and quantitative research with the objective of assisting the Party to recover from its unexpected 1970 defeat and secure victory at the polls when the time came.

In this effort, I was assisted greatly by the establishment of a small team of polling advisors including Lyons and Davis), Clarke and a young LSE don, Dr Bernard, now Lord, Donoughue (later to head to Policy Unit at No. 10), who had been seconded to the team at the insistence of Harry (Lord) Kissin, who had put up most of the money to ensure the paltry sum voted by the NEC was augmented sufficiently to provide for serious, rather than token, research. I also had hung around my neck by the NEC an academic advisory group who mostly got in the way, some of whom had more their own interests at heart rather than the Labour Party's.

Early in the week following the narrow victory for Labour at the polls on 28 February 1974, Donoughue rang to invite me to lunch at No. 10, to review my work in the run-up to and during the election, I supposed. 'Friday?', he suggested. 'Can't', I replied, 'already have a lunch date on Friday.' 'I'll have to ring you back,' he said. He did, an hour or so later, suggesting the following Tuesday. Not until I arrived at the appointed day for my first visit to No. 10 did I realise that I'd turned down lunch with the Prime Minister the Friday before. There were nine people present: 'Today is the first day of the next General Election', said the PM, to what he called the 'insiders'.

I went back that afternoon to start work on the planning of the polling for the next election, which was to be on 10 October. Thanks largely to my very able assistant, Angela Mais, who had worked with me day and night during the campaign, we had kept every scrap of paper, notes, memos, sets of computer tabulations and other documents. We pulled them altogether, everything we had done and written for the Party and everything we could find of what all the other polling organisations had done, into two fat volumes which we designated the 'Green Book', containing all the published poll data, and the 'Red Book', of Labour's private polling. These were in fact the father and mother, seven generations back, of this book.

The Nuffield books play an enormous role in the current history of political Britain. Stretching back to 1945, they are largely the work of Dr

David Butler, who has made the study of elections his life's work. They draw to some extent on polling evidence, but also on the gossip of the day, what politicians recall happened, usually to their own aggrandisement, and what Butler and his co-author(s) witness. Inevitably they contain errors, despite the efforts the authors make to check and double check the facts. Believing that the Nuffield books lacked the space to properly portray the increasing importance of political communications in the election campaigns, and the witness of two to be good but a dozen better, I instigated with the help of a former MORI colleague, Dr. Martin Harrop, the series of weekend meetings of the players in the election campaigns, the back-room boys and girls, which later became the Essex Political Communications seminars, the first, at the University of Newcastle, written up as *Political Communications and the British General Election of 1979*.[1]

Early on in my work for the Party, Shirley Williams, then a Member of Labour's NEC, for personal reasons convinced Clarke that all of my private polls for the Labour Party should be lodged at the survey archives at the University of Essex, embargoed until after the election following. This has meant that all of the MORI work for the Labour Party, including the 'Red Books' of every general election from February 1974 through 1987 (and 'Green Books' up to and including 1997) are in the public domain. As yet, they have not found the scholar who will examine them and the post-election surveys of Labour Party Candidates and Agents, to distil from them lessons hard learnt by the Party. The Labour Party no longer has such a liberal policy, but then nowadays they play for keeps.

This book began life the week following Labour's famous victory on 1 May 1997. By the end of a fortnight's holiday, booked to escape from the pressure of the general election, over 25,000 words had been written in a kind of catharsis-driven effort to get the trauma of a general election experience off my chest. It contributed to the 1997 'Green Book'. It informed Butler and Kavanagh.[2] It was read by a few others, but ignored

[1] Worcester, R. and Harrop, M., *Political Communications: The British General Election of 1979* (London: Macmillan, 1982).

[2] Butler, D. and Kavanagh, D., *The British General Election of 1997* (Basingstoke: Macmillan, 1997).

by most. Nick Jones was first in print, soon to be followed by Butler and Kavanagh themselves and by collections of essays edited by Andrew Geddes and Jonathan Tonge, by Pippa Norris and Neil Gavin, and by David Denver et al, and eventually by Anthony King, and by Ivor Crewe, Brian Gosschalk and John Bartle[3]; but few delved into the numbers which supported some political conjecture, and would have destroyed some myths ('the most boring media election', 'Goldsmith's Referendum Party lost the Tories 22 seats', 'It was the fault of the constituencies', 'Labour stay-at-homes were greater than the Tories', 'neither Major or Mawhinney are to blame for the Tories' campaign defeat', 'Labour's campaign was flawless', and so on), which if the evidence is examined, turn out to be just that, myths, promulgated by mythmakers burnishing their own role or defending against blame.

So after two years and the publication of a dozen or more books from the superficial to the self-promoting (and, just occasionally, worthy), we decided to put the evidence before the interested political junkie, who will read one more book about the 1997 election, in an effort to find out what really happened to cause Labour's landslide.

With great admiration for the work done by Iain Dale and John Simmons in setting up Politico's Bookstore, to which I have introduced both the BBC World Service and numerous American 'boys on the bus', and supportive of the cut-the-cackle publishing enterprise they have begun, we offered our manuscript to Iain to publish instead of the more established publishers with whom we have heretofore been associated. He read the text, looked at the many tables and graphs, and agreed there were things here that were new, different, and important to be recorded about what happened in 1997. It was a watershed election, capping the transformation of Britain's Labour Party. We hope that the findings of our polls will help to illuminate what happened, and why, to the benefit

---

[3] Jones, N., *Campaign 1997: How the General Election was Won and Lost* (London: Indigo, 1997); Geddes, A. and Tonge, J. (eds.), *Labour's Landslide: The British General Election of 1997* (Manchester: Manchester University Press, 1997); Norris, P. and Gavin, N., *Britain Votes 1997* (New York: Oxford University Press, 1997); Denver, D., Fisher, J., Cowley, P. and Pattie, C., (eds.), *British Elections and Parties Review* Volume 8: The 1997 British General Election (London: Frank Cass, 1997); King A. (ed.), *New Labour Triumphs: Britain at the Polls* (Chatham, NJ: Chatham House, 1998); Crewe, I., Gosschalk, B. and Bartle J., *Political Communications: Why Labour Won the General Election of 1997* (London: Frank Cass, 1998).

of politicians, political apparatchiks, academic psephologists, political scientists, political journalists, and even a few interested voters.

Finally, let me pay tribute to Dr Roger Mortimore, truly the co-author of *Explaining Labour's Landslide*, for if I started this book, he finished it, made sure my rush of interpretation and conjecture of consequences were supported by the data, polished my prose and curbed my excesses, and in every way demonstrated his safe pair of hands that I have so relied on since he joined me from Oxford six years ago as my political assistant and Editor of *British Public Opinion* newsletter.

Also, thanks to our other colleagues on the political team at MORI, Brian Gosschalk, Managing Director, Simon Braunholtz, now running MORI Scotland, Simon Atkinson (Simon A.), successor to first myself, then Brian, then Simon B. as head of the Political Unit at MORI, and to Jessica Elgood, Mark Bunting, Cara Lavan and Charlotte Levitt, members of the political unit at MORI during the election, and to the MORI staff, the Field & Tab team that backed us up throughout the campaign and the years preceding for the face-to-face polling and to the gang at On-Line Telephone Surveys who did the same for the telephone polls, and, finally, to my wife Margaret, who while she does not entirely understand why I spend holidays on the computer bashing away, indulges me in the freedom to do so.

Robert M. Worcester
May 1999

Introduction

The General Election of 1997 was a seminal event With a swing of more than 10% in votes from Conservatives to Labour, and the government losing 177 seats including seven defended by Cabinet ministers, it was one of those rare moments, that occur in British history only a handful of times in a century, when the tide of political opinion decisively turns.

In 1997, Labour had its highest ever number of MPs (26 more than Attlee won in the 1945 landslide); its overall majority (179) in the House of Commons was larger than the number of Conservative Members remaining (165). It wasn't a 'Canadian-style wipe-out' across the entire country, but as we forecast, it was in the Celtic fringe, and there were no Conservative MPs elected whatsoever in either Scotland or Wales, and in addition none in most of the major conurbations in England. The 419 seats won by Labour was the highest by any party not running as part of a coalition[1], and the Conservative share of the vote that party's lowest, in any general election since the first after the Great Reform Act, when Earl Grey defeated the Duke of Wellington.

It was also an important election for opinion polls, for two very different reasons:-

On the one hand, it was generally seen both at the time and in retrospect as an election when the private opinion polls and focus groups conducted for the political parties, especially Labour, were more influential than ever before. This certainly shaped Labour's approach to the election and contributed to its victory[2].

---

[1] At the 1931 election, the 554 national government candidates returned included 470 Conservatives. Otherwise the 412 Tory victories at the 'Zinoviev Letter' election of 1924 was the highest since the Liberals won 441 seats in 1832. See Craig, F., *British Electoral Facts 1832–1987* (Aldershot: Parliamentary Research Services, 5th edition, 1989).

[2] See Gould, P., *The Unfinished Revolution* (London: Little, Brown, 1998).

1

On the other hand, public opinion polls, conducted for and published in the media were effectively 'on trial': because the polls were thought of as having 'failed' and 'got it wrong' in the previous, 1992, British election. The media made less use of polls to understand what was going on than in recent previous elections, and instead devoted much space to speculating on how accurate the polls would be. In fact, though in 1992 they were certainly far more inaccurate than the pollsters would have preferred, they were still in the right ball-park; scientific polling of the public, whatever its imperfections, is still the most reliable way to assess what the public thinks and what the public is likely to do (as any historian ought to realise from the persistent unpredictability of elections before opinion polls were invented). But too many influential 'opinion leaders' who should have known better took the polls' error in 1992 as an excuse to believe (or say they believed) that the polls were worthless and that their own instincts were a much better guide to British public opinion and the likely behaviour of the electorate in the election.

Politicians and pundits alike failed to believe the answers given by the British public in answer to polls during the 1992–7 Parliament and especially during the 1997 election campaign itself, when the polls continued to indicate that Labour was sweeping to a landslide victory. One widely reported sceptic was the (former) Prime Minister, John Major, who described them as 'rubbish'[3] and 'a million miles adrift of reality'[4], and further stated 'I've never commented on polls [sic] whatever they may be. By and large they are of no real use in determining what people are going to do on election day.'[5]

He and others in his party found out on 1 May 1997 that they weren't rubbish after all. The polls had accurately diagnosed the collapse of the Tory vote (to the nearest percentage point on the final average), and had read all of the parties' positions accurately, within the limits of statistical reliability.

By contrast, pundits who preferred to ignore the polls, and judged

---

[3] MacAskill, E., 'Tories' turning point? Or still trailing points?', *Guardian*, 22 April 1997.
[4] Allardyce, J., *The Scotsman*, 5 April 1997.
[5] Curtice, J., 'Making sense of the polls' position', *Guardian*, 24 April 1997.

which way the political wind was blowing by sticking their fingers in the air, were ludicrously adrift.

We all now know the result of the 1997 election. But the reasons for that result are still a matter of debate, and the terms of that debate are still to some extent being shaped by the beliefs and suppositions that arose when the media pundits were ignoring or decrying the polls rather than soberly examining their findings. But, despite the mistrust of many at the time, the polls were still conducted, for the parties themselves, for the media outlets who were prepared to believe that the pollsters might be professional enough at their jobs not to make the same mistakes twice, and even for some media whose editors were quite convinced that the polls were entirely wrong, but couldn't resist them anyway as news stories. MORI interviewed some 30,000 electors during the six weeks of the formal election campaign, and hundreds of thousands during the five years beforehand. And, now the election is over and the result has vindicated the competence of the pollsters and the veracity of the electors they interviewed, the data survives. The private polling for the parties, of course, will mostly stay private for some years yet; but the polling for the media is all in the public domain, and available for analysis to give a unique insight into the reasons behind the election result[6].

This, then, is a book about British public opinion at the time of the 1997 British General Election, seen through the eyes of the British electorate, systematically and objectively measured through the technique of opinion polls. Polls are only a measuring tool. Books already published on the election have already looked at many aspects of Labour's victory. There are interviews in exhaustive detail with all the participants – ministers, candidates, party apparatchiks and spin-doctors down to the canvassers in the constituencies.

The Nuffield College study of the election[7], indeed, spoke to the pollsters and carries a chapter on the opinion polls, but its focus is on

---

[6] The full results of all polls conducted by MORI during the election campaign are published in a four-volume set of MORI 'Green Books' (Worcester, R. and Mortimore, R., *British Public Opinion: The British General Election of 1997*, London: MORI, 1997) and the data are lodged at the ESRC Archives at the University of Essex.

[7] Butler, D. and Kavanagh, D., *The British General Election of 1997* (Basingstoke: Macmillan, 1997).

how and how well the polls were conducted, in how efficiently they measured the result; it barely at all considers what the polls actually found. But for all the significance of the roles of John Major or Tony Blair, Peter Mandelson or Neil Hamilton or Philip Gould (and all, as we shall see, played a very significant role), the people who really decided the result of the 1997 General Election were the thirty million or so Britons who actually went to the polls and marked a cross on their ballot papers on 1 May. Talking to ordinary people, representative members of the British public, is precisely what opinion polls do. Understanding what drives these people as they vote is what the polls were designed to do. This book is about them.

Why the Tories lost the 1997 British General Election

Elections are 'fought' during 'campaigns', with 'strategy' and 'tactics', 'battlebuses' and 'footsoldiers'. Every war has its elements of strategy and tactics; no less the 1997 election. A strategic genius can manoeuvre to pick his battlefield and his initial dispositions so that his opponent, out-flanked, enfiladed or simply outnumbered, is already a certain loser before the first shot of the tactical phase is fired. A strategic dunderhead – or a monumental slice of bad luck – can achieve exactly the opposite. This was the fate of the Conservatives during the Parliament which led up to the 1997 election. The result was effectively determined at five strategic points in the long campaign which began soon after John Major's stunning and unexpected victory in 1992, long before the tactics of the short campaign came into play. Four were avoidable, the fifth chance:

- By taking sterling into the European Exchange Rate Mechanism at an unsustainable exchange rate, the government set in train a chain of events that destroyed the Tories' chance to benefit politically from economic recovery.
- By failing to call a referendum on the Maastricht treaty, they lost the chance to transfer responsibility for Europe from their party to the people of Britain and thereby side-step the divisions over Europe that tore the party apart.

- By allowing the question of 'sleaze' to become the keynote of the Parliament, a blight on the party's image which owed far more to indecisive leadership and ill-advised moral crusades than to the true level of misbehaviour among Conservative MPs, they took on themselves the crucial burden of mistrust which had been a prime cause of Labour's narrow defeat in 1992.
- Then, when already trailing badly, by keeping John Major as leader when he gave them the chance, they lost any opportunity to wipe the slate clean and recast their image as they had done in 1990,
- And by the sudden death of John Smith, opening the way for Tony Blair's election, Labour's renaissance as an electable party was completed, ensuring that voters felt free to run the risk of making the Tories pay for their failings.

In fact, the 1997 British General Election campaign itself, the 'tactics' if you will, as opposed to the 'strategy', was 'lost' by Labour: they shed votes throughout it, mostly to the LibDems (the real 'winners') while the Tories were making modest net gains from returning waverers. But by then it was far too late: an irrelevant battle won when the war was already lost. In this election, there were millions of voters, some 4.5 million according to our reckoning, who were so opposed to the Conservatives remaining in office that they were actively going about telling their friends and workmates not to vote Conservative, without even being asked their views. Their principal objective was to get the Conservatives out and John Major replaced, and they didn't care much how they did it. Too many lifelong Tories, to say nothing of the bulk of the 'floating' voters, had already made up their minds. Others, while they kept an open mind to the last minute, had already had an indelible impression of the parties' relative merits printed upon them, and their eventual decision was all but inevitable. A less inept Conservative campaign might still have made the margin somewhat closer, but it wouldn't have altered the outcome. It was 'time for a change'.

Opinion Polls – Why and How We Do What We Do

Taking the Temperature of the Electorate

The 1997 election was the occasion for perhaps more concentrated and vocal attacks on the use of political opinion research than has ever been the case in Britain before. Partly this stemmed from parts of the media (notably in the hierarchy of the BBC) who have always been suspicious of polling, and took the opportunity of the pollsters' embarrassment at the 1992 election to pursue their vendetta. But equally, pressure came from participants in the political process themselves, perhaps mainly because the polls were telling them what they did not want to hear. Particular concern centred around the suddenly increased prominence of polling and of the closely-related technique of focus groups in directing party political strategy, especially in moulding the 'New Labour' direction of Tony Blair's Labour party.

For the Tories, the polls' results were bad news that they did not want to hear, and which they felt they had to rubbish in order to appear to be in with a chance. For Labour, the polls carried too good a story, and they feared complacence and voter apathy. For the Liberal Democrats alone they carried really promising news for a change, and instead of fearing the usual third-party squeeze, they saw the possibility that defecting Tories did not need to vote Labour against their conscience to get the Tory out, and that natural Labour supporters in marginal constituencies where Labour stood no chance of defeating a sitting Conservative could vote tactically for the LibDem candidate and get what they wanted also, to oust the Tory.

These techniques were often portrayed as being an alien import from the United States – where, it is perfectly true, many of those involved in the private polling either as practitioners or clients had acquired valuable

7

experience. We were heading, we were warned, for government by opinion poll and policy making by focus group; the whole process was profoundly undemocratic and unprincipled, it was implied, a kind of sorcerous divination akin to King Saul consulting the Witch of Endor.

We didn't hear much of the other side of the case.

What are opinion polls for? As in the case of the media, to inform, to entertain, to educate. And as a by-product mainly, but occasionally specifically, they can be a carrier of information to the opinion former, a channel of communication between the masses on whose behalf the country is governed and the elites in the magic circle of Westminster, Whitehall and Fleet Street. In the case of the political parties' own private polls, they may also help inform the parties' strategists how best to present their case or direct their campaigning energies.

There was little new about the message coming from Labour's focus groups: what had changed was the Labour Party's willingness to listen. It was as long ago as the summer of 1988 that I wrote about the transformation that would be required for Labour to come back from the death that is Opposition in the House of Commons in the British Parliamentary system[1]. Appropriately enough, it was in a little-read journal called *New Socialist*, now defunct.

In that article, I stated things that were not popular at the time:

'Protestations from the left against polls cannot explain away or confuse the fact that the Conservatives' policies, legislation and action has caused a massive drop in trade union membership, a massive increase in share owning, a steep rise in the sales of council houses, and a shift from jobs in factories, in lorries and in the mines to jobs in offices (and on the dole). And real voters, casting real votes, in real ballot boxes, in three successive elections, have shown by the exercise of their franchise that on balance these policies, legislation and action are what more of the electorate wants from what has been on offer from the contending political parties.

'The elements of political choice that determine the voting behaviour of the marginal voter, the swing voter that determines not only who wins but the size of the winning party's majority in the House of Commons, are principally three: the images attributed to each party as being seen to

[1] Worcester, R., 'Polls Apart', *New Socialist*, Summer 1988, p. 39–41.

8

be fit to govern, united, etc.; the image of the leadership of the parties as caring, understanding of the problems facing Britain and her role in the world, listening to the electorate, etc.; and the perceived understanding and acceptance or consonance of the elector's ideas of the parties' stands on issues of importance or salience to the voter.

'The message to the main parties is clearly defined . . . the Tories are vulnerable in that more than seven in ten of their own supporters believe that an ideal society would be characterised by caring for others being more highly regarded than wealth creation and that nearly four in ten Tories profess the belief that an ideal society would provide for a social and collective provision of welfare; for Labour it is that a third of their supporters are vulnerable to appeals to their belief that an ideal society favours increasing efficiency at the expense of jobs and one that allows people to make and keep as much as they can.'

Somebody read that article. In fact, Patricia Hewitt, quite an outstanding political mind, read it closely, and indeed pointed out an error in the article which needed correction in the following issue. She was then of course in Neil Kinnock's office, working closely with Peter Mandelson. Nine years on, she was a candidate (elected for the first time in 1997, and to nobody's surprise quickly promoted to ministerial office), while Mandelson was the directing genius behind the strategy, including liberal use of polling information, that brought Labour its first election victory since 1974.

Opinion polls have no axe to grind, no incentive to manipulate or guide the decision-making process of the voter or subvert the political principles of a party's policy makers. They are there not to persuade a person to act in one way or another, to think or vote in a certain way. They are there to provide information about what others think. Many politicians and some newspaper proprietors and editors are guided by their own desire to see a certain election outcome. Opinion polls are not, and there is no incentive for them to be.

Opinion polling is widely misunderstood. It can provide understanding, analysis and tracking of the behaviour, knowledge, opinions, attitudes and values of the public. By measuring this, within the limits of the science of sampling and the art of asking questions, surveys can determine what people do and what they think. Through the media, polls can then be used to inform others of this information, for their own use in whatever way they may wish to use it.

There are many for whom the phrase 'opinion poll' means no more and no less than an attempt by survey research to predict the result of a forthcoming general election. This is an error. Although that is one possible function of an opinion poll, it is only a tiny fraction of the use to which opinion polls can be put during an election, and election polling in its turn is a tiny fraction of our work as survey researchers. Opinion polling is simply one branch of the wider discipline of market research, using the methods developed for that purpose to measure public opinion. To quote Butler and Rose, writing forty years ago in *The British General Election of 1959*[2]:

> . . . their [opinion polls'] main value does not lie primarily in election prediction. The sampling of opinion can yield a vast amount of information of the greatest political and social importance – and such information, to be valuable, need not be nearly as precise as election forecasts must be. Through opinion polling, political parties and students of politics can find out in detail the views of different sections of the public, instead of simply guessing at them, or making inferences. Voting is only the end product of a series of influences. Polls will also be most valuable in discovering, not how people are going to vote, but why they vote as they do.
>
> 'Polls can reveal how well informed the public is about any issue and whether it has strong views; they can also reveal what people do and what media of communication they are exposed to. There has never been anything comparable to sample polls as a tool for advancing understanding of mass political behaviour.'

Private Polling

Nor are the techniques of private polling for the political parties, which became a media obsession for the first time in 1997, either an 'Americanisation' of British politics, or particularly new. Almost all the techniques

---

[2] Butler, D. and Rose, R., *The British General Election of 1959* (London: Macmillan, 1960).

that the private pollsters were using are ones that have been used not only in private polling but even in public polling for the media for years. The only thing that was unusual about 1997 was that, perhaps for the first time in this country, pollsters were being properly used and the Labour Party strategists, at least, were deriving the full benefit from their skills and taking notice of their findings. That, at least, *was* a lesson learned from America!

In essence, private polling differs from public polling only in its function: to help the client to win the election, and nothing else. Before that is dismissed as too cynical, let me add that no pollster does his client any good whatsoever, in the longer term, by doing anything other than being completely honest in the choice of questions (no holds should be barred), in the depth of the analysis (no conclusions rejected because they are not 'p.c.'), in the directness of the presentation (but kept to a close circle, preferably), or in the budgeting of the work.

Private pollsters need:

- The resources to do the work they believe needs doing;
- The freedom to ask the questions that committed party workers and political volunteers feel might blight their preference for appointment or promotion if they are seen to be doing the asking;
- Continuity of work flow, so that the 'long campaign' research informs the election campaign itself;
- Access to and the confidence of the party leader.
- Political nous.

Without these five things, their work will be compromised by the ambitious, watered down by the frightened, hampered by the mean, and will end up wasting their client's money. For pollsters are in one of the few businesses where you are paid to be honest; if you are any less, you do not serve your client professionally, or well.

It was in 1969 that I was first approached to do the private polling for the Labour Party, an assignment that was to last for two decades. It was not so much in my first (1970) General Election that I became an 'insider' in the Campaign Strategy Committee, but in the run-up to the February 1974 election when Harold Wilson wrested power back from Ted Heath's unpopular 1970–1974 Government. I recall well what it was like working with Percy Clarke, Peter Mandelson's predecessor of thirty years ago.

Percy Clarke had just three people in the 'Communications Department' – himself, his mistress (later wife) Doreen Stainforth as 'Broadcasting Officer', and their secretary. Compare that to the hundreds of people, paid and unpaid in the Communications Centre on Millbank in 1997.

Professor William Schneider, then at Harvard and not yet the world-famous American elections analyst for CNN, approached me to say that two of his outstanding students were headed for Oxford to do a post-graduate year abroad. One was E.J. Dionne, now the *Washington Post*'s star columnist, the other Doug Schoen, President Clinton's co-pollster for the 1996 American Presidential election. The reason they came to work at MORI during the two 1974 elections was that when they went to Transport House to the Labour Party headquarters they were told that the Labour Party didn't take volunteers (and certainly not Americans) and that if there were jobs there to be done they would be British, paid the going rate for the job negotiated by the union. The Labour Party's loss was MORI's gain.

One finding from our early in-depth work for the Labour Party was especially memorable, and that was the public's desire for a political party that 'represented all classes'. Percy Clarke advised me to bury that finding and not show it to the Campaign Committee under Wilson, as 'The Labour Party is the Party of the Working Class, and we don't want and don't need middle-class support to win British elections'. Of course in those days two-thirds of the electorate were working class; now barely half are.

Against all my pleading to allow me to do focus groups, already a well-accepted supplement to polling in American election research, Percy said he didn't need me to do that, as all that provided he could get from a few hours at his local Labour club. We only did a few in the 70s, and not until 1983 was I allowed to spend their money on serious qualitative research. A far cry from the continual drip feed of focus group findings provided by Philip Gould to Peter Mandelson (and Tony Blair) in 1997!

At the February 1979 meeting of the National Executive Committee I was asked to present the findings of work done for the Party by the General Secretary Ron Hayward. The then Party Treasurer, Norman

Atkinson, responded to my presentation showing that the Labour Party then did not have the support of rank and file trade union members. 'Why, 20 members of my General Management Committee and I can do a better job of assessing British public opinion than you can, Bob Worcester', he said. I took quiet satisfaction several years later when his General Management Committee de-selected him in favour of Bernie Grant.

Then picture this: the first meeting of the Campaign Strategy Committee in the 1983 General Election. I have by then been the polling advisor to the Labour Party for five general elections, and a fixture at these daily 8 a.m. meetings. Wilson and Callaghan, Harry Nicholas, Ron Hayward, Reg Underhill, Percy Clarke and many others have left the scene, and others, Michael Foot, Denis Healey, Roy Hattersley, John Silkin, John Golding, Jim Mortimer and Joyce Gould and Neil Kinnock, have come on. Only Peter Shore and Tony Benn, from memory, have been round that table as long, by then, as I.

I have just finished delivering the results of the first wave of private polling: one member of the committee, from the left, says he cannot believe my figures, which show the Conservatives with a 14-point lead over Labour. 'Why do you say that?', I enquire. 'What do the public think is the most important issue?', he asks. 'Unemployment', I answer. 'And which party has the best policies on unemployment?' he asks. 'Labour', I reply. 'So how can we be 14 points behind? I've always gone on the opening night of the campaign to a meeting in [Wigan], and there have never been more than 80 there before, and last night there were 120! And they were standing on their chairs cheering. How can we possibly be 14 points behind? I can't believe your figures!'

On the Sunday before polling day, I was asked to deliver an extended review of the state of public opinion to the *apparatchiks*, the researchers, spin doctors and speech writers, who toiled in the back rooms of Walworth Road in that ill-fated campaign. I went through the woeful litany of national and local results from all of the sources, public and private, that I had by then accumulated. At one point I gave in passing the party's standing in a North London, Labour-held seat, showing the Tories likely to win by nearly 10,000. 'But that's just the kind of seat we're going to have to win if we're going to win this general election', said the National Agent (of all people). At that my patience snapped: 'Look', said I, 'the question is not whether you are going to win this general election; the question is whether you're going to run third!' On the Thursday, the Tories won by 44% to 28% for Labour (16 points ahead), with the Liberal Democrats at 26%, a very close run for third place.

That was perhaps the low point in private polls' history of impact on general elections since their entry in 1959. It was the worst-led, worst-run, worst-managed election campaign in living memory. I was not given any budget for polling until late February, for an election that began two months later. The Labour Party flew blind (and deaf, if not dumb) during the 'long campaign', and willingly, deliberately and even cheerfully flew in the face of public opinion poll findings and other evidence that they were about to be given the worst drubbing of any political party in Britain in post war history.

Contrast that to the campaign fought by Harold Wilson from mid– 1972 to 28 February 1974. (Worth remembering, perhaps, that Wilson, a former Oxford don, was a trained statistician.) In July 1972 the NEC gave me the go-ahead to conduct qualitative and quantitative research, that included laying down a base-line for a panel study which enabled Wilson and his entourage to plan for and carry out the campaign that took him to the premiership in the first week of March nearly two years later, and then, a further seven months on, to a working majority on 10 October 1974. In that election we employed all of the tools, save one, that are now used in private polling for a political party. Reviewing MORI's private polling 'Red Book' of the February 1974 campaign, Richard Wirthlin – former Presidential advisor and Reagan's 'Pollster-General of the United States' – described it as 'ten years ahead of anything in America'. It used focus groups, in-depth interviews, psychological projective techniques, panel studies, multivariate analysis, target segmentation and psychographic analysis, tracking studies, and fast feedback from the interviewers on the ground. Only people-metering (measuring the on-going reactions of an audience as they watch a TV programme or political broadcast) had yet to be introduced. After Wilson, never again was I to have a political client who used research systematically and objectively, with sufficient budget to do the work in the first place and sufficient wit to understand and value it in the second.

Wilson also employed bright people to liaise with me, especially Bernard (now Lord) Donoughue, then a lecturer in the Government Department at LSE, later Wilson's head of the Policy Unit. His first job for Wilson was to work with a small team with me, meeting fortnightly during the long campaign, and later weekly, to study issues and formulate questions, reflect on Tory activities and strategies, and work out tests of public reaction, study sub-group details of findings, and above all think about what the private poll data was showing, and what it meant for the Party and its Leader.

This became a very knowledgeable group, steeped in the methodology and findings of the public polls, and quick to see where there were gaps to be filled in what was available from the public polling, and where they should be augmented. It extended my reach, and that of my team, and brought to bear a dedicated team of volunteers with political experience and nous. Contrast this to the experience in December 1986, when we were told by the Party's principal spin doctor that there would be no questions asked about party election broadcasts, as he did not want any information on the table that would raise questions about what he wanted to do. At the Campaign Strategy meeting in February 1987, when asked by the Deputy Leader of the Party about election polling plans, I questioned this, to be told by the Leader of the Party 'Of course we want questions about the PEBs'. I saw the spin-doctor's eyes narrow; 'I'll get you', was the message behind his stare – and he did.

The various interested parties in the Labour NEC often had their own agenda. I had questions pressed on me by the General Secretary, the National Agent, Percy Clarke, Tony Benn, other NEC members, the Wilson entourage, and a committee of 'academic advisors' lumbered on me by the likes of Shirley Williams; while often well-meant, they were an obstacle to what I was trying to do, provide information obtained objectively and systematically to enable my client to do what it was supposed to do, win the next general election. Instead, individual egos and hidden agendas seemed to get in the way, then as later. What differentiates public polling for the newspapers and television from private polling for the political parties is the end use of the data. Private

15

polling for a political party should have the same objective as the party itself, one objective, and one only: to win the election. Parties lose sight of this, and so do some, perhaps most, party leaders, senior officials and officers. Harold Wilson didn't. When the head of the information sub-committee of the NEC, to whom I was supposed to report, Tony Benn, found that I proposed to ask in a questionnaire about the influence of Enoch Powell on the electorate in the summer of 1973, he forbade me to ask questions about any 'personalities'. When I next met with the Leader, I asked him if he didn't want the information. 'Of course I do', snapped Wilson, 'ask the questions, and just give me the answers'.

Many of Labour's post-Wilson errors were being repeated by the Tories in 1997. They did no regular polling before appointing ICM in the late summer of 1996, and then the work was handled too secretively by Chairman Mawhinney and his Central Office minions. Butler and Kavanagh report[3] that though rolling daily polls were being conducted, John Major was quite unaware of this until three weeks into the campaign! Things weren't like that in Tony Blair's New Labour Party – but that is a story perhaps better told by those who were there[4].

What is public opinion and how can we hope to measure it?

There is nothing occult about opinion polling, or about that mysterious entity 'public opinion' that it hopes to measure. I am convinced that as a tree falling in the forest makes a noise whether anybody is there to hear it or not, so public opinion exists, perhaps unheard until someone listens. It seems to me that a simple definition will do: 'Public opinion is the view of a [representative sample of a] defined population.' The words in brackets delimit the difference between 'public opinion' and a 'public opinion poll'. The poll is the process by which we can listen to public opinion.

Let us begin by defining what we can, and cannot, do with survey research. Fundamentally there are five things that we can discover with

---

[3] Butler, D. and Kavanagh, D., *The British General Election of 1997* (Basingstoke, Macmillan, 1997), p 130.

[4] As it has been by Labour's political advisor, the first professional political consultant to operate in British politics, Philip Gould, in *The Unfinished Revolution* (London: Little, Brown, 1998).

the techniques we have in our kit bag (which include not only 'quanti-tative methods', the traditional poll, but also 'qualitative methods', or focus groups.) We can measure **behaviour**, what we do, **knowledge**, what we know (or think we know), **opinions**, **attitudes** and **values.** I have defined these latter terms as '**opinions**: the ripples on the surface of the public's consciousness, shallow, and easily changed; **attitudes**: the currents below the surface, deeper and stronger; and **values**: the deep tides of public mood, slow to change, but powerful.'[5]

Price in his book *Public Opinion*[6] probes these concepts, quoting Doob[7], Childs[8], Thurstone[9], Allport[10] and others to distinguish between them, and argues that opinions and attitudes have been said to differ conceptually in at least three ways. First, opinions have usually been considered as observable, verbal responses to an issue or question, whereas an attitude is a covert, psychological predisposition or tendency. Second, although both attitude and opinion imply approval or disapproval, the term attitude points more toward affect (i.e., fundamental liking or disliking), opinion more toward cognition (e.g., a conscious decision to support or oppose some policy, politician or political group). Third, and perhaps most important according to Price, an attitude is 'traditionally conceptualised as a global, enduring orientation toward a general class of stimuli, but an opinion is viewed more situationally, as pertaining to a specific issue in a particular behavioural setting.'

Later Price brings in values, quoting Rokeach[11], 'Like attitudes, values are conceptualized as evaluative beliefs, but they have a special prescrip-tive quality'[12], thus adopting the continuum idea of my more poetic definition.

[5] Worcester, R., 'Reflections on Public Opinion and Public Policy', paper to the World Association of Public Opinion Research, Copenhagen, September 1993.

[6] Price, V., *Public Opinion* (Newbury Park, Cal.: Sage Publications, Inc., 1992), pp 46–7.

[7] Doob, L., *Public Opinion and Propaganda* (New York: Holt, Rinehart & Winston, 1948).

[8] Childs, H., *Public Opinion: Nature, Formation and Role* (Princeton, N.J., Toronto, New York and London: D. Van Nostrand, 1965).

[9] Thurstone, L., 'Attitudes can be measured', *American Journal of Sociology* 33 (1928), pp 539–554.

[10] Allport, F., 'Towards a Science of Public Opinion', *Public Opinion Quarterly*, volume 1, number 1, pp 7–23 (1937).

[11] Rokeach, M., *The Nature of Human Values* (New York: Free Press, 1973).

[12] Price, V., *Public Opinion* (Newbury Park, Cal.: Sage Publications, Inc., 1992), p 55.

Opinions in my own view are those low salience, little-thought-about reactions to pollsters' questions about issues of the day. They are easily manipulated by question wording or the news of the day, not very important to the respondent, not vital to their well being or that of their family, unlikely to have been the topic of discussion or debate between them and their relations, friends and work mates. These would for most people include their satisfaction with the performance of the parties and their leaders, economic optimism and pessimism, and the salience of the issues of the day, but not voting intention.

Attitudes derive from a deeper level of consciousness, are held with some conviction, and are likely to have been held for some time and after thought, discussion, perhaps the result of behaviour[13], and are harder to confront or confound. Examples of these are the Scots' support for a separate assembly, held with some force over generations and based on strong beliefs that they are not fairly represented either in Parliament or in our system of government, perhaps attitudes to the taking of medicines or exercise, preference for forms of education, or satisfaction with local authority service delivery for services used frequently and by large percentages of citizens such as rubbish collection, street lighting and schools. With some, voting intention derives from their attitudes; but with most, it comes from their values.

Values then are the deepest of all, learned parentally in many cases, and formed early in life and not likely to change, only harden as we grow older. These include belief in God, attitudes to religion generally, views about abortion or the death penalty, family values, and the like. For many people, these include voting intention, learned in childhood from parental influence, class and peer group identification, and only likely to be shifted by the most extraordinary circumstances. This concept is of particular importance to understanding a landmark election such as 1997. Both the major parties have a solid bloc of voters whose values dictate their support for that party, and whose loyalty is unlikely to be shaken by the most extreme vicissitudes of political life – the Old Labour trade unionist, dismayed by his party's lurch to the right under Blair, may lose his enthusiasm for voting at all but would be unable to

---

[13] See Festinger, L., *A Theory of Cognitive Dissonance*, (Evanston, Ill.: Row, Peterson, 1957).

contemplate voting for a different party. Similarly, a dyed-in-the-wool lifelong Tory, even if determined that there was no alternative to ejecting John Major's government, might find it very hard to defy her values by voting Labour, and will much prefer to abstain or vote Liberal Democrat if she thinks the deed can be done without her active complicity.

What polls (and I use the term more or less interchangeably with 'surveys', although there are those who use 'polls' only to describe 'political' soundings) cannot tell us well are likely future actions of the public generally and especially the future behaviour of individuals. Polls are not particularly good at exploring concepts unfamiliar to respondents, and they are also better at telling us *what* rather than *why*. The reason for this should be obvious: the respondent is often not clear as to the 'why' himself, and may only have a simplistic or even misleading understanding of the forces that are driving him. So if we just ask 'Why did you do that?', he or she is unlikely to be able to give us a complete answer. Of course, we have techniques to get round this problem. One of these is qualitative research and especially focus groups[14], which major on the interaction of the group rather than the question-and-answer, 'expert'-on-respondent, format of the individual depth interview; but the results of qualitative research, while often revealing, cannot necessarily be categorised or enumerated. We can explain the actions of individuals, but this only offers clues rather than solutions to the forces that move entire populations – 'public opinion', if you will. More productive of robust explanations is multivariate analysis, examining the relationship between different factors in the same group of voters, and it is this at which most analytical election polls are aimed, implicitly or explicitly.

Similarly, polls are not ideal at predicting voting behaviour (or any other form of behaviour), since the respondent often cannot predict it himself. In this case, however, polls tend still to hold sway since, though certainly imperfect, they are better than any of the alternatives. Election prediction is really a function of the psephologist or pundit rather than the pollster – although polling data is usually the most important factor

---

[14] Some of the projective techniques used in qualitative research are not too distantly related to the tests used by psycho-analysts and, indeed, their basic aim is not that dissimilar either – in both cases, though for different reasons, we want to find out what makes our subjects 'tick'.

to be taken into account in making the prediction, and many pollsters (including us) are also psephologists or pundits. Polls are useless at telling us much about the outcome of an election weeks or even months or years in the future. Nonetheless, the voting intention question is valuable for what it summarises about people's attitudes and values at the moment.

Public Opinion in a Democratic Society

But why do we carry out our polls, and why should politicians, the media or anybody else want to pay us to do so? In a democracy, public opinion has a fundamental role; and even apart from its significance to democratic theory, no government can safely ignore it. David Hume said in 1741 that 'All government rests on public opinion', and Aristotle stated centuries earlier that 'He who loses the support of the people is a king no longer'. Somewhat more recently Abraham Lincoln said that 'Public Opinion is everything' and went on to avow that he saw his role as the elected leader of the United States as being to find out what his electorate wanted and, within reason, to give it to them. Even so dictatorial a leader as Napoleon I admitted 'Public Opinion is the thermometer a monarch should constantly consult'.

The eighteenth century statesman Edmund Burke's belief that his vote in Parliament was determined by his own judgement rather than the wishes of his Bristol electors is often quoted admiringly by those who would dismiss poll findings: in his speech on his election for Bristol in 1774, he declared:

> '. . . his unbiased opinion, his mature judgement, his enlightened con-
> science, he ought not to sacrifice to you, to any man, or to any set to men
> living. These he does not derive from your pleasure, – no, not from the
> law and the Constitution. They are a trust from providence, for the abuse
> of which he is deeply answerable. Your representative owes you, not his
> industry only, but his judgement; and he betrays, instead of serving you, if
> he sacrifices it to your opinion.'[15]

---

[15] Burke, E., Speech to the Electors of Bristol, 3 November 1774.

However, it is seldom recalled that later in that Parliament he wrote to the Sheriffs of Bristol

'The completeness of the legislative authority of Parliament over this kingdom is not questioned; and yet many things indubitable included in the abstract idea of that power, and which carry no absolute injustice in themselves, yet being contrary to the opinions and feelings of the people, can as little be exercised as if Parliament in that case had been possessed of no right at all.'[16]

Neither is it recalled that he later said that 'The people are the masters'[17], and, or that addressing the electors of Bristol at the Bristol Guildhall during the next election, Burke said,

'. . . when we know that the opinions of even the greatest multitudes are the standard of rectitude, I shall think myself obliged to make those opinions the masters of my conscience . . . No man carries further that I do the policy of making government pleasing to the people. But the widest range of this politic complaisance is confined within the limits of justice. I would not only consult the people, but I would cheerfully gratify their humours'.[18]

But within three days after this, it became clear to Burke that Bristol did not desire so independent a member as himself to represent them; they wanted a cunning agent. Declining the poll, he returned to London, and Rockingham found for him the pocket borough of Malton.[19] My own Burke favourite was in his letter to Miss Mary Palmer six years later: 'I never conformed myself to the humours of the people. I cannot say that opinion is indifferent to me; but I will take it, if I can, as my companion, never as my guide.'[20] He seems to have forgotten his earlier admission.

Necker, Price reminds us, minister of finance in the pre-Revolutionary France of the 1780s, popularised the phrase *l'opinion publique*, using the term to refer to a growing dependence of the government's status on the opinion of its creditors. He instituted the publication of national accounts

---

[16] Burke, E., Letter to the Sheriffs of the City of Bristol on the Affairs of America, 3 April 1777.
[17] Burke, E., Speech on the Economical Reform, House of Commons, 11 February 1780.
[18] Burke, E., Speech to the Electors of Bristol, 6 September 1780.
[19] Kirk, R., *Edmund Burke: A Genius Reconsidered*, (New York: Arlington House, 1967), p 94.
[20] Burke, E., Letter to Miss Mary Palmer, 19 January 1786.

and argued that support from the French elite was necessary for success of the government's policies. To that end he advocated full publication of state activities, thus becoming not only minister for finance, but the first to propose systematic governmental public relations, the forerunner to today's government information service, the Number 10 press office, the White House spokesman, etc. 'Only fools, pure theorists, or apprentices fail to take public opinion into account', Necker observed in 1792[21].

The first book devoted to the subject of public opinion was written in 1828, four years before the Reform Act, by William Mackinnon[22]. Tocqueville of course wrote about it in *Democracy in America*[23] during 1835–40, as did Bryce in *The American Commonwealth* in 1888[24]. But Lippmann's classic *Public Opinion* was not published until 1922[25]. Lippmann pointed out that the analyst of public opinion must begin by recognising the triangular relationship between the scene of the action, the human picture of that scene, and the human response to that picture working itself out upon the scene of the action. He used the simile of pictures inside the heads of human beings, the pictures of themselves, of others, of their needs, purposes and relationships, which he says are their public opinions. Those pictures which are acted upon by groups of people, or by individuals acting in the name of groups, are Public Opinion, with capital letters. He considered first the chief factors which limit the public's access to the facts, which he describes as 'artificial censorships', the limitations of social contact, the comparatively meagre time available in each day for paying attention to public affairs, the difficulty of making a small vocabulary express a complicated world, and finally the fear of facing those facts which would seem to threaten the established routine of men's lives.

One important point that Lippmann made is that inevitably our opinions cover a bigger space, a longer reach of time, a greater number

[21] Palmer, P., 'Public Opinion in Political Theory', in Wittke, C. (ed.) *Essays in History and Political Theory: In Honour of Charles Howard McIlwain* (Cambridge, Mass., USA: Harvard University Press, 1936).

[22] Mackinnon, W., *On Public Opinion in Great Britain and other Parts of the World*, (London, 1828).

[23] Tocqueville, A. de, *Democracy in America* (New York: Alfred A. Knopf, Inc., 1945).

[24] Bryce, J., *The American Commonwealth* (London: Macmillan, 1893).

[25] Lippmann, W., *Public Opinion*, (New York: Macmillan, 1922).

of things, than we can directly observe. They have, therefore, to be pieced together out of what others have reported and what we can imagine. Or as I have said to clients and audiences so many times in my career, we don't measure **truth**, we measure **perceptions**. But the reality of the world of public policy, as well as the media and industry, is that it is perception, not fact, that determines public opinion.

Our position on the role of polls, surveys and assessment of public opinion is one not of advocacy of any particular policy, subject or topic, but of the provider of both objective and subjective information, obtained systematically and objectively, analysed dispassionately and delivered evenly. Polls, we believe, should be *descriptive*, not *prescriptive*. Having said that, we do feel passionately about the principle that decisions about public policy (and both party policy and corporate policy for that matter) should be made in the knowledge of rather than in the absence of the knowledge of the public's view. We feel that too many politicians and for that matter managers drift too far away from those they lead, either through ignorance, hubris, or indifference. Still others fear that polls are becoming too powerful. According to a recent speech by the former Labour Deputy Leader Roy Hattersley, the opinion poll is 'a major disincentive to ideological politics'. He neither wishes to prohibit polls nor in any way limit their use, but

> 'merely observe that its [polling's] existence and increasing sophistication makes politicians believe that they can choose between principle and popularity. Politicians always thought they knew what the people wanted. [sic]. Now the newspapers tell them with apparent certainty . . . They can even identify the needs and demands of target voters . . . The newspapers . . . reinforce the popular prejudices. There has never been a time in our history when it was more difficult for a politician to say "I will lead rather than follow" . . . If the Liberal Party of 1885 had employed MORI, Gladstone would have faced a real test of courage and conscience.'[26]

Others will dismiss public opinion, as mercurial, or irrelevant, or both. Foreign Secretary Douglas Hurd wrote to me at the height of the Maastricht debate a year or two ago to say:

---

[26] Hattersley, R., 'The Unholy Alliance: The Relationship between Members of Parliament and the Press', James Cameron Memorial Lecture, 23 April 1996.

'I believe that if we had followed the polls, we would have been in and out of the Community several times in the last twenty years. On matters of principle, like the Monarchy and membership of the European Community, the job of the politician is to persuade, not automatically to follow. If he fails to persuade, he will lose his objective and fail in his profession.'[27]

I am firmly on record in agreement with the principle enunciated in Douglas Hurd's letter, and endorse the idea that the job of the politician is to lead, not follow, public opinion as it is the job of managers to manage, not necessarily endorse the results of either customer or staff attitude surveys.

But then if politicians had employed polls as informative conduits supplementing the cab driver and station master, perhaps the Liberal Party of Gladstone would not have passed into history and powerlessness, perhaps the Labour Party under Foot, Kinnock and Hattersley wouldn't have spent nearly two decades in the wilderness, clearly ideological rather than representative of the electorate, and perhaps the Conservative Party of Margaret Thatcher and John Major wouldn't have hurtled to political suicide in 1997.

Politicians **should** worry about what the public thinks; after all, Burke in his way, not to mention Mrs Thatcher, found out what it means to lose public confidence. But why should senior civil servants in central government and senior local government officials worry much about what the public thinks? The answer is (in my experience) too many don't, although over this past decade this has changed, especially in local authorities and recently in the Next Steps agencies. And in America especially, pollsters themselves should consider their responsibilities, not only to their clients, the media and the policymakers, but as well to the wider public and to the future of democracy itself, as cautioned by Julian Woodward so many years ago.

In companies, in NGOs, in trade unions, in all walks of life, survey research can and should in my view be used to inform those in positions of power over others' lives of their opinions, their attitudes and their values, in order for them to make judgements *informed* by these views

---

[27] Hurd, D., Letter to Robert Worcester, 18 January 1993.

rather than *determined* by them, and thereby make better decisions in the exercise of their power.

Still, when as respected a figure in the polling field as the American researcher Daniel Yankelovich worries that 'polls have grown ever more misleading. Far from giving leaders insight into the real concerns of the public, they often add to the disconnect that separates the leadership class in the United States from the mainstream of the citizenry,' we all must join in that concern. Polls need to be used sensibly, cautiously and with consideration.

But it is much more dangerous to ignore public opinion altogether. The words of Rousseau perhaps say it best:

> 'We have seen that the legislative belongs, and can only belong, to the people . . . The initiative for issuing laws, however, comes from the prince. To discharge this office he needs a good vantage point from which to survey the climate of opinion, a matter with which the great legislator is secretly concerned. . . . In this observational task he is helped by the activities of the censor. The prince must decide which convictions of the people are active enough to support legislation; law may be based only on prior agreement, on the sense of community which constitutes the actual foundation of the state. "Just as an architect, before erecting a great edifice, observes and sounds out the ground to see if it can support the weight, the wise legislator does not begin by drawing up laws by which are good in themselves, but first investigates whether the people for whom they are intended is capable of bearing them" '.[28]

Polling in Britain

Polling in Britain has a long pedigree. British Gallup, originally known as BIPO (British Institute of Public Opinion), was founded in 1937, just two years after its American stepfather. In October 1938 it began the series of political questions that continue today, testing the public's satisfaction with the Prime Minister (57% were then satisfied with Neville

---

[28] Quoted in Noelle-Neumann, E., *Spiral of Silence: Public Opinion – Social Skin*, (Chicago and London: University of Chicago Press, 1984) *Die Schweigespirale: öffentliche Meinung – unsere soziale Haut*, (Munich: R Piper & Co Verlag, 1980).

Chamberlain, 43% dissatisfied, setting aside the 'don't knows'), and the first national voting intention questions came in February 1939 (64% said they would vote for the Government 'if there were a general election tomorrow')[29].

Gallup's first associate in Britain was the late Dr Henry Durant, who reminisced forty years on:

'Not [George] Gallup himself, but an associate of his, Henry Field, came from the USA in 1936 looking for someone to start up part-time Gallup work from home . . . For a lordly £150 a year I did postal surveys, till the *News Chronicle* became interested. They said "We want you to forecast the by-election to show that the system works." West Fulham: Edith Summerskill was the Labour candidate. It was a Conservative seat and she upset the Conservative, as I had forecast, and by a miracle I got it on the nose within 1%; beginner's luck.'[30]

During the war, Dr Durant and his colleagues largely focused on government work, but they also continued to publish poll findings regularly in the sparse pages of the *News Chronicle* during those paper-rationed times, and when the election was called in May 1945 they were ready to predict it. As Durant remembered:

'Gallup showed us that Attlee was going to win with the Labour Party. Nobody believed us, including all the *News Chronicle* people.'[31]

Nor did Conservative Central Office believe it: according to the memoirs of Lord Moran, Winston Churchill's physician, Churchill recalled that the Central Office view was that the Tories would be returned with a substantial majority. But in the event Gallup was right, in fact slightly underestimating Labour's lead.

Gallup began in both the USA and in Britain as a means of journalism, but it quickly expanded its horizons. Durant explained[32]:

---

[29] Gallup, G., *The Gallup International Opinion Polls: Great Britain 1937–1975*, (New York: Random House, 1976), p 9, 14.

[30] Chappell, B., 'Founding Fathers: Henry Durant', *Market Research Society Newsletter*, numbers 157–8 (April-May 1979).

[31] *Ibid.*

[32] *Ibid.*

'People constantly asked us to put questions on our regular surveys, and at the beginning I was stupid enough to regard these as a nuisance: then I suddenly realised that this was a beautiful way of making money. It grew and soon had its own omnibus survey[33]: today it's one of the things researchers live off.'

In 1945, Gallup was the only player in the field, but rivals soon began to move in. In the 1950 general election, as well as Gallup's poll for the *News Chronicle*, the *Daily Mail* and *Daily Express* each conducted their own polls. The *Express* poll remained a feature of the scene for several subsequent elections, and while the *Mail* poll was not repeated it presaged the foundation a few years later of National Opinion Polls (NOP) by the then circulation manager of the *Mail*, Mick Shields. The following election (1951) saw Research Services Limited (RSL), under the late Dr Mark Abrams, enter the fray, polling for the *Daily Graphic*.

By the eighties, there were five major companies engaged in regular political polling and producing eve-of-poll election 'predictions': Gallup, NOP, Harris Research, Market & Opinion Research International (MORI) and Marplan (whose political polling section later split off to become ICM Research). All produced regular polls commissioned by and published in the media, although with occasional moves of client newspapers and broadcasters between pollsters; the longest standing relationship is still that of Gallup with the *Daily Telegraph*, which has published their monthly polls since the demise of the *News Chronicle* in 1960. In the 1997 election, Gallup also polled for the *Sunday Telegraph* and Channel 4 News. ICM worked for the *Guardian*, the *Observer*, the *Scotsman* and *Scotland on Sunday*, Harris for the *Independent* and NOP for the *Sunday Times*, Reuters and the BBC. MORI had a long media client list, with weekly polls for *The Times* and *Mail on Sunday*, polls for ITN for both *News at Ten* throughout the campaign

---

[33] An Omnibus survey is a regular nationwide survey by a research company which offers clients the chance to 'hitch-hike' a few questions on to the survey, splitting the set-up costs and costs of demographic questions with all the other clients, and is normally the most economical form of survey research for a short questionnaire. An Omnibus questionnaire will often therefore include questions on a number of widely diverse subjects. Political opinion polls for the media are often carried on Omnibus surveys, with the political questions usually coming at the start of the questionnaire.

and the exit poll for election night, and polls for the *Sun, News of the World, Independent on Sunday, Sunday Mirror,* London *Evening Standard, Economist, Times Higher Educational Supplement* and the *Local Government Chronicle,* not to mention Channel 4, Zee TV and the Weather Channel. The reader will, we hope, excuse us for this exhaustive list of clients, as we all have reason to be grateful to them: these are the sponsors of our polls, and it is to their thirst for journalistic knowledge that we owe the existence of our polling data on the election (on which this book is based).

Meanwhile, the political parties and other bodies had early begun to commission their own research. The Labour Party's polling was entrusted to RSL in the fifties and sixties and then (when Mark Abrams left RSL to become a Civil Servant before the 1970 election) entirely done by MORI from 1969 to 1989, although most of the qualitative research/ focus groups in 1987 were conducted by volunteers coordinated by Gould/Mattinson. By 1992 and 1997 the quantitative polling fieldwork was done by NOP (though Philip Gould, the party's strategy and polling adviser, conducted much of the party's focus group work himself), the impetus for the questionnaire content from Gould and from Stan Greenberg, an American pollster who had worked for the Clinton campaign in 1992 (but who lost the contract for the White House in 1996).[34]

The Tories first employed survey research in the 1958 Rochdale by-election, and in the early 1960s NOP were the Conservatives' pollsters, until Humphrey Taylor left NOP to found Opinion Research Centre (ORC, which later became Harris Research) with T.F. Thompson in 1965, with the Conservative Party as its first client. More recently the Conservatives made some use of Gallup Omnibus surveys, and have worked with the American pollster Richard Wirthlin, but at the 1997 election their polling was conducted by ICM. The Liberal Democrats, and their Liberal forerunners before them, have always had much smaller polling budgets (as, indeed, their budgets for their other campaigning functions are smaller than those of the two major parties). For the record,

---

[34] Moon, N., *Opinion polls: History, theory and practice* (Manchester: Manchester University Press, 1999).

MORI worked for 19 years for the Labour Party, and has worked for the Conservative Party (at the end of the eighties, as retained advisor to Richard Wirthlin, the Tories' pollster), Liberal Democrats, Greens, Referendum Party, UK Independence Party, Pro-Europe Conservative Party, Rainbow Alliance (which didn't pay their bill) and others through the years.

The Art of Asking Questions

Polls are a marriage of the Art of Asking Questions[35] and the Science of Sampling. The conduct of survey research is a pretty simple business really, all that needs to be done is to ask the right sample the right questions and add up the figures correctly, the latter task including proper analysis and reporting.

A good question should be relevant to the respondent, easily understood by the respondent, unambiguous in meaning and mean the same thing to the respondent, the researcher and the client for the results, relate to the survey objectives, and, added as an afterthought, not be influenced in any untoward way by the context of the questioning. (I say added as an afterthought, after seeing the *New Yorker* Magazine cartoon showing the burly Hun, armed with broadsword and clipboard, standing at the doorway of a peasant's hut, asking the question: 'Do you think Attila is doing an excellent job, a good job, a fair job or a poor job?' Little doubt as to the peasant's likely response!)[36]

There are ten basic rules of good questionnaire construction:

---

[35] Payne, S., *The Art of Asking Questions* (Princeton, NJ: Princeton University Press, 1953).

[36] Nor do such anxieties apply purely to fictional respondents in the *New Yorker*. During the run-up to the 1994 Mexican Presidential election (the first in that country to be extensively polled by independent pollsters after many years of one-party autocratic government), Dr Miguel Basáñez of MORI de Mexico carried out an experiment subsequently reported in the *New York Times* (12 June 1994). A total of 400 were interviewed in-street on their presidential preferences: 100 were told the interviewers represented the sponsor of the survey, the magazine *Este Pais*, 100 that they represented PRI, 100 PAN, and 100 PRD. (PRI, PAN and PRD being the three biggest parties.) The survey found extraordinary 'swing' depending upon who the respondent thought the pollster represented – as much as 18.5% when told the sponsor was the left-wing PRD.

1. Questions shouldn't be biased, but 'even-handed'. ('Do you support or oppose . . .?')
2. Questions shouldn't be 'two-handed'. ('Do you favour a rise in income tax and the rate of VAT?')
3. Questions shouldn't be loaded. ('In the light of the need to represent Britain's interests abroad, should the Royal Yacht be replaced?')
4. Questions shouldn't assume knowledge.
5. Questions shouldn't be leading. ('Some leading Church leaders oppose the ordination of women as priests. Do you favour or oppose . . .?')
6. Questions shouldn't be too complicated: avoid long prefaces or too many different answer categories.
7. Questions should be couched in every day language.
8. Questions shouldn't use pejoratives.
9. Questions should be asked in a neutral context.
10. Questions should not be ambiguous or vague.

My favourite question of all time, which I use in lectures on this subject, is from Gallup in 1937: '*Are you in favour of direct retaliatory measures against Franco's piracy?*' which in eleven words broke five of these fundamental rules[37] – it's a wonder that as many as 22% said 'no' to such a loaded question!

The Science of Sampling

The next job is to find a representative sub-section of the population to answer the questions. This in theory is a pure science, a merely mathematical exercise. But, of course, as well as getting the mathematics right we have to solve the practical problem of how we can get to put our questions to our mathematically perfect group. Our task is to select around 1,000, or 2,000, individuals from across the country whose views

---

[37] i.e. rules 1, 4 (Franco? Who he?), 7 ('retaliatory measures'), 8 ('piracy') and 10 (the 'retaliatory measures' again – one man's direct retaliatory action is a punch on the nose, another's a nuclear bomb).

will be in the same proportion as if we had been able to ask all the 40+ million adults in the country – in other words a 'representative sample'.

One of the questions we are most frequently asked is 'How can a sample of only 1,000 people be representative of the British public?' In 1992, a Gallup survey found that 63% thought that 'from a survey of 1000 or 2000 people', it is not 'possible to give a reliable picture of British public opinion'; probably this figure was somewhat inflated by the then-recent 1992 election, when the polls had appeared to fail to read the result correctly, but even in July 1988, 51% had been equally sceptical[58]. Wilhoit and Weaver explained how George Gallup himself used to answer that argument:

> 'George Gallup effectively uses the spoon of soup analogy to disarm sampling critics. He points out that with the proper stirring, a cook can taste just a spoonful to tell how the entire pot of soup is doing. Sampling is . . . a bit more complicated than preparing a good pot of soup, but the basic mechanics and ideas of sampling are easily within the grasp of reporters and editors.'[39]

A representative sample, as such, is perfectly possible in theory; our task is to find one in practice. Random sampling, also called probability sampling, is the simplest and 'purest' method and depends on, in theory, giving every single member of the 'universe' being sampled – in the case of an election poll, every single registered elector in the country – a mathematically equal chance of being interviewed. This could be done, for example, by systematically selecting names from the electoral register selecting every nth name, and sending somebody to interview them. Indeed, for some government surveys where time and cost are no object, this is effectively what happens (though these days it would be more usual to select addresses from the Postcode Address File (PAF) rather than names from the electoral register). If this is the case, it is a matter of relatively simple arithmetic to calculate the probability that the characteristics of the sample represent the characteristics of the whole population within any given margin of error.

---

[38] *Gallup Political and Economic Index*, Report 385 (September 1992).
[39] Wilhoit, G.C., and Weaver, D.H., *Newsroom Guide to Polls and Surveys* (American Newspaper Publishers' Association, 1980).

But absolutely pure random sampling is not normally a practical option. Imagine trying to interview a thousand adults scattered all over the country, many of them living miles from the nearest other person on the list. If you want to interview them face-to-face, an interviewer has got to physically get to their home. And what if they are out, or too busy to do the survey now? The interviewer will have to come back later, perhaps several times. And what if they just won't co-operate at all? We can't just leave them out or forget about them, because the people we can't contact or people who won't do the interviews might easily be alike in other ways – they might be older than average, or concentrated in remote parts of the country. Or they might all vote Conservative. If any of these are true, then a survey which ignores them will end with a skewed result.

There are various modifications that can be made to tackle these disadvantages. Most face-to-face random samples these days will be 'clustered', using a multi-stage random sample – instead of picking names at random from the whole country, we might first pick a random selection of parliamentary constituencies and then sample the population from them. That way, each of our interviewers could be sent to a single constituency with an equal number of names to interview, all within a practical geographical area. The sample might also be 'stratified' at any of its stages – we might divide up the constituencies by region, to ensure that our final selection represented all parts of the country fairly, and we might control for the result of the last election in each constituency, so that our sub-sample was politically representative. At the individual stage, we might break down the population into categories, for example age bands, based on our knowledge of how the population is really distributed, to make sure that all groups are accurately represented. And, finally, we will probably rely on 'weighting' to correct the effects of failure to contact our targeted respondents or their refusal to be interviewed: if, for example, more over 65s than any other age group wouldn't talk to us, we would compensate by upgrading the weight we give to the answers of the over 65s who did respond, so that in the final figures that age group would be reflected in its rightful size. All of these modifications would make our job easier; but all of them also increase the statistical margin of error.

The method of quota sampling, which has been used for most election polls in Britain in the last few decades, goes one step beyond this. It begins, like a highly stratified random poll, by dividing the population up into many small compartments, each to be measured separately with the final task being to put all the pieces together again to see the whole picture. In essence, quota sampling is an attempt to replicate the results of a well-designed random sample without all the inconveniences of the random method, and it rests on the idea that if the compartments are small enough it won't matter too much which individuals are picked because the overall result will be the same – instead of giving our interviewers a list of individuals to interview, we can simply tell them what type of people to interview, and leave the choice up to them. The details of course are a lot more complicated than that – we explain below exactly how the MORI quota sampling worked in 1997 – but the justification, empirical rather than theoretical, is that when the process has been carried out without obvious errors it has generally seemed to work.

This has been proved persistently over the years in elections. Perhaps the best test of the robustness of the quota polling method independent of an election (with its possibility of late swing) was at the time of the American bombing of Libya in 1986: three polls were conducted independently at about the same time by different polling organisations for different clients, with different sampling points, different interviewers, and different question wordings, but found virtually identical results.

For election polling, we have traditionally used quota sampling rather than random (probability) sampling. This is not because we have any inherent objection to probability samples as such; indeed, MORI does a substantial proportion of its survey research using probability samples. Nor is it, as some of our academic critics seem to think, because quota sampling is 'cheap'. It is because we believe that for the specific purpose of polling in a general election, probability samples are less, not more, effective than quota samples.

The principal reason is time. To achieve a reasonable response rate from a random sample is naturally time-consuming, needing repeated attempts to contact and interview some individuals. Probability samples given less than a week to conduct fieldwork rarely rise above a response rate in the fifties, in terms of the percentage successfully interviewed;

33

even three weeks' fieldwork gets samples in the low sixties, and the seventies is thought excellent by most government agencies. But we don't have one week, let alone three weeks, in an election. During the campaign, we are trying to take a snapshot that measures the voting intention of the electorate at a specific point in time, after the public has had the chance to react to one event or speech or broadcast and before another comes along to give a new stimulus – at MORI, most of our election polls will be completed in a single day from first interview to last (and being printed in the paper less than 24 hours later). This is even truer of the final, 'prediction' poll. Electors change their minds during an election campaign – after all, that is what campaigns are for – and to get the most up-to-date measurement so as to make the best prediction we need to interview as late as possible.

All the major national opinion polls in the 1992 election were quota samples interviewing face-to-face, in most cases in-street. In almost all cases the data from these polls were weighted, either to achieve more precise conformity with the quotas, or to introduce extra control variables. Up to the election of 1992, these methods had been universal among British pollsters for a number of years, and had achieved entirely satisfactory results. As we shall see, in 1992 something went wrong, and the question of what exactly had gone wrong became a dominant one in the 1997 election – not so much to the pollsters, for we were all confident that we had put our houses in order and were producing reliable results, but to the journalists who reported our polls and the editors who employed them – to say nothing of the party spin-doctors whose job, of course, was to be prepared to rubbish the polls as effectively as possible whenever it was in their party's interests.

Special problems raised by election polling

In election polling, finding the right question can be particularly hard. Of course, we ask the 'How do you intend to vote at the General Election?' question. But that doesn't by any means necessarily tell us what that voter will do – especially if polling day is still some time away. We are often, in effect, trying to predict how a respondent will vote when that respondent himself genuinely does not know, or when he thinks he knows but will later change his mind. What is worse, voting behaviour is a variable that is particularly strongly correlated with some of the forms of inadvertent bias most likely to be introduced into a poorly designed or conducted survey: availability and willingness to be interviewed, for example, are both highly correlated with likely voting behaviour – the groups of the public that these days are likeliest to be hard to get hold of or reluctant to agree to be polled tend to be disproportionately Conservative. In other words, if we don't get a perfectly representative sample of the public, that is quite likely to make a bigger difference in a voting poll than it would in, say, a survey of consumer behaviour. Finally, we are faced with the expectation that we achieve a level of accuracy in our measurement far more demanding than in any other function that the survey industry is ever asked to perform, and indeed more demanding than its statistical basis can possibly justify.

We should perhaps expand on this last point, because it gets to the essence of what election polls are for, and what we hope to achieve with them. The published opinion polls during an election are, almost invariably, commissioned by the news media to assist in their function of reporting the course of the election. It is not unrealistic to draw the analogy between the press coverage of an election and the coverage of a sporting event. (Indeed, if evidence were needed, take the case of the *Guardian* – the leading feature writer in their election coverage is Matthew Engel who, when he is not covering elections is the editor of Wisden, the Cricketer's Almanac.) The pollsters' part of this function is to give them the latest score, and perhaps other match statistics; but the function of our final poll, published on the morning of the election, is to allow our clients to print the final score on their front pages before the final whistle has been blown.

And the only tool with which we can do this, the opinion poll, is admittedly only as good as the vagaries of sampling allow. If all else goes perfectly, we can expect to be within 1% of the truth ten times out of twenty. Of the other ten times, nine times we will at least be within 3%[40]; but once in every twenty, on average, we will be further from

---

[40] This is what the hackneyed but simplistic '3% margin of error' actually means – that we expect

reality than 3%, what is often called a 'rogue poll'. (Note that there is nothing discreditable in producing a rogue poll – it is not a sign of incompetent polling as some critics might like to suggest, but an inevitable consequence of the inexorable laws of mathematics under which we operate. Without occasional rogue polls there can be no polls at all. The art is to learn to spot a rogue poll and discount it.)

We, the pollsters, admit these limitations – in fact, we cry them from the rooftops at every opportunity, because it serves nobody to exaggerate our capabilities. Unfortunately, the media have a tendency to ignore these limitations, brushing aside our protestations and hyping the findings in the interests of getting 'a good story'; and, if this leaves them with egg on their faces, the usual reaction next is to try to pass the blame on to the pollsters. As we shall see, these tendencies were exemplified in the elections of 1992 and 1997.

Polls are an expensive form of journalism. But there is no substitute for them. Yet that is no excuse for trying to portray them as what they are not. As David Butler and Richard Rose noted as long ago as 1959, 'What is also needed is a higher degree of education about the limitations and possibilities of the polls and perhaps more information and humility from some of their sponsors.'[41]

Fifteen years later, Rose, writing in *Britain at the Polls* in 1974 pointed out[42]:

'The chief conclusion that this writer would draw from the performance of the polls (and the press) is that there is need for fundamental rethinking about polls by those who sponsor them. Each newspaper editor currently sponsoring a poll should ask himself a simple question: Why am I doing this? If it is "to get tomorrow's news today", he should realise that the risks of getting the story wrong are real, especially at a time when the party system and the electoral system are not working as predictably as in the quarter-century since 1945.

---

our measurement to be within (plus or minus) 3% of the real figure 95% of the time – but usually closer than that, and 5% of the time further away.

[41] Butler, D. and Rose, R., *The British General Election of 1959* (London: Macmillan, 1960).

[42] Rose, R., 'The Polls and Election Forecasting in February 1974' and 'The Polls and Public Opinion in October 1974', in Penniman, H., (ed.), *Britain at the Polls* (Washington, DC: AEI, 1974), pp. 109–130, 223–239.

'Ironically, the press could provide more political information for its readers if it returned to the original concept of the polls as a device for assessing opinion, rather than for forecasting behaviour. An error margin of 3 or 5 percentage points is of little consequence if one wishes to ascertain how the country divides on matters of policy, or abortion. It is technically simple (and economically attractive) to take the results of a single poll and use them in several different stories reporting popular attitudes about issues of the day. In fact, before the surge of interest in forecasting polls, the now defunct *News Chronicle* published brief stories several times a week giving Gallup Poll reports of popular opinions about issues without regard to voting intention.'

Many responsible newspapers and journalists follow such precepts. To them we owe the data that follows, but others have yet to start the fundamental rethinking that Professor Rose recommended quarter of a century ago. If only the rest of the media, obsessed with the election-as-horserace idea, could follow the example of the enlightened few.

How do we do it?

Those are the principles. Let's look at how it actually works in a little more detail. To choose who we interview in MORI's political polls, we use a two-stage sampling method. First, we choose a number of randomly selected 'sampling points' (175 in our regular Omnibus, 85 in our *Times* election polls, 255 in our final *Times* poll), strictly defined geographical areas, chosen so that together their residents make up an accurate sample of Great Britain. The sampling points may be very small – in our *Times* election polls we used single census enumeration districts (EDs), typically consisting of a couple of hundred addresses at most. To each of those sampling points we send one of our trained interviewers, with a 'quota' – instructions about what sort of people to interview, how many men and how many women, how many in each age group, how many who own their homes and how many in council houses, and so on, to ensure that their group of respondents – 13 in each quota during the election – is representative of all the people who live in that locality. (Each interviewer has a different quota, individually tailored to the population characteristics of that particular area, which ensures that not only do we interview the right sort of people, but we do it in the right places.) The interviewer then finds the appropriate number of adults, as dictated by his or her quota, and interviews them – in their own homes. The questionnaire may be printed on paper, using the traditional pen and clipboard and with the interviewer faxing back the results to our data processors, where they are entered into the computer; or, increasingly these days, the questions may have been programmed into a hand-held computer (CAPI, computer-assisted personal interviewing) which guides the interviewer through the interview – the answers are entered directly as the interview proceeds, and at the end all the data can be sent back to the office by modem, ready for immediate analysis without needing to wait for the laborious process of typing the answers in from a paper questionnaire.

What are the questions? The political questions which fill this book come first, as soon as our 'respondents' have told the interviewer enough about themselves to ensure that they fit into the quota. All these questions, of course, have been discussed and agreed with our client. Then, in an Omnibus survey, there will follow other questions on a multitude of topics for other clients – some of which may later be published, others of which will remain confidential for the private information of the clients who commissioned them. In ad hoc election surveys, however – most of the surveys reported in this book – there were only election questions, and the questionnaires were fairly short (typically not taking more than five or ten minutes to complete).

Finally, the interviewer will ask the detailed demographic questions – everything from age to marital and work status, the number of cars in the household and which newspapers the respondent regularly reads. These have two purposes – they enable us to carry out detailed analysis of the answers to the other questions on the survey, so we can isolate or compare the opinions of, say, women with children or of *Mail on Sunday* readers; but they also give us information about the overall composition of our sample so that we can correct any imbalances and ensure that, as far as is practically possible, our survey really is representative of the entire British adult population. (This is achieved by 'weighting' – computer adjustment of the figures so that any given group of respondents contributes its proper share to the overall figures to reflect its size in the whole population.)

When the data has all come back to us in London, our computers whirr and spew out the collated results, and we pore over them checking for errors until we are entirely satisfied, and ring our client to tell him or her that we have the results. (Although often, especially in the heat of a election, the client will have already been ringing us to ask if by any chance we have the results yet, hours before we had said they could expect them!) Then comes a period of close liaison between the polling team and the journalist, squeezing out every last bit of juice from the data and ensuring that he or she has not inadvertently misinterpreted or misreported anything in the poll. In fact, as one of MORI's standard contractual conditions, we insist on seeing the actual copy and any graphics beforehand so we can check them word for word and figure for figure against the poll. At last the process is complete and the newspaper rolls off the presses – Thursday morning's papers, printed on Wednesday night and telling of a survey that may have done most of its interviewing on Tuesday evening, and conceivably with questions agreed only on the Monday.

(Indeed, at a pinch it can be done faster than that, especially by using telephone polling. In our series of snap reaction polls, for ITN *News at Ten*, we were agreeing questions in the early afternoon, our telephone arm On-Line Telephone Surveys was interviewing, and we were reporting back in time to broadcast the results that same evening. But such rushed methods are risky, less certain of finding an entirely representative sample in such a keyhole window of time, and we wouldn't want to rely on that alone for our final election prediction.)

Strategy: The Long Campaign
9 April 1992–16 March 1997

Measuring why do voters vote as they do

Elections are rarely won or lost in the four (or in 1997 six) weeks between the outgoing Prime Minister visiting the Queen to get permission for a dissolution and the moment when the last vote is cast to decide whether he or his opponent will return to Buckingham Palace to kiss hands and be commissioned to form a new ministry. Many voters, for sure – as we shall see – wait until the last minute before they finally make up their mind who they will support; but it is the impression that they have gained of the parties and their leaders, their policies and their abilities, in the months and years before that tend to be the determining factors for most voters, not the brief glitz of the Party Election Broadcasts or the manifesto promises that only a minority of voters will even bother to read, let alone put their trust in. In some elections, as in that of 1997, these long-term strategic factors are so overwhelming that an experienced eye can see them long in advance and predict the effect they are likely to have on voting behaviour. Once upon a time there was no way to measure such factors except by experience and educated guesswork. But in the modern political scene, the electors are being constantly polled, not only during an election but in 'peace-time' as well, and not only asked about voting intention but tested with questions covering a wide range of political factors.

The techniques of private polling: looking backward

Much of this polling is being done privately for the political parties, and the results may not be published for years (or they may be published only selectively, giving a misleading impression in the partisan interests of their owners.) But we have a second way to look behind the curtain of the private polls. MORI has conducted private polls in the past, but was not working for any of the major parties in 1997.

Many of those same techniques that we would have been using for the parties' private information were instead at the disposal of our media clients, notably *The Times*, and we can report to the public what we would have reported instead to Peter Mandelson or Brian Mawhinney – data probably similar to what they were actually getting from their pollsters.

One exception is the use of 'qualitative' research techniques or 'focus groups'. By their nature focus groups are more productive of ideas and indications than of solid fact (though they should not be despised for that reason); consequently they are rather less valuable to a journalist reporting the political scene than they would be to party strategist trying to manipulate it, and we weren't commissioned by any of our media clients to run focus groups for their benefit. Some of the newspapers commissioned focus groups from other polling firms during the election, but even at the best the reporting of these came over as not much more revealing than a well-presented vox pop. The parties were using these more productively. A *Private Eye* report of leaked focus group findings from the Conservatives' private polls shortly before the election gives a good idea of one of the established methods, use of projective techniques to help group members articulate their underlying ideas.

'This is according to the new breed of Tory number-crunchers who have abandoned the rigour of conventional polling for the psephological equivalent of astrology. Their system involves asking focus groups daft questions such as: "If John Major were a biscuit, what kind of biscuit would he be?"

'The prime minister turns out to be a Hob Nob – oaty, conventionally-English, a safe choice; while Blair is a Bath Oliver – a deeply pretentious biscuit; a toff trying to look plain. The Labour leader figured even lower in the public estimation when the researchers got into the bathroom. The question: "What kind of toilet paper do you think Tony Blair would use?" got the cynical reply: "He'd *say* he uses recycled, but he really uses Andrex." '[1]

---

[1] 'HP SAUCE: In the Tearoom', *Private Eye*, 7 March 1997.

Private Eye underestimates the potential value of this sort of research to an astute political strategist. Similar techniques could also have been used to broaden the media coverage of the election (rather than the way the *Financial Times*, in particular, did use them).

The Political Triangle

Rather than the use of qualitative (focus group) techniques, my research for the Labour Party in the six elections I worked for them was mainly quantitative ('opinion polls' in the normal sense). In the middle of the period running up to the February 1974 election, I developed a model of the British elector, reported in my book *British Public Opinion*[2], based on the belief that most people vote their values, learned at their parents' knee, from their friends and their workmates, from their teachers and their priests. Derived both from American polling experience and from Butler and Stokes' 1969 analysis of the British voter[3], it helped me to look beyond the individual questions pressed on me by individual members of Labour's National Executive Committee with axes to grind.

The model drove the questionnaire in the first panel base-line conducted for the party (data from which was later lodged together with panel recalls at the ESRC Archives at the University of Essex). It enabled the Party to see which groups would be moved by which messages in the run-up to the February 1974 election, used by the Labour leader to guide his own speeches, the selection of which Shadow Cabinet Minister to feature in party press conferences in the final week, which themes to focus on in Party Election Broadcasts and which messages to put forward in popular newspapers. Shades of Mandelsonian manipulation, over two decades before.

The model begins with the individual elector, and the forces impinging on his or her decision-making processes, determining whether or not the elector would vote and, if voting, which party to vote for. It

[2] Worcester, R., *British Public Opinion: A Guide to the History and Methodology of Political Opinion Polling* (Oxford: Basil Blackwell, 1991), pp 49–50.
[3] Butler, D. and Stokes, D., *Political Change in Britain* (London: Macmillan, 1969).

encompassed demographic and family factors, environmental consider-
ations, issues, direct party and indirect media pressures, and local factors
as well. It eventually postulated that all elections are won and lost not by
these people, many of whom are politically dedicated, or living in non-
marginal constituencies, or in most cases both. The people my client, the
Labour Party, was most interested in, or should have been, were those in
the electorate who were the 'swing' voters, or 'churners', who happened
to live in marginal constituencies, and who numbered no more, probably,
than one million voters. These I characterise as 'X', floating in the space
between the three sides of the triangle, like iron filings and a magnet,
attracted and repelled by their perceptions of the political parties' policies,
party image and leader image, and on balance, more influenced by image
in Britain today than by issues. It was first described by the equilateral
triangle, as shown overleaf (1979). Then the Falklands War showed me
how something could pull that triangle out of shape, into the isosceles
triangle represented by the 1983 model. This then evolved into a scoring
exercise, asking the public collectively what it was that focused their
minds at election time. This led to the 1987 model, and took in people's
values, the three-dimensional 1987 model adding weights derived from
survey findings of how the electorate judged for itself its relative
importance of the three factors – issues, leader image and party image –
and the 1992 tetrahedron.

The model not only forms the basis of any private polling that MORI
does, but provides the backbone of our public polling programme for
the media. Our principal polling series these days is sponsored by and
published in *The Times*: the basic questions (voting intention, leader
satisfaction, economic optimism and 'most important issues facing Britain') are carried monthly, together with a varying selection of extra
questions from month to month which may address the particular issues
of the day but also feature at regular intervals the key components of the
political triangle – leader image, party image and attitudes to the parties'
policies on salient issues. Thus we can present much the same analysis as
would be our basic starting point if we were working for one of the
parties, and we can track back attitudes right through the Parliament
from the moment in 1992 when the nation returned John Major to
office with a majority of 21.

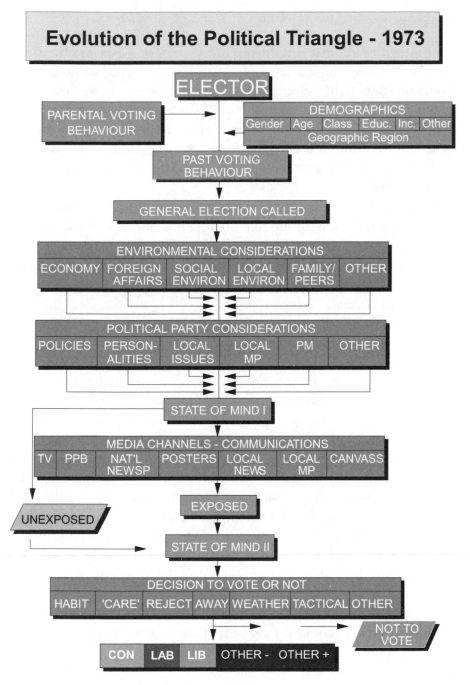

Figure 1: The MORI model of the British voter, 1973

Issues

The issues question that is tracked monthly in *The Times* asks the British public in an open-ended question, 'What would you say is the most important issue facing Britain today?', and follows up with a second question 'What do you see as other important issues facing Britain today?' and the answers are taken down, unprompted, on a code-frame on the interviewer's questionnaire. The time series is shown below (figure 4) going back over the period of this Parliament for the five leading issues.

To me, while this question is of historic interest, and looks at the entire electorate's view of the role of Britain in the world and problems the country faces, what is of political moment is which issues are most able to influence the individual's voting behaviour, for I believe that there are four conditions that must be met for an issue to become electorally important.

First, it must be salient to the voter; if you do not care about housing policy, then the best housing policy in the world will not affect the way you vote. Second, the voter must be able to perceive differences between the parties on the policies or issue which he or she feels important: even if a voter thinks that housing policy is the most important issue and rates it above all others in determining how he or she casts his or her vote, if there is nothing to distinguish one party's policy on housing from another, there is nothing to help that voter choose between parties at the ballot box. Third, the voter must feel that the party in power can do something about the issue: in 1983 the public overwhelmingly thought that unemployment was the most important issue, and that Labour was the party with the best policies on unemployment; but as well as believing the Labour Party incapable of governing, the public also thought that the problem of unemployment was a world-wide phenomenon, and beyond British political parties' capability of solving, so thought there was nothing the Labour Party, if in power, could do about it. Fourth, that the party in power *would* do something about the issue. Polls show that three people in four favour the banning of fox hunting with hounds. No one thinks that the Tory Party in Government would ever do anything about this

46

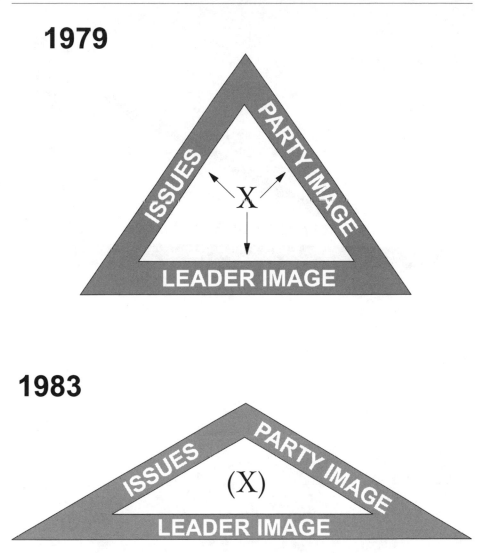

1979

1983

Figure 2: The evolution of the political triangle 1979–83

issue anyway, even though it might be salient to a number of voters, who perceive differences between the parties on the issue, and who know that the party in power could, if it wished, do something about the issue.

Therefore, we use a different question to determine the electoral impact of issues, asking 'What are the issues that are very important to

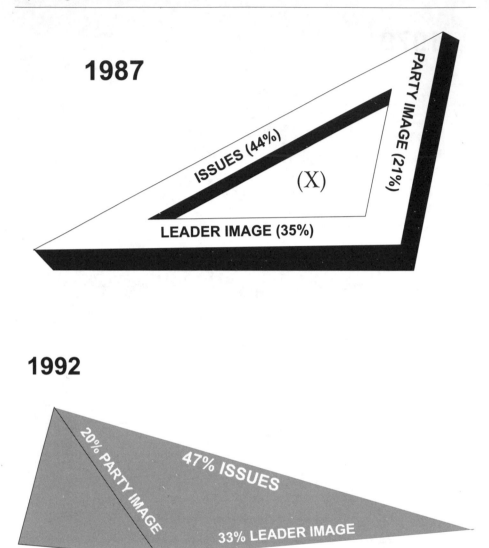

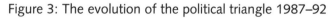

Figure 3: The evolution of the political triangle 1987–92

deciding how you will vote at the general election?', and then we go on to ask those who rate the issue as 'very important' which party has the best policy on that issue.

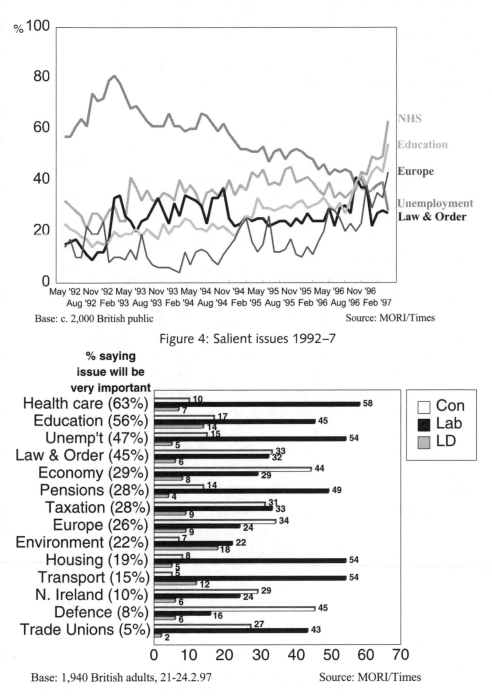

% 100

80

60   NHS

                                      Education

40   **Europe**

                                      Unemployment

20   **Law & Order**

0

May '92 Nov '92 May '93 Nov '93 May '94 Nov '94 May '95 Nov '95 May '96 Nov '96
    Aug '92 Feb '93 Aug '93 Feb '94 Aug '94 Feb '95 Aug '95 Feb '96 Aug '96 Feb '97

Base: c. 2,000 British public   Source: MORI/Times

Figure 4: Salient issues 1992–7

% saying issue will be very important

Health care (63%)

Education (56%)

Unemp't (47%)

Law & Order (45%)

Economy (29%)

Pensions (28%)

Taxation (28%)

Europe (26%)

Environment (22%)

Housing (19%)

Transport (15%)

N. Ireland (10%)

Defence (8%)

Trade Unions (5%)

☐ Con
■ Lab
▨ LD

0 10 20 30 40 50 60 70

Base: 1,940 British adults, 21-24.2.97   Source: MORI/Times

Figure 5: Best party on key issues, February 1997

49

Leader Image

Over the past decade, we have used factorial correspondence analysis, a multivariate analysis technique, put onto a 'perceptual map' to help us define the relative positions of the three party leaders on attributes both positive and negative which people in focus groups tell us are important about their leaders. In February 1990, the year she fell from office, Mrs Thatcher was seen as 'good in a crisis', but was thought by more people than thought so of the other two leaders, Neil Kinnock and Paddy Ashdown, as 'inflexible', 'narrow-minded', 'out of touch with ordinary people', and 'talks down to people'. No wonder that her party thought that if she were not replaced, they would lose the next election, so replace her they did.

John Major came into Downing Street in November of 1990, and the country was involved immediately in the Gulf War. By the following February, Major was seen as 'capable', 'good in a crisis' and 'has sound judgement'. At the time of his election, he announced he would eschew spin doctors and image makers, and that he would be seen as he really was and not what somebody made him up to be – 'I am what I am and people will have to take me as I am. Image makers will not take me under their tutelage.'[4] As the trends show, over time his image became much like Mrs Thatcher in trousers – except that he was thought neither 'capable' nor 'good in a crisis'. As the years went by, this image became more and more fixed in the minds of the electorate, and the coming and going of John Smith did little to change the basic perception that John Major might be a 'nice guy', but he hadn't captured the hearts and minds of his electors.

These became set in concrete during the last two years of his leadership of the country, and carried on right up to the eve of the election. The head of the planning staff at Number Ten, Norman Blackwell, saw these perceptual maps, as did Danny Finkelstein at Central Office, but dismissed them as irrelevant in the contest to come, when the

---

[4] John Major interview on BBC Radio Peterborough, November 1990, quoted in Jones, N., *Soundbites and Spin Doctors: How Politicians manipulate the Media – and Vice Versa* (London: Indigo), p 40.

innate conservatism of the British people, buttressed by the realisation of the sound economic management provided by the Conservative Government, and threatened by the twin terrors of the trade union bosses and constitutional change, would pull off the greatest recovery since the original Easter. They were, of course, deluding themselves. Later, Blackwell admitted he knew we were right; Finkelstein still lives in hope.

Party Image

The third dimension of the Political Triangle is the image of the party as fit to govern, a good team, etc., which again we illustrate with perceptual mapping. There too the Tories were in deep trouble, going back to the beginning of the decade. They began as 'professional in its approach' with a 'good team of leaders' and was a party that 'kept its promises'. Having said that, it was also seen as 'too dominated by its leader', 'out of touch with ordinary people' and perhaps too 'extreme'. By contrast, the Kinnock-led Labour Party was a 'divided party' (and divided parties don't win British elections), was seen as 'willing to promise anything to win votes', but was 'concerned about people in real need', 'looks after the interests of people like us' (a powerful supporting image for a party to have), and was felt to 'understand the problems facing Britain'.

Year by year the Conservatives lost its positive attributes and hardened the perception the public had of the negatives, until only the negatives were left. Yet the Party continued in its sleepwalking towards the Labour landslide that was to come, oblivious of the obvious and doing little to repair the evident damage. They seemed not to have heard that politics is about perception, and it was the management of their perceptions that was lacking. They should have known of the sayings of the first Century slave-philosopher Epictetus: 'Perceptions are truth, because people believe them'.

Even up to the very month before the election began, the image of the Conservative Party was all negative, and yet Prime Minister, Deputy Prime Minister and Party Chairman convinced themselves, or at least whistled a merry tune, that suggested they did not foresee what was to

51

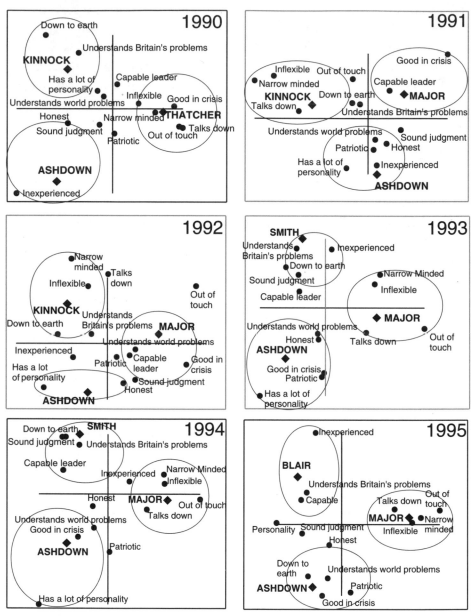

Base: c. 2,000 adults 18+ each February
Source: MORI/The Times

Figure 6: Leader Image 1990–5

befall them. Time and time again one or the other would rubbish the polls, saying 'we beat them in 1992, and we'll beat them again'.

How the election was lost before 1997: four predictions

I'd done my sums in the summer of 1995 in preparation for a speech to the Sunday night fringe meeting of the Liberal Democrats in Glasgow that September. The electoral arithmetic had been clear for years. The 'core vote' for the Labour Party, tested nearly to destruction in 1983, was 30%. In that election, the Labour Party had presented the worst regarded leader with the most unpopular policies, especially on unilateral nuclear disarmament, with a party divided and thought incapable of governing, and still got 28%. The 'core vote' for the Tories was 30%, again to be tested nearly to destruction in 1997, with an even less popular leader, even more unpopular policies, and a party conspicuously divided over Europe, and in the event they got 31%. The 'core vote' for other parties including the Liberal Democrats, Liberals, Liberal SDP Alliance, Nationalists, Greens etc., was around 20%, tested in the Euro-Parliamentary elections of 1989, when with the Liberals and the SDP in the process of divorce, the Greens got 15% of the vote, and other parties including the few votes that year for the Liberals, added to just over 20%. Thus 80% or so, perhaps plus or minus 5%, of the aggregate electorate's votes are predetermined by their unchanging values, or by habit, custom, conviction, and inertia with the present first-past-the-post system of voting, leaving 20%, or say between 15% and 25% of those who vote, to play for in the run-up to and during the election campaign.

Seeing that the standing of the parties in the third quarter of 1995 was 26% Conservative, 56% Labour, 14% Liberal Democrat (remarkably similar to now), I tried to think what was driving the minds of the electorate, and concluded that despite its economic performance, the twin errors that John Major's Government was making – complacently relying on improving economic performance and failing to transfer responsibility for Maastricht from the Cabinet to the people via a referendum – would prove fatal to its chances of re-election. There was

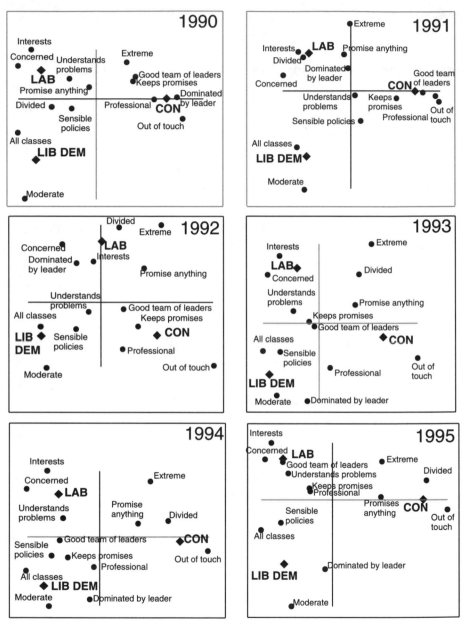

Base: c. 2,000 adults 18+ each year
Source: MORI/The Times

Figure 7: Party Image 1990–5

Party Image - Sept 1996

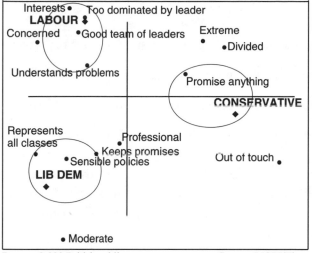

Base: c. 2,000 British public   Source: MORI/Times

Leader Image - Oct 1996

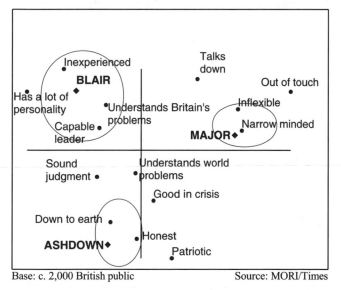

Base: c. 2,000 British public   Source: MORI/Times

Figure 8: Party and Leader Image, Autumn 1996

little sign of recovery. What many people wanted was the Government out of office and John Major replaced as Prime Minister.

At that Liberal Democrats' conference meeting, more than a year-and-a-half before polling day, I made four predictions about the coming election:

- **That the general election would be held on 1 May 1997;**

- **That it would be the lowest turnout since the War;**

- **That the Liberal Democrats would do well, not badly**, and

- **That the Conservative deficit against Labour would narrow**, I thought to about six per cent, but that Labour would still win by what then I described as 'a landslide'. I thought then that the Labour majority would be about 41, which on historic terms would have been described as a 'Labour landslide', of proportions second only to those of Attlee's 1945 victory.

On the first three of my predictions, I was dead right, on the fourth partially so – the deficit did narrow (to about only half of what the polls were showing that autumn), but not nearly as much as I expected, and Blair's eventual victory was a landslide on anybody's terms. (Professor Anthony King on the BBC on election night said it was more like 'an asteroid hitting the planet and destroying practically all life on Earth', a comment he then quoted in *New Labour Triumphs*, shyly attributing it to 'one television pundit'.[5]) At the same time I also made a fifth prediction, concerning what would happen after the election – to which we shall return later (p. 252).

What was I basing my predictions on? I expected that the general election would be held on 1 May 1997, because there was nothing in my crystal ball that would improve the Government's standing with the electorate sufficiently to put them back in the lead, and they would have to play for time, their mandate running out on 22 May 1997. With local government election day being fixed on 1 May, they would be forced to

---

[5] King, A., 'The Night Itself', in King A. (ed.), *New Labour Triumphs: Britain at the Polls* (Chatham, NJ: Chatham House, 1998), p. 1.

go then, and probably not before unless they had just given up. John Major's character would not allow that.

I expected a low turnout because many 1992 Conservative Party supporters wanted to see the Government defeated and John Major replaced. As they would see from the state of the polls closer to the day that that was likely to happen, they would realise that to get the outcome they wanted they did not have to vote against their core beliefs and values, which remained conservative. They could safely stay at home (especially if they lived in safe seats where their vote would only be a gesture anyway). Further, for the same reason that some would stay at home, others would vote for the Liberal Democrats as they learned that the vote for the Liberal Democrat in Con-LibDem marginals was the most effective way to get what they desired, the Government out of office and John Major replaced as Leader of the Conservative Party.

I also reasoned that once reluctant Tories saw from the polls that they could, after all, still vote for their local Tory candidate without risking the re-election of John Major's Government, many would decide after all to do so – hence the gap in the polls would narrow. It did, a little. But I wasn't reckoning with the Tories reinforcing rather than weakening their image of being the most divided party this century, over Europe, and of being the party of sleaze, or with their having the most haplessly-run campaign since Labour's 1983 debacle.

It wasn't really until the Wirral South by-election (27 February 1997) that I realised that the polls weren't going to narrow so much, and that a ten-point win rather than six was in the offing, and I upped my forecast to an overall majority for Labour of 81. This was my position going into the election, and the position of the average of the Reuters' panel of pundits, academic onlookers and poll pickers and psephologists (see below, p. 215). Little did I know then that the election would be called early, with the hope of the Prime Minister that he would be able to launch the campaign surfing the good economic news in its first week and reduced unemployment rates as well; little did he know that his first fortnight's strategy was to be swamped in sleaze (followed immediately by the decision of that grand strategist of the Tory Party to send a man dressed in a chicken suit out to peck at the heels of Tony Blair, the nadir episode in British politics) as the Hamilton/Bell Tatton constituency was to become the 'Jennifer's

Ear' of the 1997 election campaign, and dominate the news for three-and-a-half weeks of the six-and-a-half week campaign.

How had the Tories got themselves to this low ebb by 1995? They had already made four crucial mistakes.

Table 1: The Long Campaign 1992–7

1992
April
• General election – Conservative majority of 21
July
• Danish referendum on Maastricht votes against
• John Smith elected Labour leader
• First sex scandal allegations against David Mellor
August
• British troops sent to Bosnia
September
• 'Black Wednesday': pound forced out of ERM and devalued
• David Mellor resigns
• French referendum on Maastricht narrowly in favour
• EC foreign ministers agree to ratify Maastricht
October
• Closure of 31 coal mines announced
• British troops in Croatia
November
• Commons passes Maastricht paving motion
• Scott enquiry into Matrix Churchill affair set up
December
• Emergency EC summit in Edinburgh to resolve doubts over Maastricht treaty

1993
January
• Start of Single European Market
• Bank base rates cut to 6% (lowest since 1977)
February
• Inflation rate falls to 1.7% (lowest since 1968)
• Duke of Westminster resigns Tory whip over leasehold reform proposals
March
• Government defeat in Maastricht debate
• Budget: some taxes raised, VAT extended to domestic fuel
May
• Asil Nadir flees to Northern Cyprus
• Newbury by-election (28% swing to Lib Dems, Tory vote halved) and County Council elections (Tories lose control of 15 councils, retain only 1)
• Second Danish Referendum on Maastricht votes in favour
• Norman Lamont sacked. Kenneth Clarke Chancellor, Michael Howard Home Secretary

June
- In the Lords, Lady Thatcher says she would never have signed Maastricht treaty
- Michael Mates resigns over links with Asil Nadir

July
- Government defeated in Commons after 23 Tory MPs rebel over Maastricht Bill
- Major's 'Bastards' comment leaked
- Christchurch by-election (35% swing to Lib Dems – highest against Tories since WW2)

August
- UK ratifies Maastricht treaty
- Emergency meeting of EC finance ministers effectively suspends ERM

September
- *The Times* cuts its cover price to 30p, beginning the newspaper price war
- Labour conference re-affirms commitment to Clause Four but accepts One Member One Vote

October
- Major's 'Back to Basics' speech at Tory conference

November
- Maastricht comes into force: EC becomes EU
- Government admits clandestine negotiations with IRA
- First 'unified' Budget

December
- MPs vote to allow Sunday Trading
- Downing Street Declaration on Anglo-Irish agreement

1994
January
- Tim Yeo resigns (sex scandal)
- Alan Duncan resigns (controversial housing deal)
- Earl of Caithness resigns (domestic scandal)
- District Auditor charges Westminster City Council Tories with gerrymandering
- Arms deal over Pergau dam revealed
- David Ashby resigns (gay sex allegations)

February
- Death of Stephen Milligan in bizarre sexual circumstances
- Hartley Booth resigns (sex scandal)

March
- UK accepts compromise reducing national veto power in EU Council of Ministers: Tony Marlow calls on Major to resign

May
- Local Government elections (Tories lose over 400 seats and 18 councils)
- Michael Brown resigns (gay sex scandal)
- Channel tunnel opens
- Death of John Smith

June
- European Parliament elections (Tories 29% of vote) and Eastleigh by-election (21% swing to Lib Dems)
- Austria votes to join EU

- UK vetoes Jean-Luc Dehaene as EU President at Corfu summit
- Germany bans British beef

July
- DTI confirms it is investigating Lord (Jeffrey) Archer over insider trading allegations
- Graham Riddick and David Tredinnick accused of accepting 'Cash for Questions' in *Sunday Times* entrapment
- Jacques Santer unanimously approved as EU President
- Cabinet reshuffle: Gillian Shephard replaces John Patten at Education, Michael Portillo Employment Secretary, Jeremy Hanley becomes Party Chairman
- Blair and Prescott elected Labour leader and deputy leader

August
- IRA announces cease-fire

October
- Blair tells Labour conference of plans to change Clause Four
- Finland votes to join EU, Norway votes against
- Loyalist paramilitaries in Northern Ireland declare cease-fire
- Tim Smith resigns over 'Cash for Questions' payments from Mohammed al Fayed
- Neil Hamilton resigns over similar allegations. Nolan Committee appointed.
- Jonathan Aitken accused over payment of bill at Paris Ritz

November
- Government drops plans to privatise Post Office
- High Court rules Pergau dam deal illegal
- Cedric Brown (British Gas Chief Executive) reported to have been given 75% pay rise
- Sweden votes to join EU
- Whip withdrawn from 8 Tory Euro-rebels after confidence vote on EU bill; another MP resigns the whip in protest
- Budget: VAT on fuel to be increased

December
- Government defeated on budget proposal to raise VAT on fuel
- Dudley West by-election: 29% swing to Labour

1995
January
- Austria, Sweden and Finland join EU

February
- Allan Stewart resigns (violence at a demonstration)
- Charles Wardle resigns (EU immigration policy)
- Baring's Bank collapses

March
- Robert Hughes resigns (sex scandal)

April
- Scottish Local Elections (Tories win 81 of 1,159 seats)
- Richard Spring resigns
- Jonathan Aitken issues libel writ against the *Guardian* and Granada TV
- Two Tory MPs suspended from Commons over Cash for Questions
- Whip restored to 8 Tory Euro-rebels
- Controversy over decision to spend £13m of lottery money to buy Churchill papers
- Labour membership vote to amend Clause Four

May
- Local Elections (Tories lose 1,800 seats and 59 councils)
- First report of Nolan Committee
- Perth & Kinross by-election (SNP gain from Tories on 12% swing)

June
- Major resigns to fight election as party leader, Redwood resigns to fight Major

July
- Major re-elected leader
- In Cabinet reshuffle, Michael Heseltine deputy PM, Malcolm Rifkind Foreign Secretary, Brian Mawhinney Party Chairman.
- Littleborough & Saddleworth by-election (Tories fall to third place)

October
- Alan Howarth crosses the floor to join Labour
- Michael Howard controversially sacks Derek Lewis, director-general of Prison Service
- Budget: 1p income tax cut

November
- Sir James Goldsmith launches Referendum Party

December
- Emma Nicholson defects from Tories to Liberal Democrats

1996

January
- Labour's all-women shortlists declared illegal

February
- First privatised rail services begin
- Canary Wharf bomb – end of IRA cease-fire
- Scott Report on Arms to Iraq published and debated
- Peter Thurnham resigns Tory whip to sit as Independent
- Mortgage rates lowest since 1965

March
- Government admits link between BSE and CJD. EU bans all British beef exports.

April
- Staffordshire South East by-election – 22% swing to Labour

May
- Local elections (Tories lose over 500 seats)
- District Auditor declares Westminster Council Tories guilty of using public money for gerrymandering, and surcharges them £31m
- Britain adopts policy of obstructing EU business to get beef ban lifted

June
- Rod Richards resigns (sex scandal)
- David Davis denies reports that he offered to resign over Europe policy differences

July
- Labour launches 'pre-manifesto' with five pledges
- David Heathcote-Amory resigns over Europe

October
- Lord McAlpine defects from Tories to Referendum Party
- Peter Thurnham takes LibDem whip

November
- Budget. 1p cut in income tax. Budget details leaked to *The Mirror*.

December
- David Willetts resigns for misleading standards committee

1997

January
- Jerry Hayes denies gay relationship
- Gordon Brown announces Labour will stay within Tory spending limits for two years
- Sir George Gardiner deselected as candidate; he subsequently defects to Referendum Party

February
- Wirral South by-election – 17% swing to Labour, as predicted by constituency polls

17 March: Election date announced as 1 May 1997

The loss of the economic talisman

The first strategic error, even before the 1992 election, was entering the European Exchange Rate Mechanism (ERM) at an impossible exchange rate, which led inevitably to 'Black Wednesday', 16 September 1992. After a frantic but vain (and expensive) attempt to shore up the position, Major and Chancellor Lamont were forced to let sterling plummet out of the ERM, showing up the Treasury backed by the entire might of the British economy as being less potent on the international markets than George Soros (and filling the Soros pockets accordingly). This humiliation, just five months into the parliament, damaged any chance the government might have had of making political capital on the basis of economic recovery.

Yet the Conservatives persisted in assuming that achieving a strong economy was the trump card that would swing the votes to them – economic determinism – and prove the polls wrong. Led by Michael Heseltine, many expected, or so they said, that a grateful British public would reward them for their cautious, and successful, management of the economy. 'When did the British voting not follow economic optimism?' they asked; 1 May 1997 was the answer.

MORI measures the EOI or Economic Optimism Index ('consumer confidence' or 'feel-good factor') monthly. EOI had risen sharply in the last few months before each election since the Tories came to power,

Table 2: Economic performance and 'time for a change'

Q. Which of the statements on this card comes closest to your own views?

	%
The Government has built strong foundations for Britain's economic recovery, and they deserve to win the election	20
The Government has built strong foundations for Britain's economic recovery, but at this election it is time for change	28
The Government has failed to build a strong economy, but they deserve to win the election	5
The Government has failed to build a strong economy. At this election it is time for change	38
None of these	4
Don't know	6

Source: MORI/*The Times*
22 April 1997
Base: 1,133 British adults

and this encouraged them to think that the economy had the potential to help them again, if they could harness their fortunes to it. In most past elections a rise in the EOI tended to go with a rise in the Government's popularity in the opinion polls, and vice-versa; in statistical terms, there was a high correlation between the two variables.

In the six months preceding the 1997 election, by contrast, there was a *nil* correlation. In the event, as in past elections, the EOI *did* rise — from −9 in December 1996 to +13 the weekend before the election, peaking at +28 (a record) a fortnight after Labour's victory. But it didn't help the Tories at the polls; other factors pertained. One possible hypothesis is that the EOI rose during the run up to the election because the public anticipated a Labour victory.

The Conservatives persisted in assuming that achieving a strong economy was the trump card that would swing the votes to them and prove the polls wrong. In fact, it never worked for them. Perhaps the single most revealing question MORI put to the electorate during the 1997 campaign coupled the assessment of the Tories' economic perform-ance with whether they deserved to win the election.

A majority of those who had an opinion, 48% of the total, agreed 'The Government has built strong foundations for Britain's economic recovery'. Remember, 43% of the vote would probably have been

Table 3: The government and the economy

Q. **On balance do you agree or disagree with the following statements?**

	Agree	Disagree	Don't know
In the long term, this government's policies will improve the state of Britain's economy	36%	47%	17%
Labour would do a better job of running the economy than the Conservatives	42%	35%	23%
The Conservative Government has been responsible for the recent improvements to the state of the economy	42%	42%	16%

Source: MORI/*Independent on Sunday/Sunday Mirror*
2–3 April 1997
Base: 1,069 British adults 18+

enough to return the Tories with a fingertip majority. Yet far fewer than half of those who agreed the government deserved credit for economic performance would go on to agree they deserved to be re-elected; the majority still thought it was 'time for a change'. That was result alone was enough to ensure the Tories were doomed.

We found similar results in our panel survey for the *Independent on Sunday* and *Sunday Mirror* a couple of weeks earlier (2–3 April). Respondents were evenly divided on whether the Tories were responsible for an improvement in the economy. Furthermore, they did not hold unrealistic expectations of Labour: although more thought they would do a better job than disagreed, the margin was narrow.

But their confidence in the future under the Tories was much shakier – only 36% thought the Tory economic policies were good for the country in the long term, while 47% disagreed. Perhaps they were heeding the mandatory warning of the share adverts, that past performance is not necessarily a guide to future performance? Most revealingly of all, however, while prepared to accept that the Conservatives were responsible for a strong economy, that same sample preferred Blair to Major by 39% to 27% as most capable Prime Minister, and expected to vote Labour rather than Conservative by 55% to 30%. Three weeks later, when we re-interviewed the panel, they had swung still further away.

The evolution of this situation could be clearly seen in MORI's regular monthly polls during the previous parliament. There was little correlation between the Economic Optimism Index (EOI or 'Feel-Good Factor') and either the Conservative share of the electorate's support or its lead (deficit) over Labour in the last few months before the election. While in prior contests the EOI has been highly correlated with voting intention, after 'Black Wednesday' the relationship entirely broke down. This led to the conspicuous failure of the Government's economic standing with the electorate, from which they never recovered.

In fact, the Tories' faith in economic determinism should already have been shaken, for it wasn't that which snatched them victory in 1992. Conventionally, we measure the strength of the relationship between two variables such as voting lead and EOI by the crude index of correlation, r^2 (R-squared). In 1983, with the Falklands War a recent memory, nevertheless the r^2 between the EOI and the Conservatives' lead over Labour was 0.45, that is 45% of the variation in the electorate's voting intention in the six months leading up to the election could be explained by the 'feel-good factor'. In 1987, it was no less than 90%. In 1992 however, it was only 6%, and in 1997, less than 2%.

This is not to suggest that there was no correlation between EOI and voting intention at any time during the Parliament, but it was not a consistent one. As the chart shows, a regression run over the whole five years finds nil correlation. The old relationship had broken down, and a new relationship took time to re-establish itself. The break coincides closely with Black Wednesday, and it is not unreasonable to suppose that might be the cause (though so much else was simultaneously going wrong for the government that September that it would not be entirely implausible to ascribe it to other causes, or simply to the combination of events). But over the period from January 1995 to October 1996, the correlation was almost as strong as it was in the mid-eighties, with 65% of the voting intention lead (or, rather, deficit) explicable in terms of changes in economic optimism. But this relationship disappeared again when the Tories needed it, in the last six months before the election.

However, there is more to understanding the value of that relationship to the Tories than the simple correlation indices. The first point to note is that the EOI has risen sharply in the last few months before each election since the Tories came to power, and indeed this was true again

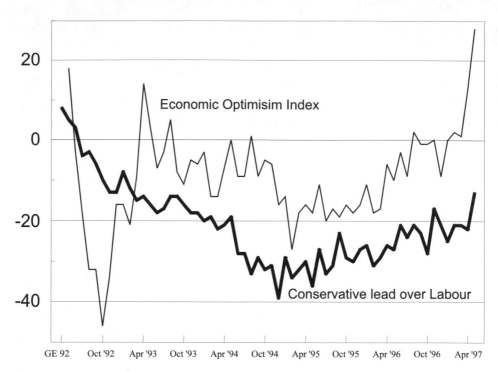

Figure 9: Correlation of voting intention with economic optimism 1992–7

in 1997; this meant that the EOI had the potential to help the Tories, if they could harness their fortunes to it.

Equally important is the nature of the relationship between the two variables – in technical terms, the regression equation that can be derived from them, how much the Conservative lead can be expected to rise for each percentage point improvement in the EOI. In 1987, the regression co-efficient was 0.4999 – in other words, for every one point improvement in the EOI the Tories could expect a half-point improvement in their lead over Labour. In 1992 it had been much lower, only 0.099, so that they needed a ten-point improvement in the EOI to achieve a one point improvement in the lead; not much use even if the r^2 of the relationship had been high (it wasn't). Between January 1995 and October 1996, the coefficient was 0.47, almost as high as in 1987 – apparently very encouraging.

The difficulty was that the Tories were starting from a much lower base, and needed a bigger improvement in the lead to get on level terms.

In 1987 the equation predicted that the Tories and Labour would be neck-and-neck if the EOI was no worse than −8, and a positive EOI would give the Tories a working majority. In 1995–6, by contrast, the equation predicted that the EOI needed to reach +46 simply for the Tories to reach parity with Labour, yet the highest our monthly figure had ever reached since we started measuring it in 1979 was +23. Much less hopeful! Then, on top as that, as we have seen, the correlation broke down in the last six months anyway – the Feel-Good Factor was not going to win John Major the election.

In the event, as in past elections the EOI *did* rise – from −9 in December 1996 to +13 the weekend before the election, peaking at +28 a fortnight after Labour's victory. The MORI Financial Services 'Mood of the Nation' Index, which is indexed on April 1993=100 and takes into account actual unemployment and fear of redundancy as well as economic optimism, also rose throughout the first half of 1997, reaching record heights after the election. But it didn't help the Tories.

In fact, if we look behind the figures we can see why. Until the last few months before the election, those expecting the economy to improve in the next year were predominantly Tories (as is usual – it is supporters of the government that have most confidence in it.) But in the last few months this changed – now Labour supporters were as optimistic as Tories! Why? Because even the Tories didn't really trust their government to improve things further, but Labour's confident hordes anticipated victory at the polls and economic recovery brought about by their own, Blair government.

Divisions over Europe

Next came the refusal of a referendum over the Maastricht treaty. If the Prime Minister, Chancellor and Foreign Secretary had transferred responsibility for the decision to sign Maastricht from themselves to the people, they could have avoided the awful divisions that tore the Tory Party apart. Time after time I argued they should. John Major said he couldn't get it through the Cabinet. Canny Ken Clarke asked 'How do you know we'd win?'. Douglas Hurd wrote to me to say that to consult

Table 4: Public attitudes to the Maastricht treaty

Q. Do you think the Government should or should not hold a public referendum on whether to agree the Maastricht treaty or not?

Q. If there were such a referendum, would you vote for or against the ratification of the Maastricht treaty?

	5–6 Jun 1992 %	10–13 Jun 1992 %	14–15 Sep 1992 %	17–19 Sep 1992 %	20 Oct 1992 %	23–27 Oct 1992 %	11–15 Dec 1992 %	5–6 Feb 1993 %	25–29 Mar 1993 %	20–24 May 1993 %	11–12 Jun 1993 %
Yes, should hold	75	71	61	71	72	66	67	73	67	67	73
No, should not hold	20	18	16	19	17	18	16	16	17	15	18
Don't know	5	11	23	10	11	16	17	11	16	18	9
Vote for	34	35	24	26	24	26	25	30	27	28	31
Vote against	39	30	22	44	40	37	34	36	35	32	42
Neither/don't know	27	35	54	30	36	37	41	34	38	40	28

Source: MORI
Base: c. 1,000 or c. 2,000 British adults in each survey

the public in a referendum was 'not done'. A referendum would have been popular enough, most of the public were demanding one – never fewer than three in five in our polls over the period (see table). But its real value would have been in the chance for amicable settlement between opposed cabinet factions.

Part of the difficulty the Tories might have had in winning a Maastricht referendum must be attributed to the failure of the EC itself to properly manage public opinion in their 'selling' of Maastricht. The Treaty was complex, obtuse, in parts unreadable, with little thought for how it would 'play in Peoria' and apparently no consideration for the adoption process to ensure its passage, ignoring its impact on public opinion. Certainly no-one that was aware of the findings of Eurobarometer (the European Commission's own regular poll) or who had read my 1989 article in the *European Business Journal*[6] would have chosen Denmark, even more reluctant Europeans than the out-of-step British, in which to test the water! No wonder the first referendum result was a defeat for the Danish Government and for the 'managers' of Maastricht.

Contrast the 'a-management' (as opposed to 'mismanagement') of the

---

[6] Worcester, R., 'The attitudes of Europeans to the European Community', *European Business Journal*, volume 1, number 4 (Autumn 1989).

Maastricht referendum exercise to the careful manipulation of British trade union ballots in the previous decade, when Mrs Thatcher's government's forced on a reluctant union movement the requirement for them to ballot their members to retain the right to have a political levy. (Sauce for Mrs Thatcher's goose certainly not the sauce for her gander when consulting the public!) What happened was that the Labour Party and the TUC and individual powerful trade union barons connived to set up group of Labour-supporting trade unionists, the Trade Union Co-ordinating Committee (TUCC) under the chairmanship of Larry (now Lord) Whitty, later to become General Secretary of the Labour Party. This group ensured that the ballots were held first in those trade unions where support for the political levy was highest, to ensure that when the more reluctant memberships were polled they were eighth, ninth, or later in the queue, after resounding majorities had been recorded, and widely publicised, from the more enthusiastic, compliant and political unions. The parallel would have been for the 'managers' of the Maastricht process to have organised themselves to obtain early victories from the countries known to be the most pro-Maastricht, most in favour of European expansion and transfer of sovereignty, perhaps Ireland, Portugal, Netherlands, Luxembourg. How much might that have improved Major's chances of selling it to the British people as well?

Even so, they might have won it. In June 1992, when MORI first measured Europe-wide attitudes to Maastricht for *The European*, the British then were marginally in support, 54% to 46%, leaving aside the 'don't knows'. This was still the case in mid September, just before 'Black Wednesday', but in a poll taken for *The Times* in its immediate aftermath that memorable week, MORI found a huge swing against ratification of the Treaty, 62% opposed it and 38% were in favour. Opposition then widened so that by the end of September some 68% were opposed. By the end of October the balance was still opposed, but had moderated to 59% opposed, 41% in favour. The Eurobarometer figures (after reallocating the undecideds in proportion to those expressing a view) matched those tracked by MORI.

But Major decided not to take the risk, and instead had to take the responsibility for the decision, and the consequences. From that point on, the atmosphere in the Conservative party quickly deteriorated.

69

Before long, Major was incautiously referring in public to some of his own cabinet ministers as 'bastards', and nine of his MPs submitted to losing the party whip rather than toe the Euro-tolerant line (technically depriving the government of its overall majority).

As already explained, we regularly measure the public's perception of party image, asking them which of a list of descriptions (some positive, some negative) fit their impressions of each party. Survey by survey from the late eighties the Conservatives lost their positive attributes and hardened the perception the public had of the negatives, until only the negatives were left. Perhaps most damaging of all these attributes is the perception of being 'divided'. Divided parties don't win British elections. Between July 1992 and late September 1992, the period over which the Maastricht issue blew up, the proportion identifying the Tories as divided doubled from 17% to 34%. By July 1993, it hit 50% and never dropped back below 40% in the next four years before the election.

Yet, though Europe was the cause, Europe in itself was not an election winning or losing issue: it simply wasn't important enough to enough voters. When we asked electors, in July 1995, which issues (from a list) they thought would be very important to them in deciding which party to vote for, two-thirds picked 'health care' and more than half 'education'; fewer than one in five said Europe would be very important, and of those that did only a quarter thought the Tories had the best policies on Europe. Over the next two years, with Europe and the Tories' divisions over the question frequently in the news, the position got no better: by the time of the election, a quarter of electors thought it was an important issue but only one in five of them thought the Tories had the best policies.

In fact, the Tory image on Europe was so ambivalent that it could hardly have helped them even if it had been higher on the agenda. A recent article by Geoffrey Evans in the *British Journal of Political Science*[7], analysing data from the British Election Panel Study on perceptions of the parties in 1996, showed that people who perceived the Conservatives as anti-European tended to themselves be pro-European, while those

---

[7] Evans, G., 'Euroscepticism and Conservative Electoral Support: How an Asset Became a Liability', *British Journal of Political Science*, Volume 28 Part 4 (October 1998), pp 573–90.

who perceived the party to be pro-European were more likely to be anti-European[8]. (Neither of the other parties had the same handicap.) The divisions on Europe had not simply made it harder to exploit the issue but had actually turned it into a more dangerous one.

Had the referendum on Maastricht been held, it would not have saved the Tories from defeat. But it might have spared them the humiliation of a 179 Labour majority.

The swamp of sleaze

If Black Wednesday was a failure of economic management and party divisions on Europe one of political management, Major's third failure was essentially one of image management. The issue was 'sleaze'. Serious as some of the allegations against individual MPs and ministers were, its real impact was one of image. Senior ministers were not implicated personally. Nobody questioned the probity of Major or Heseltine, Rifkind or Clarke. But they were smeared by association and made ridiculous by their colleagues (and in Major's case by his having appointed those colleagues). Sleaze was the keynote of the 1992–7 Parliament, and the damaging issue which the Tories found it hardest to shrug off. But in electoral terms, this was almost a phoney war. Sleaze as such probably swung few votes outside Tatton (see below). Laurel and Hardy once made a film entitled 'The Battle of the Century'. The first reel suggested it would be a boxing picture, but the title had nothing to do with boxing. Like the Battle of the Century, the Battle of the Sleaze was really about custard pies.

In the great sleaze war, Major's most dangerous opponent was not the Labour Party but the Press, and what he lacked most was a competent

---

[8] Anthony Heath and his colleagues, working from the same data as Evans, completely missed this vital insight, concluding erroneously 'a more eurosceptic line . . . would have been of little electoral advantage to them. The Conservatives were already well-placed on Europe, their perceived position being closer to that of the average voter than was that of any of the major parties.' Heath, A., Jowell, R., Taylor, B. and Thomson, K., 'Euroscepticism and the Referendum Party' in Denver, D. et al (eds.), *British Elections & Parties Review* Volume 8: The 1997 General Election (London: Frank Cass, 1998), p 109.

spin doctor. As the Labour MP Tony Wright noted, 'Not one resignation has been forced by information uncovered by MPs. The Commons has become a mere echo chamber for noises off'.[9] We might ask how the Tories came to lose the support of much of the Press, especially Murdoch's *Sun*, which had been so virulently supportive in 1992. Some commentators, indeed, would want to argue that the switching of the *Sun* (and of the *Sun*'s Sunday sister the *News of the World*, as well as the *Daily Star* and *Evening Standard*) from Conservative in 1992 to Labour by 1997 was a crucial factor in swinging public support. But that certainly puts the cart before the horse. The populist Tory press had little choice but to switch their formal support to stay in tune with their readers, who had already long before the election abandoned Major in droves. That movement was partly started, of course, by press scorn for the failures of the government at a period before they had irrevocably switched sides. But what choice had they? Could the editor even of the *Sun* be expected to defend the Tories over Black Wednesday? The editorial line had always been as much anti-European and even xenophobic as specifically partisan Tory in any case, and this was a government humiliation caused by being pro-European. On Maastricht, similarly, the government left the *Sun* rather than vice-versa.

But it was over sleaze that the press coverage really bit, and in this there is little need to look for any serious editorial or proprietorial policy. No paper can afford to miss a good story. Of course, a 'good story' also needs to be a legitimate story, or the press dare not use it. Thirty years ago, perhaps, the sex lives of Tory MPs would not have been a legitimate story unless there was some extra element giving a cast-iron justification (as the security implications did to the Profumo affair). But for the press of the nineties, intrusive stories about the private lives of public figures are the norm – frowned upon officially, and apparently disapproved of by the public themselves, but sure-fire circulation boosters nonetheless, and with the toothless Press Complaints Commission the only restraint. So the newspapers need not so much justification as pretext.

When the David Mellor story broke, it must have seemed heaven-

---

[9] Quoted in Doig, A. and Wilson, J., 'Untangling the threads of sleaze: the slide into Nolan', *Parliamentary Affairs*, Vol 48 no 4 (October 1995), pp 562–79.

sent: not just an undeniably titillating story, but involving perhaps the single person that most editors would have wanted as a legitimate victim in an ideal world. For it was Mellor who had lectured the press on their excesses and warned them that they were 'drinking in the last chance saloon'. It was Mellor who still held over them the threat of more draconian regulation and an end to their right to intrude into public figures' private lives, as being the responsible departmental minister. And by the same token, it was politically impossible for the responsible minister, Mellor himself, to dare to attempt to suppress the story without looking the most arrant hypocrite and appearing to have more to hide than had already been revealed.

Perhaps none of this passed through editors' minds when they began the hounding of the Heritage Secretary. At any rate, many may feel that the start of the affair does not show British journalism in its best light. The press campaign for his dismissal began in July 1992 with sexual revelations of an extra-marital affair with an actress (on the 'public interest' justification that his affair was making him too tired to perform his governmental duties properly), then moved swiftly on to ridicule (alleging – in the public interest, of course – that he had sex wearing a Chelsea football shirt). Later, he having kept his place in the Cabinet through this storm, more serious allegations emerged of having accepted free hospitality from a friend with PLO connections that raised questions of conflict of interest and seemed to throw possible doubt on the integrity with which he made decisions. These allegations forced his resignation on 24 September (adding to the government misery in the week following 'Black Wednesday'). But the tabloid press made no bones about what they thought was the most interesting aspect of the affair: the *Sun* headline that announced Mellor's resignation referred back to the most lurid of the sexual allegations and suggested that it was this, rather than the more substantive question, that had forced the Prime Minister's hand. It was Mona Bauwens that brought down David Mellor, but the tabloid press were united in giving the credit to Antonia de Sancha.

And so started the great hunt for sleaze. Even at this early stage, we can see the behaviour which was to characterise the next 18 months' coverage, the blurring of distinctions between allegations of public corruption (a perfectly legitimate subject for journalistic investigation, of course) and the purely private sexual misbehaviour of ministers, the exposure of which was not really in the public interest but which nevertheless could be made to interest the public.

But our concern is not to dissect the ethics of the press. The *Sun* and all the rest behaved predictably in the circumstances. Our question must be, what if anything could the Tory leaders have done about it? And what effect in the long run did the whole sordid mess have on the 1997 election?

The Mellor affair, perhaps unfairly, made John Major look bumblingly indecisive and too easily bullied. The Prime Minister having once allowed the media to force one of his ministers out of office could never be entirely convincing about his refusal to let it happen again, and so, inevitably, the Press started looking for further opportunities.

The Mellor incident may have been a blow Major could not have avoided, and both Matrix Churchill and Asil Nadir were embarrassments that were essentially hangovers from the previous regime, the impact of which might have been containable, but the next development was undeniably an error, an avoidable and devastating one – the introduction of 'Back to Basics' and the importance of the family as a policy theme at the 1993 Conservative Conference. This simply declared open season on ministers, giving the Press the cast-iron justification that they craved for investigating the sex lives of Conservative politicians – no longer forced to scramble for specious justifications that such prurience was in some way in the public interest (an argument that never convinced most of the public). They were now able to accuse any Conservative who endorsed the policy (even implicitly by silence) of hypocrisy unless entirely pure himself. It seems improbable that Mr Major and his Cabinet can really have believed that every one of his MPs was whiter than white and able to withstand aggressive press investigation – his whips (whose job it is to know about any peccadilloes of MPs that might damage the party) should surely have told him otherwise. 'Back to Basics' was thus an avoidable and extraordinarily foolish mistake. Admittedly Back to Basics wasn't originally meant to cover sex. But again, a good spin doctor would have caught it. Unfortunately the Tories always gave the impression of being forced to rely on spin paramedics.

The legitimation of sex exposé as the investigation of Tory hypocrisy seems to have been important in pulling the public mood into line with the direction the tabloids wanted to take. By January 1994, when the press was beginning to exploit 'Back to Basics' as an excuse for sex stories about Tory MPs, 75% agreed that the press is right 'to expose ministers or MPs who say one thing in public but behave in a sharply different way in their private lives'. On the other hand, when the issue of hypocrisy was not raised, the majority were tolerant: though 41% agreed that 'if it is discovered a minister has committed a serious moral or financial indiscretion in their private life, they should resign', 53% opted for the alternative that 'if these matters are entirely private and not illegal, that as long as they perform the job well as ministers, they should not be required to resign'[10]. These attitudes, incidentally, seem fairly stable over time: at the time of the Lambton-Jellicoe scandal in 1973, 53% told Gallup 'Cabinet ministers should be able to lead their private lives as they wish', while 42% took the contrary view that 'their private lives should be above reproach'[11].

What now happened unabated was the deliberate blurring by some sections of the media between sleaze proper (that is, corruption or misuse of office) and other more venial misdemeanours (especially of a sexual nature): this enabled the Press to find enough scandal to keep the story running, and indeed in itself encouraged them to do so. After all, sex sells more newspapers than fingers in the till.

'Sleaze' became an all-encompassing term for any accusation of dishonest or disreputable behaviour, or even more widely to cover cases that at worst were nothing more than perfectly legal and ethical, if slightly unpalatable, greed for pay rises − as when the pay of British Gas Chief Executive Cedric Brown became dragged into the argument as a case of 'snouts in the trough'. (Note that British Gas, though privatised by the Tories and providing a public utility, is a private company and its pay levels are not the responsibility of the government, and that Brown was not some Tory placeman or a former civil servant who had slipped into

---

[10] MORI poll for the *Sun*, conducted 10–11 January 1994.
[11] Gallup, G., *The Gallup International Opinion Polls: Great Britain 1937–1975*, (New York: Random House, 1976), p 1253.

some comfortable niche he had built with public money, but had worked his way up from the shop-floor. John Major, an enthusiastic reader of Trollope, might notice in the Cedric Brown case certain parallels with the plot of *The Warden*.)

By 1995, Dunleavy, Weir and Subrahmanyam noted[12] that 'the concept of sleaze . . . married together quite disparate areas of near wrongdoing across several parts of public life which had previously been considered entirely separately'. They categorised these perceptions and allegations into eight groups, which we may summarise:

- Financial wrongdoing by ministers and MPs, shady deals and the misleading of others;
- Lobbying of government and the intermediary role of certain MPs;
- Packing of 'quangos' with partisan supporters;
- Quango jobs and honours for individuals or companies backing the Tories financially;
- Directorships or lucrative consultancies for retired ministers and civil servants, in companies with which they had had dealings while in office;
- Party fundraising from controversial (especially foreign) sources;
- Sexual misbehaviour (and associated accusations of hypocrisy where the politician involved had been associated with taking a high moral tone on family matters);
- Salary increases or share options for 'fat cats' in the privatised public utilities.

'These eight aspects of public life', they continue, 'were never closely bound together by any other concept before sleaze came into widespread use to cover them all.'[13] Without the impetus of 'Back to Basics' and the enthusiasm of the popular press for sex scandals, it has to be considered possible that that binding together might never have happened, and that the overall impact on the image of the government might have been substantially less.

---

[12] Dunleavy, P. and Weir, S. with Subrahmanyam, G., 'Sleaze in Britain: Media Influences, Public Response and Constitutional Significance', *Parliamentary Affairs*, Vol. 48 no 4 (October 1995), p 603.

[13] *Ibid.*, p 604.

Table 5: Sleaze – what the public would ban MPs from doing

Q. **Here is a list of things that some MPs do. Which, if any, do you think MPs should be allowed to do? And which, if any, do you think MPs should be banned from doing?**

	Should be allowed %	Should be banned %	Net allow %
Carrying on a trade or profession (e.g. as a farmer, lawyer, dentist etc) while being an MP	45	33	+12
Being paid to write articles for newspapers and magazines	35	43	–8
Having any paid job outside Parliament	28	48	–20
Being the paid representative of a non-commercial interest group (e.g. the Police Federation)	22	44	–22
Being sponsored by trade unions towards election and campaigning costs in their constituencies	21	48	–27
Speaking or voting on issues which affect commercial interests or private companies from which they receive payments	4	73	–69
Speaking or voting on issues where they stand to gain financially	4	77	–73
Receiving fees from specialist lobbying companies to promote their clients' interests at Westminster	2	76	–74
Receiving fees from private companies in return for lobbying on their behalf at Westminster	3	78	–75
Asking questions in parliament for money	3	83	–80
Other	1	1	
Don't know	8	3	
None of these	21	3	

Source: MORI/Joseph Rowntree Reform Trust, 21 April–8 May 1995
Base: 1,758 adults

What effect did sleaze have on the public mind? Did they care? Did it swing their votes? The public have long held the view that corruption in public life is an unusually heinous evil. In 1980 more people (73% of British adults) considered 'politicians accepting gifts for services rendered' to be 'morally wrong'[14] than thought the same of the use of cannabis (70%), racial discrimination (61%), adultery (60%), blood sports (59%) or pornography in the cinema (55%).

---

[14] MORI/ *Sunday Times* poll of 1,930 British adults, 24–29 January 1980. The question asked 'Q. *Here is a list of activities that some people might consider to be immoral. Which of them, if any, do you personally consider to be morally wrong?*' Of the list of 17 activities, more respondents selected 'politicians accepting gifts for services rendered' as morally wrong than any other.

The line on what is acceptable is drawn very strictly: in 1994 almost half the public said they would condemn accepting even free lunch at a restaurant or bottles of wine or whisky at Christmas.[15] Indeed, their disapproval goes far beyond matters that could normally be considered corrupt or even controversial – not only would 48% ban trade union sponsorship of candidates and 44% being the paid representative in Parliament of a non-commercial interest group such as the Police Federation, but we found that by 1995 43% would even ban MPs from being paid to write articles for newspapers and magazines.

The public are happy to admit that they expect a higher standard of behaviour from politicians than from others: 70% said in January 1994 that 'we, the public, are right . . . to expect MPs to behave according to a higher standard of moral behaviour and financial honesty than ordinary people.

The clear distinction drawn by the public between matters of corruption and mere sexual misbehaviour is reflected by their attitude to the role of the media in investigating these cases. In August 1992, before the full barrage of sleaze stories had really got going, MORI found that 40% of the public thought it was justifiable for the press to invade the privacy of a politician in pursuit of a story. Asked about more specific cases, only 49% thought the newspapers were right to publish the story of David Mellor's affair, 39% to publish the five-year old story of Paddy Ashdown's affair (revealed during the 1992 election campaign), and 26% to publish the story that Virginia Bottomley had been (many years before) an unmarried mother.

The distinction drawn by the public was even clearer when we asked which misdemeanours should be resignation issues for ministers and MPs, and which should not; few of them seem to hold to John Redwood's view that 'if a man is likely to betray his wife he is equally likely to betray his country'[16]. Only 32% thought that an MP revealed as a practising homosexual and 34% that an MP who committed adultery should be required to resign his seat, whereas 88% would want the resignation of an MP making money legally but unethically.

---

[15] Gallup poll for the *Daily Telegraph*, October 1994.

[16] Quoted in Smith, T., 'Political Sleaze in Britain: Causes, Concerns and Cures', *Parliamentary Affairs*, Volume 48, number 4 (October 1995), pp 556–7.

Table 6: Sleaze – what is a resignation issue?

Q. **For each of the following circumstances, please tell me whether you feel that a Government minister should or should not be required to resign as a minister?**
Q. **Now would you tell me whether or not you think that an ordinary MP should or should not be required to resign as an MP?**

	Minister			Ordinary MP		
	Should %	Should not %	No opinion %	Should %	Should not %	No opinion %
Committed adultery	41	53	6	34	60	6
Was a practising homosexual	32	61	7	32	63	5
Was convicted of drink driving	62	33	5	61	34	5
Engaged in financial sharp practice which made him/her rich by exploiting a weakness in the law	90	9	1	88	10	2

Source: MORI On-Line/*The Sun*
10–11 January 1994
Base: 820 British adults 18+, interviewed by telephone

The press campaign had its effect. The public's perception was that sleaze in the worst sense was very widespread. In October 1994, a horrifying 64% agreed that 'most members of Parliament make a lot of money by using public office improperly'. There was also a widespread belief that corruption extended to government abuse of its powers of patronage: 63% believed that the government preferred known Conservative supporters and people who had donated funds to the party when making appointments to 'bodies like regional health authorities', only 17% thinking such appointments were made strictly on merit; and 47% had the impression that the government was packing quangos with Conservative supporters, only 11% disagreeing.[17] At the time of the Pergau dam controversy, almost a third (29%) believed 'from what you know of the Scott Inquiry and the arms-and-aid deal with Malaysia' that the government 'is corrupt and/or abuses its power'.[18]

Gallup tracked for a long period the percentage of the public who thought 'The Conservatives these days give the impression of being very sleazy and disreputable', and the percentage who took the same view of

[17] Gallup poll for the *Daily Telegraph*, October 1994.
[18] ICM poll for the *Guardian*, March 1994.

Table 7: Trust in ministers and politicians

Q. Now I will read out a list of different types of people. For each, would you tell me whether you generally trust them to tell the truth or not?

| | 1983 | | Nov 1983 | | 25–28 Apr 1997 | | Net change 1993 –97 |
	Tell truth %	Not tell truth %	Tell truth %	Not tell truth %	Tell truth %	Not tell truth %	%
Doctors	82	14	84	11	86	10	+3
Teachers	79	14	84	9	83	11	–3
Television news readers	63	25	72	18	74	14	+6
Professors	n/a	n/a	70	12	70	12	0
Judges	77	18	68	21	72	19	+6
Clergymen/priests	85	11	80	13	71	20	–16
Scientists	n/a	n/a	n/a	n/a	63	22	0
The Police	61	32	63	26	61	30	–6
The ordinary man/ woman in the street	57	27	64	21	56	28	–15
Pollsters	n/a	n/a	52	28	55	28	+3
Civil servants	25	63	37	50	36	50	–1
Trade Union officials	18	71	32	54	27	56	–7
Business leaders	25	65	32	57	29	60	–6
Journalists	19	73	10	84	15	76	+13
Politicians generally	18	75	14	79	15	78	+2
Government Ministers	16	74	11	81	12	80	+2

Source: MORI

the Labour Party. At the end of 1994, the figure peaked with 73% saying the Tories gave the impression of sleaze, while 21% thought the same of Labour. Over the last year before the election, the figure hovered between 61% and 68% for the Tories, ending at 63% in the poll taken over the week of the Hamilton nomination furore (26 March–2 April). Incidentally, Labour by no means escaped unscathed in the public perception – their sleaze score was as high as 26% in August-September 1996, though back down to 19% by the March-April poll[19].

Nor did the public show much gratitude to the fourth estate for their exertions. In November 1993, they ranked journalists even below ministers for trustworthiness.

---

[19] Gallup Political and Economic Index December 1994, April 1997.

Because the sleaze issue was not solely damaging to the Conservatives – and to some extent all politicians were tarred with the same brush – it may be questioned how much direct influence it was likely to have on votes. The standing of Parliament as a whole was undoubtedly tarnished by the continuing allegations (even though those accused by the media were almost exclusively Tory). When Gallup asked in October 1994 'From what you know, do you think Conservative MPs are more likely to behave in this way [accepting money and gifts when they should not have done] than Labour and other Opposition MPs or not?', 49% said they thought the Tories were no worse than any other MPs, and 47% agreed that 'The Conservatives are no worse than most. My vote at the next general election won't be affected by all the current talk of sleaze', the same proportion who disagreed and thought they were 'less inclined to vote for [the Conservatives] than I was before'.[20]

Nevertheless, there tended to be strong correlation between voting intention and respondents' views of government probity, suggesting that this was an issue that was swinging votes, even if unconsciously. An ICM survey for the Joseph Rowntree Reform Trust after the Scott enquiry reported found 63% thought ministers broke the UN embargo on arms to Iraq, and a virtually unanimous 92% thought ministers had misled the House of Commons. But when asked whether the misleading was intentional or unintentional, more than two-thirds of non-Tories thought it was deliberate whereas only a third of those intending to vote Conservative thought the same[21].

And it surely damaged Major's standing. Even though the Prime Minister himself was not personally implicated in any of the sleaze allegations, the public was dissatisfied with the way he handled the situations. 47% thought that he had handled David Mellor's affair badly (and 28% that he had handled it well), 55% that he had dealt badly with the allegations of insider share dealing against Lord Archer, 55% also that he had dealt badly with enquiring into the Mark Thatcher affair. 64% thought that he had handled badly the question of allowing former

---

[20] Gallup poll for the *Daily Telegraph*, October 1994.
[21] Dunleavy, P. and Weir, S., 'Now Labour must open up', *Guardian*, 21 February 1996. ICM interviewed 752 adults on 16–17 February 1996.

Cabinet ministers to accept posts with companies they did business with while in government. Worst of all, 67% thought he had handled the question of party funds received from Asil Nadir badly, and just 7% that he had handled it well.[22] Furthermore, many voters must have assumed Major's complicity in such activities as packing quangos with Tories and other government abuses of power which, as we have seen, a substantial proportion of electors believed to have been taking place.

Other polls found a clear distinction between the opinion of those Tories who had stayed loyal to the party and those who had voted Tory in 1992 but now intended to vote for some other party (the 'switchers'). After the Scott report was published, Tory loyalists were almost evenly split on whether William Waldegrave and Sir Nicholas Lyell ought to resign, but the switchers wanted both to resign by a ratio of ten to one[23]. We have to conclude that there was sleaze was having some direct effect on vote. But more significant must have been the indirect effect on image.

Arguably, 'Back to Basics' was the most damaging of the three strategic errors the government had made by the end of 1993. Black Wednesday may have struck more directly at voters' pockets, Maastricht may have raised issues of greater political principle, but sleaze, like custard, sticks: you look very silly as you wipe it out of your eyes. The legitimisation of sexual investigation by giving the newspapers a pretext to justify it did not merely widen the scope of the journalistic investigations and improve their selling potential, but it made its effect on the government more damaging. A government smeared with the taint of financial corruption may be hated, perhaps even held in contempt; but such misdemeanours cannot approach the scope for ridicule offered by the indignity of ministers and MPs being caught with their trousers round their ankles. When public opinion stops merely disliking a government and starts laughing at it, its defeat may already be assured. When a government is laughed at, it cannot pretend to credibility or competence; nothing it does or says will be taken seriously. So the blow that Black Wednesday

[22] Gallup poll for the *Daily Telegraph*, fieldwork 26–31 October 1994.
[23] Kellner, P., 'Voters want heads of Scott ministers', *Sunday Times*, 18 February 1996. The figures were from an NOP poll for the *Sunday Times*, conducted on 15–16 February 1996.

struck in the field of economic management was reinforced and widened over the whole gamut of government responsibility.

Leadership

The fourth and final strategic error was in not replacing John Major as leader when he gave them the chance, by voluntarily initiating a leadership contest.

In the Spring of 1990 the Conservative Party lagged the Labour Party by 23% in the polls. What did they do? They changed their leader, Margaret Thatcher for John Major, they changed their policies, especially by dropping the hated poll tax, they changed a third of their Cabinet, and they changed the Party Chairman. In 1992 they won the General Election, albeit by such a narrow margin that if one person in two hundred who voted Tory had voted for the second party in their constituency, it would have been a hung Parliament.

In the Spring of 1994, the Conservatives lagged the Labour Party in the polls by 22%. What did they do? They kept their Leader, they kept their policies, they kept their Cabinet. They changed the Party Chairman, twice, and got it wrong both times. Throughout this period the Prime Minister complacently stressed the improving economic situation and his confidence that once the British public were aware that inflation was down, unemployment was falling and the economic management by his Government was sound, that the public would return them, gratefully, to office for an unprecedented fifth term. The senior members of the Government repeatedly ignored the worsening political poll findings, repeating how they'd proved the polls wrong in 1992, and they'd do it again. Heseltine's cry: 'We'll win by 60'.

Of course, it was not just the polls the Tories were defying. When politicians want to dismiss poll findings, they are wont to talk clichés about 'real votes in real ballot boxes'. But throughout the parliament, the real votes in real ballot boxes were telling them the same as the polls. At by-election after by-election, Newbury, Christchurch (how could the Tories conceivably lose Christchurch?), Eastleigh, they were humiliated by the Liberal Democrats. When there was finally a by-election in a

Tory seat where Labour was the challenger, Dudley West, in December 1994, the swing was an unprecedented – unbelievable – 29%. In the 1993 county council elections, the Tories lost 478 seats, and clung on to just a single council (Buckinghamshire). In the 1994 local elections, they were reduced to the equivalent of 27% of the national vote, losing another 440 seats, and a month later at the European elections managed only 28%, their lowest share in history in a national election. John Major's response? 'I believe it has been clear for some years that many people are simply not frank when asked questions by opinion-pollsters.' How frank did he want them to be? In May 1995, a few weeks before Major offered himself for re-election, the Tory share hit rock bottom, 25%, and they lost almost two thousand councillors (more than 2,000 if the effects of introducing new unitary authorities are included), slipping behind the Liberal Democrats into third place in both number of seats held and numbers of councils controlled. 'Real votes in real ballot boxes'; quite.

We regularly measure leader image. (See the perceptual maps on p. 52.) John Major came into Downing Street in November 1990, and the country was involved immediately in the Gulf War. By the following February, Major was seen as 'capable', 'good in a crisis' and 'has sound judgement'. At the 1992 election he outscored Neil Kinnock (that is, had a higher score on positive attributes and a lower score on negative ones) on ten of the fourteen characteristics we test. Perhaps most critically, 35% thought he was good in a crisis (Kinnock just 14%) and 47% that he understood world problems (Kinnock 31%). He also scored well as a capable leader (47% to Kinnock's 36%). His weakest point was that 35% thought he was out of touch with ordinary people (only 18% thought the same of Kinnock); he also trailed on being down to earth, understanding the problems facing Britain and having 'a lot of personality'. All in all, though an election-winning hand in 1992, very vulnerable against a well-rated opponent if his image of competence were to slip.

His image did indeed slip. Over time he became much like Mrs Thatcher in trousers, except that he was thought neither 'capable' nor 'good in a crisis'. His image became fixed in the minds of the electorate: John Major was perceived as a 'nice guy' (as had been Michael Foot),

Mid-term Blues? (1987-1992)

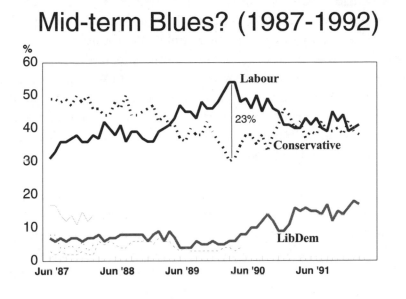

Base: c. 2,000 British public   Source: MORI/Times

Mid Term Blues? (1992-7)

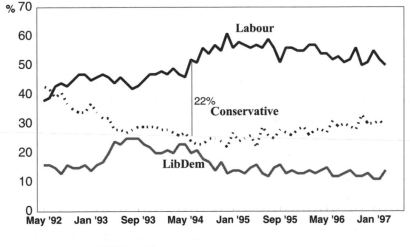

Base: c. 2,000 British public   Source: MORI/Times

Figure 10: Mid-term blues?

but electorally he had become a liability. Major's ratings as capable leader, good in a crisis and having sound judgment all fell in five successive polls from the 1992 election to July 1993. Now only 11% thought he was a 'capable leader', 7% that he was 'good in a crisis' and 6% that he had 'sound judgment'. Even the unfamiliar John Smith (whose ratings on all attributes were low, as is always the case with a new party leader until the electorate have had a chance to fix their image of him), outrated him on all three, 23% thinking him a 'capable leader', and 16% that he had 'sound judgment', though his 8% rating on 'good in a crisis' was unimpressive.

By the start of 1995, Major's new image was set, and none of his ratings were changing significantly from poll to poll; it should have been plain that it would take a miracle to rehabilitate him with the voters. Tony Blair, Labour's new leader, outscored him by 28% to 11% as a capable leader, 18% to 10% as down to earth, 14% to 6% on 'has sound judgment', and even by 22% to 19% on 'more honest than most politicians', on which John Smith had never managed to beat Major.

Major's voluntary resignation to fight a leadership battle in the summer of 1995 was therefore a key opportunity. The 'trial heats' polls showed even at that stage that Michael Heseltine (though not any other likely contender) would have started with an initial advantage, even on no more basis than being a new face at the helm; who knows what might have happened with a year-and-a-half of firmer leadership and a clean slate?

It is most unlikely that a change of leader could have revived the Tories, but at that stage it was their only chance. But the credible alternative candidates lacked the nerve or disloyalty for the challenge, and John Redwood had neither the ability to portray a reassuring public image nor the standing with his own colleagues to have any chance of success, even as a 'stalking horse'. The only concrete effect on the Conservative Party leadership of Redwood's candidacy in 1995 was to make William Hague Major's successor in 1997 (for without the two years' standing as a Cabinet minister which he was given by the vacancy at the Welsh Office that Redwood's resignation opened up, Hague could not have run in 1997.)

One positive suggestion of Redwood's campaign was that, if elected,

Table 8: Trial Heats Poll, June 1995

Q. **How would you vote if there were a general election tomorrow?**
Q. **How would you vote if there were a general election tomorrow, if . . . were leader of the Conservative Party?**

	John Major* %	Michael Heseltine %	Michael Portillo %	Kenneth Clarke %	Gillian Shephard %	John Redwood %
Conservative	31	34	29	29	29	28
Labour	55	53	56	56	57	57
Liberal Democrat	11	11	12	12	11	12
Other	3	3	3	3	3	3
Conservative seats (assuming uniform swing)	143	195	97	97	97	79

Figures for Major are taken from the standard voting intention question

Source: MORI On-Line/*The Economist*
26–27 June 1995
Base: 1,002 British adults

he would clamp down on sleaze, refusing office to all who might be an embarrassment to the party. It was probably too late in the Parliament for this to have worked anyway – the Tory image as the party of sleaze was set in stone (and in fact there were no important new sleaze allegations which arose between the leadership battle and the general election). But anyway, while this might have been an option for a new leader who to some extent would have been able to begin building his cabinet from scratch, it was not an option for an incumbent leader who couldn't sack sitting ministers without an explanation (and the likelihood of bringing out the very revelations and embarrassment that a sleaze clampdown would have aimed at averting).

Major compounded his own failings by unwise appointments to key offices. The campaigns run by Central Office and the men he appointed Chairman, Jeremy Hanley and Brian Mawhinney, were disastrously unsuccessful. Their advertising was counter-productive, they focused attention on the wrong policy issues, and their final attempt to seize the initiative at a key moment of opportunity consisted of sending out a man dressed in a chicken suit to peck at the heels of Tony Blair.

New Labour, No Danger

Going hand in hand with Tory decline was Labour recovery, driven by the election of Tony Blair as leader after John Smith's death. This had two principal consequences. When the electorate looked at Neil Kinnock they saw over one shoulder the spectre of the loony left, CND, and tax and spend; over the other, the spectre of the trade union barons. There was a trace of those ghosts over John Smith's shoulders as well. And while Kinnock had had Peter Mandelson by his side, Smith had him banished from the court. When you looked at Tony Blair, there were no ghosts, and Mandelson was back, to chair the most effective campaign in Labour's history.

We should make clear that this is not to say that Labour would not have won under John Smith. On the contrary, the way the Tories self-destructed in 1992, Labour would probably have won under Neil Kinnock; certainly, the election was already won and lost for the Tories before John Smith died. In previous elections it had been essential that Labour should be 'electable', and in the opinion of too many voters they had not been. By 1994, it was already clear that (assuming the Tories could not repeat their 1990 trick of replacing the leader and starting with a clean slate) the next election would be different – whatever the voters thought of Labour this time the Tories were not re-electable.

But in any case, Labour had already considerably modernised, both in reality and image, and this was bearing fruit. Smith's ratings, as we have already seen, were better than Major's, and Labour held a comfortable lead at the time of his death, exemplified by sweeping gains in the 1994 local elections and (under Margaret Beckett's caretaker leadership) the European Parliamentary elections. But Blair's election, his determination to force through a 'New Labour' agenda symbolised by if not really dependent upon the reform of Clause Four, and the efficiency of the campaigning machinery directed by the reinstated Mandelson, ensured that the Tories had no way back from beyond the Styx.

We can see this strengthening by looking at Labour's image in isolation (rather than in comparison with the other parties, as is measured by the perceptual maps.) If for each party we examine its average score on the nine positive attributes on our party image test, and divide it by the average score on the five negative attributes, we can get an index which gives us an overall view of how well the party is regarded. If the index is more than 1, then a party's image is on balance more positive than negative, and the higher the better. During the 1992 election campaign, the Kinnock party's image index was 1.14 and in March 1994 under Smith the figure was 1.27 – a little better but not dramatically so. Six months later, after Blair's first conference as leader, the index had shot up to 1.85.

Although the index fell back again from this high point between 1994 and the election (and slipping below 1 in September 1996), it was almost exactly replicated in the last few weeks before the election itself. As the temporary relapse coincided with the launch of the Tories' negative 'New Labour, New Danger' advertising campaign, it might be supposed that that had something to do with it, and it is instructive to look at which of Labour's image attributes deteriorated most. If the campaign aimed at destroying any one part of New Labour's image, it was its claim to be reformed and moderate, and therefore safe. Yet 'moderate' was the only positive attribute where Labour did *not* suffer over this period, and 'extreme' increased only by a statistically insignificant margin.

A failure to understand the transformation of the public mood was behind the misguided Tory advertising campaign that was at the centre of their strategy for much of the final year. No doubt they felt constrained to opt for negative rather than positive advertising – they had a big gap to make up, and it is generally received wisdom that, though disliked by the electorate[24], negative advertising has the more powerful effect. But there is no point in 'knocking copy' if your audience is not prepared to believe it. The Tories had lived for the best part of twenty years by playing on the voters' fears of Labour, memories of the 'Winter of Discontent' and of how 'Red Ken' Livingstone had staged an internal party coup to seize power for the left immediately after the election of a moderate-led Labour administration on the Greater London Council. In

---

[24] In both 1992 and 1997, we asked the public whether they thought the election should be fought by the parties '. . . putting forward their own policies and personalities' or '. . . pointing out what is wrong with the policies and personalities in other parties'. By 68% to 9% in 1992 and by 65% to 9% in 1997, they said they preferred the positive campaigning option.

Table 9: Labour Party Image Attributes 1992–7

Positives	G.E. 1992 %	Jul 1992 %	Sep 1992 %	Apr 1993 %	Jul 1993 %	Mar 1994 %	Oct 1994 %	Mar 1995 %	Oct 1995 %	Mar 1996 %	Sep 1996 %	Apr 1997 %
Keeps its promises	13	5	6	6	6	6	6	7	8	5	5	9
Understands the problems facing Britain	40	26	29	30	30	30	36	34	35	35	29	37
Represents all classes	28	20	21	21	21	22	25	27	26	27	22	31
Looks after the interests of people like us	34	22	22	25	26	26	27	29	28	25	21	30
Moderate	17	10	13	14	17	16	16	15	16	16	16	15
Concerned about the people in real need in Britain	49	35	36	37	42	38	41	40	37	37	34	36
Has sensible policies	30	17	17	19	18	21	25	23	23	25	20	27
Has a good team of leaders	29	13	14	14	14	14	21	20	23	20	17	25
Professional in its approach	24	8	9	10	10	10	16	14	18	18	12	21
Negatives												
Extreme	20	11	10	9	10	8	7	6	7	6	7	5
Will promise anything to win votes	43	34	35	35	35	34	27	29	33	30	35	31
Out of touch with ordinary people	16	14	13	13	13	12	8	10	8	10	11	7
Too dominated by its leader	26	8	9	7	7	7	6	9	16	15	21	15
Divided	24	29	32	26	22	19	16	15	15	17	25	12
No opinion		15	11	13	13	13	14	14	11	14	15	9
Av. Positive	29.3	17.3	18.6	19.6	20.4	20.3	23.7	23.2	23.8	23.1	19.6	25.7
Av. Negative	25.8	19.2	19.8	18.0	17.4	16.0	12.8	13.8	15.8	15.6	19.8	14.0
Image Index	1.14	0.90	0.94	1.09	1.17	1.27	1.85	1.68	1.50	1.48	0.99	1.83

Source: MORI/The Times

Table 10: Conservative Party Image Attributes 1992–7

Positives	G.E. 1992 %	Jul 1992 %	Sep 1992 %	Apr 1993 %	Jul 1993 %	Mar 1994 %	Oct 1994 %	Mar 1995 %	Oct 1995 %	Mar 1996 %	Sep 1996 %	Apr 1997 %
Keeps its promises	20	7	6	5	4	4	4	4	5	4	4	5
Understands the problems facing Britain	38	22	21	18	14	14	15	12	15	14	15	20
Represents all classes	20	12	10	9	8	6	6	5	6	6	7	10
Looks after the interests of people like us	21	13	9	8	9	7	6	6	10	6	7	9
Moderate	19	12	12	12	12	10	11	10	11	11	12	11
Concerned about the people in real need in Britain	18	11	9	10	8	6	8	7	8	7	7	8
Has sensible policies	31	17	15	12	11	10	10	8	9	11	11	14
Has a good team of leaders	35	24	16	13	8	7	7	6	8	9	7	10
Professional in its approach	42	24	19	16	12	11	11	8	10	11	12	13
Negatives												
Extreme	16	9	10	10	11	11	9	9	12	11	10	10
Will promise anything to win votes	41	35	41	47	52	54	51	52	51	50	49	40
Out of touch with ordinary people	51	47	53	57	61	64	63	62	62	62	56	50
Too dominated by its leader	14	8	11	11	11	9	9	10	10	10	9	10
Divided	14	17	34	30	50	44	40	47	42	48	43	44
No opinion	2	13	7	10	9	8	10	11	9	11	11	9
Av. Positive	27.1	15.8	13.0	11.4	9.6	8.3	8.7	7.3	9.1	8.8	9.1	11.1
Av. Negative	27.2	23.2	29.8	31.0	37.0	36.4	34.4	36.0	35.4	36.2	33.4	30.8
Image Index	1.00	0.68	0.44	0.37	0.26	0.23	0.25	0.20	0.26	0.24	0.27	0.36

Source: MORI/*The Times*

the 1992 General Election, these fears had still had an effect: analysis suggests that the oft-mentioned issue of taxation lost Labour vital votes not because the middle-classes feared tax rises as such, but because they didn't trust a Kinnock government not to waste them[25]. Much anecdotal evidence also suggests a key role of 'Red Wednesday', the misplaced triumphalism of the Sheffield rally a week before polling day, which many Tory candidates campaigning on the ground were convinced had saved their seats. In 1992, the voters were probably ready for the programme that Labour was promising, if only they believed the promises. As Kinnock himself put it, it was 'the triumph of fear over hope.'

The Tories' advertising has been noted since the 1979 General Election, when the 'Labour Isn't Working' poster made its mark, and the reputation of Saatchi & Saatchi. In this election however, it was undistinguished, even counter-productive. By adopting Labour's brand label of 'New Labour' in their own slogan 'New Labour, New Danger', they accepted (and spent their own money propagating) their opponents' claim to have broken with the past, and directly weakened the chances of making their scare stories stick. Philip Gould has described Labour's reaction: 'To us this was like rain in a drought'[26].

We tracked the voters' own perceptions of the issues that would swing their votes throughout the long campaign. By February 1997, it was apparent that the 'four horsemen' of the election would be health care, education, unemployment and law & order. When ITV asked me to attend the Labour Party's 'Road to the Manifesto' launch in July 1996, I was handed a 'pledge card' – not the 'pledge card' of the Labour Party of old, asking on one side for my pledge of allegiance and on the other the party's commitment to clause IV, but Tony Blair's pledge to the electorate, on the issues of health care, education, unemployment and law & order, in fact the same top four that the polls showed were of concern to voters. Meanwhile, the Tories had come up with 'New Labour, New Danger'.

'New Labour, New Danger' was launched in the run-up to the

---

[25] Heath, A., Jowell, R., and Curtice, J., 'Can Labour Win?' in Heath et al, *Labour's Last Chance?* (London: CREST, 1994), p 292.

[26] Gould, P., 'Why Labour Won' in Crewe, I., Gosschalk, B., and Bartle, J. (eds), *Political Communications: Why Labour Won the General Election of 1997* (London: Frank Cass, 1998).

Table 11: 'New Labour, New Danger'

Q. As you may know, the Conservative Party has recently launched an advertising campaign using the slogan 'New Labour, New Danger'. On balance, has this made you more favourable towards the Labour Party, less favourable to the Labour Party, or has it made no difference?

Q. And on balance, has this made you more favourable towards the Conservative Party, less favourable to the Conservative Party, or has it made no difference?

	To Labour			To Conservatives		
	All	Ex-Con*	New Lab*	All	Ex-Con	New Lab
	%	%	%	%	%	%
More Favourable	11	17	22	3	1	2
Less Favourable	4	2	2	22	29	33
No Difference	66	68	60	57	58	51
Don't Know	1	1	1	2	1	1
Not heard of	17	12	14	17	11	13
Net Favourable	+7	+15	+20	−19	+28	−31

Source: MORI/*The Times*
23–28 July 1996
Base: 1,928 British adults

(*'Ex-Con' are those respondents who said they had voted Conservative in 1992 but would not do so again if there were a general election tomorrow; 'New Lab' all those intending to vote Labour who said they had not done so in 1992.)

election, in mid–1996. It was not well received by the electorate, with more people saying that on balance it made them more favourable to Labour, not the Tories, especially among ex-Conservative voters. In July 1996, a nation-wide sample of nearly 2,000 adults was asked their reactions; the results are shown in the table above.

I have a theory about the most notorious of the Tory ads of the long campaign. One Sunday evening the Prime Minister was having his regular meeting with his advertising and PR gurus, m'Lords Saatchi and Chadlington, and Sir (now m'Lord) Tim Bell. The PM was holding his head saying that 'If we don't get Europe off the agenda, we're dead!' Maurice Saatchi replied: 'Well Prime Minister, we've been thinking . . .' and pulled out a mock up of the ad that was to become 'Satanic Eyes'.

Did it work? The evidence suggests not. It only ran on one day in August, in three papers, yet had enormous publicity, and knocked Europe off the media agenda while the papers and broadcast media focused on the merits and demerits of the ad. As advertising, it was unsuccessful; it may have achieved its PR aim.

When asked 'Has the Conservative Party's poster campaign showing Tony Blair with 'satanic eyes' made you less likely to vote Labour at the next general election, more likely to vote Labour at the next general election, or has it made no difference?', 11% said it made them *more* likely, 3% less likely, and 75% said it made no difference. Among ex-Conservative voters (from 1992), the ratio was 18:4; among new Labour switchers, 11:2.

Afterwards, 'New Labour, New Danger' was resurrected. In January 1997 we asked the public's view again, with similar results: among all voters there was a 14:5 ratio favourable to Labour and 2:32 less favourable to the Tories, and even worse among ex-Conservatives (13:6 and 0:17) and much worse among new Labour switchers, of whom by 24 to 1 said it made them more favourable to Labour and by 0, nil, to 46%, less favourable to the Conservatives. In February came the posters and broadcasts of the weeping lion ('It will all end in tears'); ORB's panel of former Tory voters, polled for HSBC James Capel, again gave it the thumbs down – 8% more of this key target group said it had reduced their support for the Conservatives than that it had increased it[27]. Tears, indeed.

Despite this evidence, Central Office continued to assert the efficacy of their message. *The Times* reported:

> 'A senior Tory strategist said last night: "New Labour New Danger is the most effective slogan we have had since Labour Isn't Working in 1979. It is working, which is why successive polls show that people do not trust Tony Blair and prefer John Major."'

Which polls, we wonder? Certainly not ours.

This self-delusion was no doubt fed by the refusal of M&C Saatchi to test their broadcasts and poster campaigns in the normal way, with focus groups, apparently to maintain confidentiality and the element of surprise. A prominent opponent of this dangerous strategy, according to *The Times*, was Norman Blackwell, head of the Downing Street Policy Unit,

---

[27] Pierce, A., 'Tory adverts "are not working"', *The Times*, 21 February 1997.

but his objections were ignored[28]. Reports after the election claimed that the advertising strategy was also opposed by Brian Mawhinney, but pushed through by Maurice Saatchi:

> 'The two men fell out so badly they only spoke when they had to . . . Most of their rows were over the Conservative Party adverts. "As the campaign wore on, Saatchi wanted to use much more aggressive adverts attacking Blair but Mawhinney wouldn't have it," said one Tory insider. . . . In the end . . . Saatchi used different tactics to try to get his way when Dr Mawhinney rejected ads, claimed one Conservative official. "He would leave it right to the last minute, present virtually the same thing again with an alternative that was so hopeless he knew it would never be used. . . . Saatchi treated Mawhinney with contempt." '[29]

The Tory campaign seems to have done nothing to shake public trust in Labour. The Blair revolution in the party's image was established.

Other strategic factors

Besides these five key moments, not much else went right for the Tories between 1992 and 1997. The BSE crisis – 'mad cow disease' – was a running sore throughout the Parliament, though its genesis dated back to the Thatcher governments. The Courts took a more interventionist view of judicial review of ministerial decisions than ever before, Michael Howard as Home Secretary being particularly in the firing line, arguably more the effect of a development in legal philosophy than anything new in the way the government was governing. In Northern Ireland a cease-fire, which had seemed to promise much, collapsed, not to be re-established until after Blair's election. None of these events can have helped the Tories' image, though they were probably blamed by few for Ulster.

A further obstacle to Conservative success was a structural one – the electoral system was tilted against them in the sense that, had both parties won equal numbers of votes, Labour would have won significantly more

---

[28] Pierce, A., 'Tory adverts "are not working" ', *The Times*, 21 February 1997.
[29] 'Ads that upset Mawhinney', *The Express on Sunday*, 4 May 1997.

seats, and that Labour could secure an overall majority in the Commons with a far narrower lead in votes than could the Tories.

Over the years the bias has swung from one party to the other and back again, and there is normally not much the parties can do about it[30]. However, in this respect the 1997 election was different, because it was the first to be fought on a newly-redrawn set of constituency boundaries. This represented another missed opportunity for the Tories.

All other things being equal the Conservatives can expect to benefit substantially from any boundary review, because it corrects the periodic bias which builds up as Labour seats get smaller in electorate and Tory seats get larger. (Most inner-city seats, which tend to lose population, are Labour held, most suburban and commuter belt seats, which are growing, Tory, so the average Tory MP tends to represent more electors than the average Labour MP after the boundaries are a few years old[31]).

But getting this, entirely deserved, advantage depends on playing the game properly. Boundary revisions are settled by the neutral boundary commissions, who make judicial decisions on the basis of guidelines laid down by law after public enquiries to hear the evidence and consider the alternatives. They cannot take into account what they, and everybody else, know to be the case, that the political parties making representations and presenting evidence at these enquiries do so almost entirely in the pursuit of partisan advantage; whichever party can best present their own preferred scheme as fitting most nearly the criteria on which the decision must be made will get their way.

In the review that produced the boundaries used in 1997, it was Labour that got its way nearly every time. Research shows that far more of Labour's boundary proposals were accepted than Tory ones – not because of bias but because they were better prepared and argued[32]. As a

---

[30] In any case, viewed by comparison with Proportional Representation, the disadvantage that the 'First Past the Post' system currently imposes on the Tories in their competition with Labour is much smaller than the disadvantage it imposes on the LibDems fighting against both of them.

[31] This generalisation applies to England. The situation is exacerbated by Labour being much stronger than the Tories in Scotland and Wales, where the electorates are systematically smaller, but this is not corrected by boundary revisions as it follows from the Parliamentary Constituencies Act which governs the whole process.

[32] For details and discussion of all the issues surrounding the work of the Boundary Commissions,

result, the boundary review did almost nothing for the Tories – Rallings and Thrasher's estimate is that it gave them a net gain of just 5 seats over Labour[33], making little dent on the 38-seat bias against the party that had existed in 1992[34].

The new boundaries once finalised also contributed to Labour's campaign of ridicule against the Tories. With some constituencies changed or abolished and others newly created (and therefore lacking sitting MPs), MPs of all parties had the opportunity and perhaps incentive to move to safer seats for the next election. Those Tories who did so were accused of taking part in a 'chicken-run' – being so lacking in confidence of holding seats with small majorities that they had chickened out. Some of these accusations seem fair enough, but in other cases were a little stretched – it seems harsh to blame Brian Mawhinney and Stephen Dorrell, both of whose seats were split between two new ones, for choosing to contest the safer though smaller portion. As for Norman Lamont, his seat disappeared altogether (four Tory seats in Kingston and Richmond were reduced to three, and he was the loser in the game of musical chairs between the incumbent MPs), but the spectacle of his increasingly desperate attempts to find a foothold elsewhere was damaging, if only for the suspicion that Major's personal antipathy was causing Constituency Associations to reject a senior and well-qualified candidate. (Lamont eventually landed in the apparently safe Harrogate and Knaresborough, but, when the election came, even that proved to be below the high tide mark and he was swept out to sea with the rest.)

But in fact the public seems to have been largely oblivious. Just before the campaign got underway we polled in Loughborough, Stephen Dorrell's old seat, for the *Mail on Sunday*, asking among other things whether voters happened to know the names of the candidates for the

---

see McLean, I. and Butler, D. (eds.), *Fixing the Boundaries: Defining and Redefining Single Member Electoral Districts* (Aldershot: Dartmouth, 1996). The effectiveness of the parties in making their submissions to the Boundary Commissions is assessed in Johnston, R., Pattie, C., Rossiter, D., Dorling, D., Tunstall, H and MacAllister, I., 'Anatomy of a Labour Landslide: The Constituency System and the 1997 General Election', *Parliamentary Affairs*, volume 51 number 1 (1998).

[33] Rallings, C. and Thrasher, M., *Media Guide to the New Parliamentary Constituencies* (London: BBC/ITN/ PA News/Sky, 1995), p 2.

[34] Curtice, J. and Steed, M., 'The Results Analysed', in Butler, D. and Kavanagh, D., *The British General Election of 1992* (Basingstoke: Macmillan, 1992), p 351.

constituency. Only 2% could name the (prospective) Tory candidate, Kenneth Andrew, while 32% mistakenly thought that Stephen Dorrell would be fighting the constituency again. (By contrast, 14% knew the name of Labour candidate Andrew Reed[35].) So chicken runs do not seem to have made much impact. Except for that lost chance to rebalance an electoral system that chance and population movement had gerrymandered against them, it is unlikely that the Tories really suffered from the introduction of new constituency boundaries.

Conclusion: How they stood by the start of 1997

By the time the strategic phase was played out, the election about to be called and the short-term tactics of the campaign itself begun, the election was already effectively lost. The squandering of their reputation for economic management, disunity over Europe and the clinging fog of sleaze had destroyed the Conservative Party's image as being fit to govern. As Daniel Finkelstein notes, 'Rightly or wrongly, they saw us as arrogant, smug, sleazy, weak, incompetent and divided.'[36] Blair by contrast was popular, trusted, and backed by an efficient campaigning organisation. The outcome of the election was certain, going back two years, probably four to 'Black Wednesday'.

Nevertheless, many Tories affected to disbelieve that, and to disbelieve the polls as well. After all, they argued, the polls had got it wrong in 1992, and there was nothing to corroborate their findings now. Cloud cuckoo land. Ian Lang wrote to us after the election: 'I don't know why we were surprised; you told us what was happening.'

What wasn't clear until the Wirral South by-election, on 28 February 1997, was the magnitude of the coming Labour landslide. All four of the regular polling companies' most recent published poll before Wirral South showed the Tories' share of the national vote between 30% and

---

[35] MORI On-Line interviewed a representative quota sample of 602 Loughborough constituents by telephone on 19–21 March 1997.

[36] Finkelstein, D., 'Why the Conservatives Lost' in Crewe, I., Gosschalk, B., and Bartle, J. (eds.), *Political Communications: Why Labour Won the General Election of 1997* (London: Frank Cass, 1998).

Table 12: Wirral South

	1992 GE %	Sun/ MORI poll of by-election voting intent 14–16 Jan 1997 %	Mail on Sunday /MORI poll of by-election voting intent 6–7 Feb 1997 %	By-election result 27 Feb 1997 %	Sun/ MORI poll of general election voting intent 28 Feb– 2 Mar 1997 %	Sun/ MORI poll of general election voting intent 19–20 April 1997 %	General election result 1 May 1997 %
Conservative	50.8	36	35	34.4	38	36	36.4
Labour	34.6	52	54	52.6	54	54	50.9
Liberal Democrats	13.1	12	10	10.1	7	8	10.4
Other	1.5	*	1	2.9	1	2	2.2
Conservative lead	+16.2	−16	−19	−18.2	−16	−18	−14.5
Swing		16.1	17.6	17.2	16.1	17.1	15.4

Source: MORI/*The Sun/Mail on Sunday*

34%, with an average of 32% – certain defeat, but only if the polls were right. Wirral South offered the corroboration that had been lacking – a result right in line with MORI's polling in the constituency, showing no pool of 'shy Tories'. The voters of the Wirral had told us the truth. They had swung by 17%. And, they said, most of them were going to do it again on 1 May. We believed them. A landslide was on the way.

Tactics: the short campaign 16 March–1 May 1997

The strategic manoeuvring over, the battlefield in front of us. The rival generals marshal their forces and prepare to fight. One side, as in 1997, may have already achieved a decisive advantage. But the battle has still to be fought, and the details of its outcome will depend upon the sizes of the forces, upon their armament and their skill in using it, and upon the tactical decisions of their leaders, as well as upon the initial dispositions to which the strategic phase has brought them.

While the commanding generals, Major, Blair and Ashdown, were in the field, their three-star operations chiefs, Mawhinney, Mandelson and Holme, were alternatively directing the tactics and briefing the media from their bunkers in London. The weapons at their disposal were diverse: at the national and regional level, multi-million pound budgets to spend both on the strictly limited number of TV Election Broadcasts available and on newspaper and poster advertising, the editorial assistance of friendly newspapers and the skill of their planning and their spokesmen in turning the attention of the neutral broadcasting media (and of those parts of the newspapers whose contents are dictated by news values rather than the editorial or proprietorial line) in the directions most favourable to their party's case. (In all but the last of these functions, which is more dependent upon skill than resources, the Liberal Democrats were disadvantaged by comparison with the two bigger parties and, indeed, by comparison with Sir James Goldsmith's generously-funded Referendum Party). These are the artillery and cavalry of the election war.

Meanwhile at the local level, the infantry is at work. Here legal spending restrictions are in force, and much remains as it was in bygone days: the burden of the work falls on the armies of voluntary helpers usually referred to as 'grass-roots party members' (paid canvassing is of course illegal), and the task involves the hand-to-hand fighting of the election – targeting the delivery of the message to the individual voter. Leaflets must be stuffed into envelopes or put through letterboxes. Voters must be canvassed. The candidate must tread the streets, shaking hands and kissing babies. Nevertheless, modernisation is intruding at the local level as well. The traditional election meeting is almost dead, for most voters would rather watch the Prime Minister and Leader of the Opposition put their case on television than sit in a draughty hall listening to their local candidate. A computer now probably logs the canvass returns, the same computer which will print address labels for the election addresses and allow the targeting of different messages at different sectors of the electorate. The leaflets to be posted through letterboxes may be supplanted by video cassettes (the Referendum Party's distinctive innovation), and much of the canvassing may be done by telephone rather than in person. The candidate, though still tramping the streets, is kept 'on message' with daily briefings by fax or pager from his party headquarters in London.

All this is a complex operation. But how effectively do the parties operate it, and how much difference does it really make to the voters? Let us begin by seeing what the parties did.

Table 13: Campaign Calendar

WEEK ONE
Monday, March 17th
- Election called
- Major says he is willing to take part in a head-to-head TV debate with Blair

Tuesday, March 18th
- *Sun* announces support for Blair
- Labour promises minister for jobs
- Blair and Ashdown attack Major for proroguing before Downey report on sleaze can be published

Wednesday, March 19th
- Headline unemployment figures fall below 1.75 million to 6.2%, lowest since 1990
- Rifkind warns single currency will split EU

Thursday, March 20th
- Underlying inflation rate fell from 3.1% to 2.9% in February
- Last Prime Minister's Question Time dominated by bitter clash over sleaze
- Interim report by Sir Gordon Downey exonerates 15 MPs but leaves accusations against 10 Tories unresolved

Friday, March 21st
- *Guardian* publishes summary of unpublished Downey report evidence

Saturday, March 22nd
- Speaker announces new rules for MPs' expense claims

WEEK TWO
Monday, March 24th
- Ex-Scottish Office Minister Allan Stewart resigns as a candidate in Eastwood
- Official figures published showing an accelerating rise in living standards

Tuesday, March 25th
- Tories announce plan to introduce pupil tests at 14
- Blair announces plans to create an anti-drugs supremo

Wednesday, March 26th
- IRA bombs Wilmslow railway station
- Tim Smith announces he will stand down in Beaconsfield

Thursday, March 27th
- *Sun* accuses Piers Merchant of an affair with a 17-year old night-club hostess
- Conservatives call press conference to accuse Labour of 'running away from' a leaders' TV debate

Saturday, March 29th (EASTER SATURDAY)
- Sir Michael Hirst resigns as Scottish Conservative Chairman amid fears of a sex scandal
- Beckenham Tories back Piers Merchant

Sunday, March 30th (EASTER SUNDAY)
- Launch of Channel 5
- *Sunday Telegraph* reports transcripts of the Downey sleaze inquiry, leaked to it by Neil Hamilton

WEEK THREE
Monday, March 31st
- Major supports use of 'draconian powers' against MPs found guilty of misconduct
- Lady Thatcher attacks Blair in *Daily Telegraph*
- Major calls Blair a 'chicken' for not accepting his challenge to a TV debate, and Central Office announces it will hire a man in a chicken suit to follow Blair and make the point

Tuesday, April 1st
- Liberal Democrats lauch campaign portraying Blair and Major as Punch and Judy
- Blair describes single currency as a 'big if'

Wednesday, April 2nd
- Launch of Conservative manifesto

Thursday, April 3rd
- Launch of Labour manifesto
- Tory 'chicken' attends a series of Labour events, and clashes with the *Daily Mirror*'s 'headless chicken' and 'fox'. Two bears and a rhinoceros also appear.
- IRA plants two bombs on M6; M1 and M5 also affected

Friday, April 4th
- Launch of Liberal Democrat manifesto
- Blair compares the powers of a Scottish parliament with those of a local council

Saturday, April 5th
- IRA bomb scare cancels Grand National

Sunday, April 6th
- Martin Bell agrees to stand as independent anti-sleaze candidate in Tatton
- Major attacks Labour's policy U-turns in *Frost on Sunday* interview

WEEK FOUR
Monday, April 7th
- Blair refuses to rule out privatisation of air traffic control system
- David Dimbleby interviews Blair on *Panorama*
Tuesday, April 8th
- **Dissolution of Parliament**
- Tatton Tories adopt Neil Hamilton as their candidate
- Report into *E coli* food-poisoning outbreak condemns government
Wednesday, April 9th
- Policy Studies Institute attacks lack of information available to the voter
Thursday, April 10th
- Paul Sykes claims support from 150 Tory candidates opposed to the single currency
Friday, April 11th
- *The Times* challenges Major and Blair to take part in a TV debate
Saturday, April 12th
- Riot in Whitehall during demonstration over sacked Merseyside dockers
- HSBC report claims UK unemployment is 14%
- Mo Mowlam revealed to have been suffering from a brain tumour
Sunday, April 13th
- Referendum Party's rally at Alexandra Palace

WEEK FIVE
Monday, April 14th
- Major attacks Blair as a 'hypocrite' over his decision to send his son to a grant-maintained school
- Dame Angela Rumbold rules out joining the single currency
Tuesday, April 15th
- Labour's 'bulldog' party political broadcast
- Referendum Party draws up 'white list' of 93 constituencies it will not contest
- Two ministers (Paice and Horam) vow not to join the single currency in their manifestos
Wednesday, April 16th
- **Nominations close**
- Major's 'don't tie my hands' speech on his European negotiating policy
Thursday, April 17th
- Major offers Eurosceptics free vote on the single currency
Friday, April 18th
- Conservative advertising poster showing Blair sitting on Helmut Kohl's knee
- Two IRA bombs at Leeds and Doncaster railway stations; M6 also targeted
- Major announces surprise honours list
Saturday, April 19th
- Clarke describes fears of Eurosceptics as 'paranoid nonsense'

Sunday, April 20th
- Clarke and Howard disagree over Europe

WEEK SIX
Monday, April 21st
- IRA targets Central London transport system
- Jacques Santer attacks Eurosceptics as 'doom merchants' in speech
- Labour's 'Land of Hope and Glory' party political broadcast

Tuesday, April 22nd
- Broadcasters ban Pro-Life Alliance (anti-abortion) party political broadcast
- Perth speech: Major warns devolution will lead to break-up of union
- Labour launch 'Laurel and Hardy' poster of Major and Clarke

Wednesday, April 23rd
- ICM/*Guardian* poll shows Labour with only a 5-point lead: splash in *Mail*, *Express*, *Telegraph* (burying its own Gallup 21-point lead)
- Tories leak Labour 'War Book'

Thursday, April 24th
- Tories accuse Labour of lying over their plans for the state pension

Friday, April 25th
- Blair promises he will be a 'radical leader' in *Times* interview

Saturday, April 26th
- Labour leak Conservative briefing document for prospective candidates
- *News of the World* announces support for Blair

Sunday, April 27th
- Edwina Currie predicts a 'bloodbath'

WEEK SEVEN
Monday, April 28th
- ITV 500 debate: Heseltine takes Major's place
- Major warns 'there is only 72 hours left to save the Union'

Tuesday, April 29th
- *Times* backs Eurosceptic candidates
- EU warns UK could lose its place on G7
- Blair evokes memory of John Smith

Wednesday, April 30th
- Major warns voters, 'Don't fall for New Labour'
- Blair: voters face choice between 'party for the future and a party for the past'

Thursday, May 1st – POLLING DAY

Issues and agenda setting

We can begin with an overview of the course of the campaign and the parties' tactics. As we have explained, we had been tracking the relative salience to the public of 14 possible issues (increased to 16 during the election), asking which would be 'very important' in influencing their votes. It was soon plain that the top four issues of the election would be health care, education, unemployment and law & order. That's what Labour spokesmen concentrated on, right from the beginning when they were the chosen themes of the 'Road to the Manifesto'. During the election, what did Labour spokesmen concentrate on, their press conferences, their leader's speeches? Health care, education, unemployment and law & order, and not until the final week, when the Tories had driven up Europe in salience, to their own detriment, did Labour react by including in their final week's advertising their pledge not to take the pound into the EMU without a referendum of the British people on this issue.

Meanwhile, what of the Tories? Mr Major hoped to launch the election surfing the good economic news and the announcement of reduced unemployment rates. Little did he know that his first two weeks were to be swamped in sleaze.

Nothing that the Tories could do, nor for that matter the other parties, would get the media's attention back onto the issues of the election. It well suited Labour to continue the focus on sleaze, for they were characterised by only a fifth of the electorate as 'sleazy', while two-thirds so described the Conservatives[1]. So the Mandelson machine poured petrol on the sleaze bonfire daily. They were of course helped by the early declaration of the *Sun* for Labour, and as vitriolic as the *Sun* had been in aid of the Tories in earlier elections, so it was vicious on Labour's behalf against the Tories in 1997.

But in the face of this obviously damaging sleaze onslaught, the Tory leadership seemed transfixed like rabbits in the headlights. It was almost as if they regarded it as an Act of God. Daniel Finkelstein, one of the key Central Office strategists, opened his explanation of 'Why the Conservatives Lost':

'During the few weeks of the campaign itself a Scottish MP, who had previously resigned as a minister having been accused of threatening

---

[1] King, A., 'Voters fear Labour's crushing domination', *Daily Telegraph*, 4 April 1997, reporting Gallup data for the *Daily Telegraph*, fieldwork 26 March-2 April 1997: asked 'Do you agree or disagree with the following statement: "The Conservatives/Labour these days give the impression of being very sleazy and disreputable"?', 63% agreed with regard to the Conservatives, and 19% with regard to Labour.

somebody with an axe, was forced to resign his candidacy in a further scandal. The Scottish Party chairman, mooted as a replacement, had to stand down having been accused by colleagues of homosexual relationships with other Conservative activists. Two former government ministers were embroiled in the Harrods so-called "cash-for-questions" affair. A Parliamentary Private Secretary was photographed in a park embracing a 17-year-old Soho night-club hostess. A white-suited war hero BBC journalist, Martin Bell, decided to stand against the Tatton Conservatives with the help of David Soul from *Starsky and Hutch*. And, of course, there was the rebellion over European Monetary Union (EMU).'[2]

And all this Finkelstein sums up 'One might have been forgiven for believing that strategy, even politics, had nothing to do with it.'!

Admittedly, not all of these public relations disasters could have been prevented by Central Office – principally because the party had no effective powers to vet and eject or even discipline sitting MPs who had the confidence of their constituency parties and wanted to run for re-election. (These were the powers that Neil Kinnock had fought tooth and nail to get for Walworth Road ten years earlier against opposition from the left of the party, and which the new Hague regime in Smith Square was very quick to create in the aftermath of the 1997 landslide by setting up an ethics committee.)

We have seen already how the strategic failure to deal with the menace of sleaze allowed the momentum of the issue to grow until it was inevitable that it would be an issue of the short campaign if Labour or the Press were given any openings to make it so. But it was party indiscipline in the constituencies, or alternatively admirably stubborn but misguided refusal to drop candidates who, guilty or innocent, had had their credibility holed below the waterline, that allowed the stream of bad news to continue and overwhelm the crucial opening fortnight of the campaign when John Major was hoping to turn the tide. None of the matters Finkelstein lists came out of the blue except the essentially trivial case of Piers Merchant (accused of dalliance with the 17-year-old Soho hostess, Anna Cox) which, but for seeming part of a trend, could

---

[2] Finkelstein, D., 'Why the Conservatives Lost' in Crewe, I., Gosschalk, B., and Bartle, J. (eds), *Political Communications: Why Labour Won the General Election of 1997* (London: Frank Cass, 1998).

probably have been ignored completely. Merchant, incidentally, held his Beckenham constituency comfortably despite the 'scandal', though after the election he had to resign his seat when the press produced allegations of a second liaison with the same girl.

It must surely have been obvious that Allan Stewart in Eastwood (who had resigned over the axe incident), Tim Smith at Beaconsfield and Neil Hamilton at Tatton (the two who had resigned ministerial posts over the cash-for-questions allegations) were vulnerable to attack and that their candidacy had the potential to damage the party nationally. Why so surprised when the damage indeed occurred? Stewart and Smith both eventually stood down, but not before their cases had helped to stoke the sleaze bonfire. The sex scandal over Stewart's putative replacement, Sir Michael Hirst, was perhaps less easily foreseen. On the other hand, the Hirst allegations were reputed to have come from within the Scottish Conservative Party itself[3], and if the whole fiasco derived from internal party back-biting, the wounds were certainly self-inflicted. (Again, if the Eastwood fiasco had been an isolated incident, a braver leadership might have stood by Hirst, refusing to accept his resignation, and demanded that indiscretions in his private life were nobody's business but his own, and no bar to Conservative candidacy; admittedly, it might not have played well with the Conservative electorate of Eastwood, the safest Tory seat in Scotland, but it could hardly have been more damaging nationally, and despite a second change of candidate they lost Eastwood anyway. As we have seen, the voters are considerably more tolerant of alleged sexual peccadilloes than of allegations of financial misdemeanours or abuse of office.)

Smith, unlike Hamilton, admitted that he had received money from Mohammed Al Fayed. Even so, Brian Mawhinney felt compelled to deny that Central Office had forced him to resign: 'If you are asking was he being levered out, that is not the case . . . If his association had been happy to continue with him, he would have been a candidate of good standing, but, out of respect for the Prime Minister and not wishing to

---

[3] The *Sunday Mirror* on 30 March led its front page: 'DIRTY TRICKS: Tory lies about *Sunday Mirror* force party chief to quit over gay lover', going on to allege 'Sir Michael's senior Party colleagues misled him to get him to quit. They said the *Sunday Mirror* had a dossier . . . We had no dossier.'

be a distraction, he has made his decision.' Then, referring to the Hamilton case he went on 'We don't sit in Central Office and force candidates on associations. . . . There is a huge difference between the positions of Tim Smith and Neil Hamilton out of their own mouths. Hamilton vehemently denies he was taking money, and people are innocent until and unless proved guilty.'[4]

But the other side of the coin was that the difference between Smith and Hamilton by this stage was that Smith was no longer harming the party while Hamilton still was. The party whose constituency executives could force out Sir George Gardiner for asserting too vocally a Euroscepticism that most of his constituents probably shared refused to oust Neil Hamilton even when it must have been clear that many of his constituents believed the cash-for-questions accusations that had been levelled at him and that his candidacy was becoming a symbolic cause celèbre that the party's opponents would exploit. There was plenty of evidence, including a MORI On-Line constituency poll for the *Sun* a few days after Bell's candidacy was confirmed, on what the people of Tatton thought about the whole affair.

Of course, if they wanted to stand by their candidate that was their right – indeed, perhaps it was noble self-sacrifice and their duty if they believed in his innocence. But in that case they can hardly complain at Martin Bell's candidature (if it hadn't been him it would have been somebody else), which was the natural consequence, or suggest it was not the result of their own actions. They can at least be grateful that in the end there was not – as was at one point mooted – an independent Conservative candidate put up as well, in which case there is a distinct possibility that Hamilton would have faced the humiliation of finishing third[5].

Is there something 'unfair' about Labour and the Lib Dems standing down and endorsing an independent candidate when it simultaneously

---

[4] Speaking on *Newsnight*. Quoted in Jones, N., *Campaign 1997: How the General Election was Won and Lost*, (London: Indigo, 1997), p 169.

[5] The MORI/*Sun* constituency poll on 9 April asked Tatton electors how they would vote 'if a member of the Conservative party were to stand as an independent Conservative, opposing both Neil Hamilton and Martin Bell', and found support of 33% (of those expressing a voting intention) for Bell, 31% for the unnamed independent Tory and 23% for Hamilton.

Table 14: Tatton electors' views of Neil Hamilton's candidature

Q. **On balance, do you think that Neil Hamilton should have been selected to stand for the Conservatives by the local party on Tuesday, or not?**

	%
Should have been selected	28
Should not have been selected	60
Don't know	12

Q. **In your opinion, do you think Neil Hamilton is innocent or guilty of the accusations of financial misconduct that have been made against him?**

	%
Innocent	18
Guilty	44
Don't know	37

Q. **On balance, do you agree or disagree that an election campaign with Martin Bell opposing Neil Hamilton will prevent a full debate on all the issues in the constituency?**
Q. (To those who agree that full debate of issues will be prevented) **Who are you most inclined to blame?**

	%
Agree, blame Neil Hamilton	23
Agree, blame local Conservative party	9
Agree, blame Liberal Democrat and Labour parties	8
Agree, blame the media	4
Agree, blame Martin Bell	2
Agree, blame John Major	2
Agree, blame someone else	4
Agree, blame nobody	*
Agree, don't know who to blame	6
Total agree	57
Disagree	29
Don't know	14

Source: MORI On-Line/*The Sun*
9 April 1997
Base: 525 adults 18+ in the Tatton constituency (interviewed by telephone)

gives them a chance of dislodging a Tory MP from an otherwise safe seat and of exploiting the propaganda advantage nationally? Or is it just good tactical management, of a sort Labour had in abundance and the Tories apparently completely lacked? Finkelstein seems to take the former view. Welcome to the dirty world of modern professional politics, Danny. Even if every sleaze story ever printed about Tory MPs had been entirely untrue, the Tories had only themselves to blame (collectively as a party, if not necessarily specifically at Central Office or in Number Ten) for the degree to which it was allowed to destroy their campaign in the first few weeks of the 1997 election proper[6].

Ironically, there was a perfect demonstration of the effective, if cynical, way to silence sleaze allegations during the election. Jonathan Aitken had resigned from the Cabinet in July 1995, and issued writs against the *Guardian* and Granada TV following allegations they made against him. His case collapsed and he subsequently pleaded guilty to perjury, but that was after the election. During the election itself, no doubt partly because the case was *sub judice*, there was hardly a whisper of Aitken's name or the specific allegations against him in all the tornado of sleaze allegations; this reticence didn't save him his Thanet seat, but nor was his name used to damage his neighbours.

Compared to the slick, news-management 'control freak' world of New Labour, the Tories were left looking very old-fashioned and amateur in their approach. They were not ready for a possibility that they ought to have foreseen, and it cost them their first chance to seize the agenda.

But even when the Tories had the chance to get out from under the blanket of sleaze and set the agenda by concentrating on their own chosen issues, their focus was badly misconceived. As the sleaze bonfire seemed to be burning itself out, the Tories switched the focus to blaming Labour for scuppering the possibility of a presidential-style TV debate. How? Party Chairman Brian Mawhinney approved the sending out of a man dressed in a chicken suit to peck at the heels of Tony Blair, and thus wasted two more days as the television, the tabloids and even *The Times* couldn't resist photo opportunities of the chicken on the campaign. It was reminiscent of 'Chicken George', sent out by the Clinton team to harass George Bush in the first Clinton campaign. More Americanisation

---

[6] The evidence seems clear that the damage was to the party as a whole, and not just to those candidates against whom allegations had been made; analysis suggests most sleaze-accused candidates did no worse than any Tory might have expected in their constituency. See Farrell, D., McAllister, I. and Studlar, D., 'Sex, Money and Politics: Sleaze and the Conservative Party in the 1997 Election' in Denver, D. et al (eds.), *British Elections and Parties Review* Volume 8: The 1997 General Election (London: Frank Cass, 1998). pp 80–94.

of British politics, and not to the good. Predictably, it failed to impress the public. Two-thirds of the electorate were in favour of a TV debate taking place[7], but despite the Tory campaign, almost as many blamed the Tories or Mr Major as blamed Labour or Mr Blair for preventing it[8], and nine in ten agreed that the chicken gimmick was childish[9].

With the manifesto launches, the parties captured the agenda, and press conferences, politicians' speeches and the Party Election Broadcasts began to emerge. And no sooner had the manifestos been launched, at the end of that same week, than the confirmation of Neil Hamilton as Conservative candidate in Tatton switched the focus straight back to sleaze and to Martin Bell's decision to run against him as an Independent.

The first weeks of the election were then swamped in sleaze and plagued with chickens, and it wasn't until after Easter, with a third of the election gone, that substantive issues began to emerge. Meanwhile the Prime Minister spent the third week talking about constitutional threats of Labour's policies and especially devolution. Out of 16 issues, 'constitutional issues/devolution' ranked 16th in importance with the voters, and the issue that the Deputy Prime Minister spent most of the same week talking about, trade unions, ranked 15th out of 16.

Finally, too late to have any chance of making much impact, the Tories switched the emphasis back to Europe. This, of course, was the issue that still transfixed the Tory party. But as we have seen, Europe wasn't an 'issue issue', it was an 'image issue'. Europe did not lose the 1997 election for the Tories – but it helped to win it big for Labour.

---

[7] In a MORI poll for *The Times* on 15 April, 65% said they would support 'a public debate between the Prime Minister, John Major, and the Leader of the Opposition, Tony Blair'. 19% were opposed.

[8] A Gallup poll for the *Daily Telegraph* on 4–6 April asked 'As you probably heard, it now seems that there may not be any television debates between the party leaders during the election campaign, and the Conservative and Labour parties are blaming each other for preventing them from happening. From what you know, who do you think is to blame?', with respondents allowed to give more than one answer. Labour/Blair were named by 30%, the Conservatives/Major by 28%.

[9] The Gallup poll went on to ask 'The Conservatives are sending a man dressed as a chicken around the country to draw attention to what they say is Mr Blair's cowardice in not agreeing to a televised debate. Do you think the Conservatives are making a serious point, or is this just a childish gimmick?'. 91% said it was a childish gimmick, 6% that it made a serious point. (*Daily Telegraph*, 7 April 1997).

Labour's low key mildly pro-European policy wasn't a vote winner; but the Tories' spectacular split over Britain's role in Europe, combined with the bizarre decision to focus on Europe during the campaign, ensured that voters were reminded that the Tories were divided over the issue. Divided parties don't win elections.

Did they not do any issues polling, or did they just not pay any attention to it? (Presumably the latter: after the election Charles Lewington revealed 'John Major had understood the perils inherent in a Europe-focused campaign. . . . We were impressed by an ICM analysis showing that voters' concerns about Europe were not a primary influence in determining voting intentions'[10]; but when it came to the point, they forgot that insight as well.)

That is not to say that Europe as an issue per se was swinging no votes. But it can exaggerated: for the vast majority of voters, it was not decisive – only 22% of electors interviewed by MORI for *The Times* in mid-campaign rated Europe as 'very important' in deciding their vote, placing it only *eighth* in the ranking of importance to voters in deciding how to vote. But for a minority, who were disproportionately strong among the group of voters who abandoned their Conservative loyalty after 1992, Europe was a touchstone issue – and by two to one those, like the majority of the Parliamentary party, were Euro-sceptics rather than Europhiles.

Of course, there were numerous factors contributing to the disillusionment of so many former Conservative voters. But for many of them – on both sides of the debate – policy on Europe was a factor sufficiently important to make them rethink their loyalties. A MORI survey for the Euro-sceptic activist Paul Sykes, conducted the week before the election, found both support *and* opposition to a single European currency higher among defecting Conservatives than among any other group – only don't knows were rare. (Just 6% of Tory defectors didn't know how they would vote in a referendum on a single currency, compared with 14% of Tory loyalists and 23% of Labour voters.)

The Tories' problem, of course, was that they were too divided at the

---

[10] Lewington, C., '"You know we can't win . . . how do you think history will judge me?"', *Sunday Telegraph*, 8 June 1997

top of the party to adopt a firm policy on Europe in either direction. Every debate touching on Europe emphasised the split at the top of the party – for every vote that could be directly gained by the leadership committing the party one way or the other, far more were being indirectly lost by reinforcing the image of the party as divided, an attribute which has always been a factor in the British voter's judgment of a party's fitness to rule. Nearly half the electorate (44%) saw the Conservative Party as divided during the 1997 election campaign, while Labour – equally divided by their personal opinions on the European issue but better able to control the expression of dissent – were seen as divided by only 12%. In these circumstances, it is unlikely the voters would have trusted their promises even if they were briefly able to present a united front. It became damaging rather than helpful for the issue to be kept on the agenda at all; but this was a lesson the Conservatives seemed unwilling or unable to learn.

One circumstance which may have contributed to Central Office's difficulties over Europe was fear of the Referendum Party; but, despite Sir James Goldsmith's millions, this fear proved generally misplaced. The RP won just over 800,000 votes, but only about half of those seem to have come from former Tories – 100,000 of their supporters had voted Labour in 1992, about the same number voted Liberal Democrat, and the remainder supported minor parties or didn't vote at all. And, of course, it would be a mistake to assume that those 400,000 would have voted Conservative again had the Referendum Party option not been available.

In terms of seats, the impact was equally low. It is true that the Referendum Party vote exceeded the majority by which the Conservatives were beaten in a number of constituencies, but taking into account the fact that those votes were not all defecting Conservatives, it seems likely that *at most* Referendum candidates cost the Tories just six seats, and only three to Labour. Labour's majority might have been 173 instead of 179. This is a mere fleabite. The most likely effect is shown in the table below (the RP effect being the estimated effect of votes lost to the RP on the Conservative lead over their main challengers).

Suppose circumstances had been different, though – what if the Tories had been able to gag dissent among the Cabinet, and Major had taken

Table 15: Effect of the Referendum Party

Constituency	Winner	Majority	RP vote	RP effect	Estimated majority without RP
Harwich	**Lab**	**−1,216**	**4,923**	**−2,018**	**802***
Falmouth and Camborne	Lab	−2,688	3,534	−1,448	−1,240
Norfolk North West	Lab	−1,339	2,923	−1,198	−141
Taunton	LD	−2,452	2,760	−1,007	−1,445
Castle Point	Lab	−1,116	2,700	−1,107	−9
Lewes	LD	−1,300	2,481	−905	−395
Somerton and Frome	**LD**	**−130**	**2,449**	**−893**	**763***
Weston-super-Mare	LD	−1,274	2,280	−832	−442
Braintree	Lab	−1,451	2,165	−887	−564
Eastleigh	LD	−754	2,013	−734	−20
Harrow West	Lab	−1,240	1,997	−818	−422
Colchester	LD	−1,581	1,776	−648	−933
Winchester	**LD**	**−2**	**1,598**	**−583**	**581***
Kettering	**Lab**	**−189**	**1,551**	**−636**	**447***
Lancaster and Wyre	Lab	−1,295	1,516	−621	−674
Milton Keynes NE	**Lab**	**−240**	**1,492**	**−611**	**371***
Romford	Lab	−649	1,431	−586	−63
Kingston and Surbiton	**LD**	**−56**	**1,417**	**−517**	**461***
Northampton South	Lab	−744	1,405	−576	−168

*Referendum Party intervention decisive

the authority to adopt a European policy and stick with it? To be electorally effective it would have had to be a Euro-sceptic policy, not only because that was the preference of the majority both of loyal and of defecting Tories, but because the impact would have been much diminished if the policy was not strongly differentiated from that of the other parties. If they had been able to do so – and, equally crucially, if the electorate had been prepared to believe them – the polling evidence suggests it might have significantly increased their vote. A MORI poll in Wirral South ten days before the election found the Tories with 36% support (precisely the share of the vote they eventually won in that constituency). When we asked the sample how they would vote 'if the Conservative Party were to announce that it would not take Britain into a single European currency with the first group of countries', the same respondents said they would vote 43% Conservative, a seven point swing back. If they could have achieved that differential nationally, they might have come very close to depriving Labour of a majority and bringing about a hung Parliament.

Wirral South is an excellent example of the sort of seat where the Tories most needed to rekindle their appeal to the voters if they were to avoid humiliation. But this poll probably exaggerates the real effect a policy shift could have achieved. A poll concentrating the voters' minds on a single issue can always expect a higher response than that issue would achieve in the real world, competing for the agenda with all the other issues and, as we have already noted, fewer than a quarter of voters thought Europe would be important in deciding their vote. Of course, it could be argued that Europe was only so low in many voters' priorities because they could see no meaningful difference between the parties' policies, and more would have switched if the Tories established themselves as genuinely Eurosceptic. But there is little evidence for it. Europe performed almost as poorly on our unprompted 'important issues facing Britain today' question (which is where we would expect to find evidence of an issue concerning voters but suppressed from the agenda by party agreement), only 33% naming it in March, though it rose to 43% a week before the election (third behind the NHS, 63%, and education/schools, 54%) when the Conservative concentration on it in campaigning pushed it to the top of the voters' minds.

We should also note that any short-term benefit might have been a liability in the longer term. A united hard line on Europe might have reduced Blair's majority or perhaps even replaced it with a Blair-Ashdown coalition. But it would still not have won for the Tories, and now, years down the line, the party would still be facing the problem of which direction to move – perhaps handicapped with an additional burden of unjustified complacency. A Euro-sceptic policy would have won back some Euro-sceptic Tories, and probably some others with no strong opinions on Europe yet contempt for the vacillating indecisiveness and party divisions that made a policy impossible; but it would equally have further alienated the smaller but none the less committed band of Europhile defectors. These would not have voted for the party, anyway, in 1997, but the task now is to win them back by 2002 – difficult as that may be, it would probably have been impossible had Major fought and narrowly lost on a Euro-sceptic platform. There were enough Tory

Euro-sceptics for the party to have lost less badly on 1 May; but there were not enough of them for the party to have won.

Campaigning effectiveness: getting the message across

Unlike the Tories' hapless 'pennyfarthing' of a machine, Labour's 'troops' on the ground had a good campaign. (See table on p. 118). Labour called on fractionally more people, 12% of electors against 11% for the Tories. They out-leafleted the Tories 75% to 66%. They reached more potential voters than the Tories by billboards, 55% to 53%, and they reached as many through their party election broadcasts both on TV and on the radio. The Labour Party rang up over two million people, more than double those telephoned by the Tories, and they had more active helpers on the ground. Only on sending letters individually addressed signed by the party leaders were they equalled by the Tories. On delivering videos through electors' letterboxes they were hugely outgunned, but not by the Tories: some 22% of electors recalled their household getting the Referendum Party's video. John Banks, the Referendum Party's advertising adviser, confirmed that they were sent to almost one in four households. Much good it did them.

Labour's machine was even stronger in the marginals; in Gloucester, which Tony Blair visited so often people were beginning to talk, twice as many people were canvassed by Labour as by the Conservatives, more received leaflets from Labour, a third more had received a letter from Tony Blair than from John Major, and a fifth more were conscious of Labour's billboards than of the Tories'. Forty-one per cent of the people we polled in Gloucester for the *Sun* said Labour was making the most effort to win them over, compared with 16% who thought the Tories were. The swing there was 11.5%, as in most of the marginals above the national average.

117

Table 16: Campaign Penetration

Q. **During the past few weeks have you. . . . ?**
Q. (If yes) **Which party was that?**

	Any %	Con %	Lab %	Lib Dem %	SNP /PC %	Ref P'ty %	Oth pty %	Yes but DK which pty %	No not seen any %	DK %
Had any political leaflets put through your letterbox	89	66	75	55	9	30	13	3	9	2
Seen any party election broadcasts on TV	73	59	59	50	9	17	14	3	26	1
Seen any political advertisements on billboards	70	53	55	16	3	7	2	4	28	2
Watched the leaders debate on TV	36	30	30	23	4	2	1	2	62	2
Received a video through your letterbox from a political party	27	*	1	1	*	22	*	2	72	1
Been called on by a representative of any political party	24	11	12	5	1	1	1	*	74	1
Received a letter signed by a party leader individually addressed to you	20	10	9	3	1	*	*	1	77	3
Heard any party election broadcasts on the radio	15	10	10	8	1	2	2	2	79	6
Been telephoned by a representative of any political party	7	2	5	*	–	*	*	*	92	1
Helped a political party in its campaign	4	1	2	*	–	1	–	*	95	1
Attended a political meeting addressed by a candidate	2	1	1	*	–	*	*	*	97	1

Source: MORI/*Independent on Sunday*/*Sunday Mirror*
23–24 April 1997
Base: 941 British adults

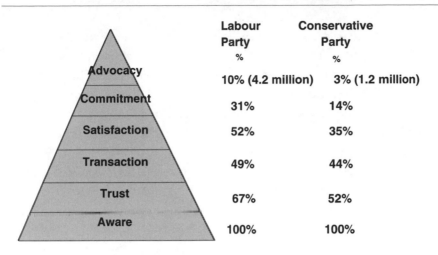

	Labour Party %	Conservative Party %
Advocacy	10% (4.2 million)	3% (1.2 million)
Commitment	31%	14%
Satisfaction	52%	35%
Transaction	49%	44%
Trust	67%	52%
Aware	100%	100%

Base: 1,133 British electors, 22 April 1997   Source: MORI

Figure 11: The relationship hierarchy

Tony's Army

But Labour's 'war machine' was not only better armed and better directed than that of the Conservatives, its power was magnified by a secondary factor. Labour's secret marketing weapon was word-of-mouth advertising, the most cost effective of the black art's tools. Over four million people, one elector in ten, enlisted in Tony's Army during the election. That is more than three times as many foot soldiers on the ground talking up the election of New Labour as Tories who advocated John Major's return to Downing Street.

Applying the MORI Excellence Model (MEM) technique developed for its work with corporate clients, MORI found that nearly one in four (24%) intending Labour voters said they supported the Labour Party so strongly they encouraged others to vote for it without being asked, while only one in ten of those who expected to vote for the Conservatives were intent on convincing their friends.

At the other end of the spectrum, four times as many people (12%) across the country said they were so strongly opposed to the Conservative Party they attempted to discourage others from voting for it without

119

being asked compared with only three in a hundred who were as strongly opposed to Labour. This meant there were over five million electors actively arguing against John Major's re-election, countered by only just over a million true blue Tories rubbishing New Labour. Twice as many young people, under 25, were rubbishing the Conservatives as advocating them, six per cent to three per cent, while the reverse was true of Labour, seven per cent to three per cent.

Combining these figures, we get confirmation that this was more a 'negative' than a 'positive' election, despite the public's avowed opposition to negative campaigning. More of the electorate was spontaneously campaigning against the Tories than for Labour.

The support of the *Sun*, the newspaper with the largest national readership, for New Labour seems to have helped mobilise support for Blair. Fifteen per cent of *Sun* readers said they actively advocated others voting for Labour, five times as many *Sun* readers as said they advocated returning the Tories to Government.

Trying to buy success: the advertising war

Spending on advertising in the 1997 election was almost certainly higher than at any election in history, a reported total of £28 million between summer 1996 and the election – £12.7m by the Tories, £7.6m by Labour and £7.7m by the Referendum Party. Most of this advertising spend was on posters rather than press advertising: £10.8m of the Tory budget and £5.2m of Labour's, though only £1.2m of the Referendum Party's.[11] Yet all this expenditure seems to have had minimal impact on voting behaviour.

The Tories continued their trend of producing posters more newsworthy than obviously effective into the election campaign. The most notorious of their advertisements, showing a tiny Tony Blair like a ventriloquist's dummy sitting on Chancellor Kohl's knee was apparently thought up by – of all people – the generally pro-European Michael Heseltine. Certainly the press coverage of this supposed insult to a foreign

---

[11] Grice, A., 'The ad campaign that got away', *Campaign*, 9 May 1997.

head of government got publicity for the image much more widely and cheaply than could have been achieved simply by booking billboard space. No doubt many of the 47% of electors who, as we noted above, were not aware of having seen any Tory posters had, nevertheless, seen coverage of the Kohl advert. But did it, or any of the other posters, work? A week before the election, only 2% of Tories said posters on billboards had influenced the way they intended to vote, while 5% of Labour and 4% of Liberal Democrats said they had been influenced.

And it is worth noting that 4% of the population, a higher figure than for any other medium, thought they had seen an election poster but didn't know which party it was for. The notorious curse of the advert more memorable than the brand it promotes applies even to political advertising.

Saatchi & Saatchi, the advertising group from which the Saatchi brothers had broken away taking the Tory account with them, had the final word immediately after the election by hiring an ad van to circle Central Office carrying the legend 'Look what happens when you change your advertising agency'.[12] By July it was reported that the party had split with M&C Saatchi, and would be inviting other agencies to pitch for the contract in time for the 1999 European Parliament elections.[13]

---

[12] Bell, E., 'Monster raving loony adverts', *Observer*, 4 May 1997.
[13] 'Saatchis can't be written off', *Daily Telegraph*, 8 July 1997.

What did the voters think affected or would affect their vote?

Campaigning methods

Having seen how the parties chose to campaign, let us now begin to ask how well it worked. Consider the voters' own perceived effectiveness of these campaining methods – which ones did they themselves feel had influenced their voting intention? Table 17 shows the position the week before the election.

Table 17: Effectiveness of campaigning methods

Q. And which of these items, if any, have influenced the way you intend to vote?

	All %	Con %	Lab %	LD %	Switchers %
Party election broadcasts	12	12	11	16	22
The television debate between the party leaders	10	10	11	14	8
Newspapers	10	12	11	6	10
The views of your local candidates	9	7	9	9	6
Political leaflets put through letterbox	6	4	5	11	20
Posters on billboards	4	2	5	4	6
Video received from political party	2	1	1	2	-
Opinion polls	2	1	3	3	6
Telephone calls from political parties	–	–	–	–	-
Other	4	5	3	1	10
None of these	61	65	61	53	37
Don't know	3	2	3	3	10

Source: MORI/*Independent on Sunday/Sunday Mirror*
23–24 April 1997
Base: 941 British adults

There was no campaigning method that more than an eighth of the electorate thought had influenced them at that point (although this probably does not take into account their ability to reinforce existing intentions, which respondents might not recognise as 'influence' yet the importance of should by no means be underestimated.) The party election broadcasts seem to have made most impact, with 'the television debate between the leaders' in next place (even though there was no formal debate) together with newspapers. (The impact of the media is examined below.) Very few thought they had been influenced by the opinion polls, and not a single respondent admitted being influenced by telephone calls, even though 7% said they had been canvassed in this way (the equivalent of two million telephone calls!).

There was little difference between the reactions of Conversative and Labour supporters except on posters on billboards, on which the Tories scored significantly worse. Labour's leaflets had slightly more effect, probably reflecting the fact they delivered more, and perhaps significantly the Tories lost out also on 'the views of your local candidates' – in an election where Labour's candidates were tightly dragooned into following the party line while the Tories (despite an extraordinary attempt by Central Office to vet the manifestos of hundreds of candidates before approving them) asserted more freedom to follow their own line, especially on Europe, the suggestion seems to be that the diversity was counter-productive.

The pattern for the Liberal Democrats is significantly different, and fits our expectation that they were picking up voters who prior to the election had not given consideration to voting for them. Leaflets were more than twice as important for them as for the other parties (even though they were able to deliver fewer), while the PEBs and the leaders' debates, the means by which the party is able to raise its TV profile during an election, were also disproportionately important. The newspapers, by contrast, had much less effect – newspapers unlike the broadcast media are not required to be balanced or to give equal space to all the main contenders, and with no newspapers backing the Liberal Democrats this was naturally a less potent means of winning over supporters.

As a final test of campaign effectiveness, however, the 'switchers' column in the table is perhaps most significant. This exploits the most valubale feature of a panel survey, that it is possible to isolate individual respondents who have changed their responses between waves of the study. The switchers are those in the *Independent on Sunday/Sunday Mirror* panel who switched voting intention between the three main parties during the first three weeks of April. Of these, 22% said that election broadcasts had influenced them and 20% that leaflets through the letterbox had been important. These seem to have been the two most effective forms of campaigning (reflecting the fact that these were most useful to the LibDems who were the main net beneficiaries during that period).

Our survey covered all the main means by which the parties organized their campaigning. However, as we have already seen, there was a further factor to be taken into account – in the world outside the party bunkers, beyond the nucleus of professional party officials and the battalions of organised but unpaid campaigners and canvassers was an army of voters who were also determined to participate on their own account.

Media coverage

But, of course, the parties put as much if not more effort into secondary or indirect forms of campaigning – basically communicating through the media and manipulating the news agenda to boost their message – as into direct methods of contact and outright advertising. It should not be assumed that there is something disreputable in this process, simply because the introduction of 'spin doctors' and modern news management techniques such as Labour's computerised 'rapid rebuttal system' have made it appear more professional than in the past. In the modern age, the media (and especially television) are the main channels of communication between the governors and the governed. In a democratic election it should certainly be within the power of the candidates to bring up and have debated those issues on which they think the election should be fought, even if the broadcasters also have a legitimate role in putting on the agenda those issues that the candidates would like to avoid but which are of relevant interest to the voters.

The parties are right to put a premium on optimising the media output, for it has a powerful effect on the electorate. Again, we can start by getting an assessment straight from the horse's mouth. A question which we put to voters after the election looked specifically at the effect of media coverage on their voting behaviour, comparing the effect of

125

Table 18: Perceived influence of media coverage

Q. For each of the following, please tell me how much influence, if any, each had on your decision about what you would do on the day of the General Election?

	A great deal %	Fair amount %	Not very much %	None at all %	Don't know %
Election coverage on TV	10	29	21	40	*
Election coverage in newspapers	6	25	20	49	*
Party election broadcasts on TV	4	19	22	54	1
Leaflets delivered by the parties	3	15	18	64	1
Opinion polls	2	10	18	69	1

Source: MORI
7–8 May 1997
Base: 1,192 British adults

the journalistic coverage of the election with that of the parties' own communications. The media is not just an observer of the election, it is a key participant. It provides most voters with most of their information about the campaign, and more voters think their vote was influenced by television or newspaper election coverage than by the parties' own election broadcasts or the campaign leaflets. We conducted 1,192 interviews with adults aged 18+ across Great Britain by telephone on 7–8 May. When asked what influenced their vote, about half said none of the five factors listed had done so, but nearly four in ten said that election coverage on TV influenced their vote a fair amount or a great deal, a third said they were influenced by election coverage in the newspapers, nearly a quarter by party election broadcasts on TV, one in six by leaflets delivered by hand to their house, and 12% by opinion polls.

The importance of the media as an intermediary is confirmed when we ask the electorate about the party manifestos. Barely half say they are likely to read them – and many of those may mean their own candidates' leaflets rather than the formal manifestos (whose sales are hardly on the scale of the newspapers). A majority of those who are interested at all in what the parties have to say are happy to admit that they prefer it in pre-digested form.

Table 19: Interest in manifestos

Q. **How likely or unlikely are you to read or look at any of the party political manifestos in this election campaign?**

	%
Very likely	21
Fairly likely	32
Not very likely	22
Not at all likely	25
Don't know	*

Q. **Which of these statements best describes your attitude to the party election manifestos?**

	%
They are important for everybody to read	36
I wouldn't read them but I would hope to hear about them in the media	46
I think they are a waste of time and I wouldn't pay any attention to them	14
None of these	2
Don't know	2

Source: MORI/*Independent on Sunday/Sunday Mirror*
2–3 April 1997
Base: 1,069 British adults 18+

The Political Triangle and Important Issues

So far we have considered the form of the campaigning message rather than it substance. To examine the effect of more substantive issues, we resort again to the 'political triangle model'.

As in previous elections, most voters felt that policies were the predominant factor in determining their votes, though to a less dramatic extent than in 1992; the significance of the general influence of the party, meanwhile, though still in third place, had increased. It is interesting to note how little real difference in motivation there was between the supporters of the three parties, though the fact that Labour supporters were a little more likely to name 'party' and a little less likely to name 'policies' may reflect the fact of a slightly negative election based more on general distrust of the Tories than a debate over competing pro-grammes of government.

To the political triangle itself we again added the questions to

Table 20: The Political Triangle 1997

Q. (To all naming a party for which they intend to vote) **I want you to think about what it is that most attracted you to the ... party. Some people are attracted mainly by the policies of the party, some by the leaders of the party and some because they identify with the party as a whole. If you had a total of ten points to allocate according to how important each of these was to you, how many points would you allocate to the <u>leaders</u> of the Party you intend voting for, how many to its <u>policies</u> and how many to the party as a whole?** *(Percentages reflect mean scores out of 10)*

	All	Con	Lab	Lib Dem
	%	%	%	%
Leaders	34	36	36	33
Policies	41	42	38	43
Party	23	22	25	23

	1987	1992	1997
	%	%	%
Leaders	35	33	34
Policies	44	47	41
Party	21	20	23

Source: MORI
Base: 1,959 British adults 18+
25–28 April 1997

investigate its three dimensions, measuring leader image, party image and best party on key issues. There was little change from what we had been seeing during the previous five years, as the charts show.

In fact, during the campaign we changed the issues question slightly, to take into account that the Prime Minister spent the third week's campaigning talking about constitutional threats of Labour's policies and especially devolution, and added these, as well as animal rights, to our list. Out of 16 issues, constitutional issues/devolution ranked 16th, and the issue that the Deputy Prime Minister spent most of that week talking about, trade unions, ranked 15th out of 16; even then the Tories could not conjure up a lead among concerned voters on trade union policy. On four of the five most important issues, Labour had a clear lead; only on law and order, historically a 'banker' for the Tories, were they slightly more trusted among those who thought it important. Overall, it could not be considered a winning hand.

The Political Triangle

1997

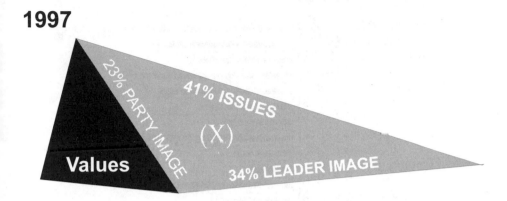

Base: 1,959 British public, 25-28 April 1997   Source: MORI/Times

Figure 12: The Political Triangle 1997

But this is the theory. By the time these variables are measured in an election, these perceptions of the parties may be as much caused by voting intention (voters who have already made up their minds preferring to think best of their favoured party) as a cause of it. More interesting are those voters whose minds were not yet made up. What really swings votes during a campaign, and before the last-minute decisions? We directly asked voters who changed their intentions between the third and sixth weeks of the campaign why they had done so (using our panel study, sponsored by the *Independent on Sunday* and *Sunday Mirror*, where we interviewed the same group of electors twice)[1]. Here (remembering

---

[1] MORI conducted a two-wave panel study for the *Independent on Sunday* and the *Sunday Mirror*, the results being published on 6 April and 27 April. In the first wave MORI interviewed a representative quota sample of 1,069 adults aged 18+ at 78 enumeration district sampling points throughout Great Britain. All interviews were conducted face-to-face in-home on 2-3 April 1997. Data were weighted to the match the profile of the population. In the second wave, 941 of the initial respondents were re-interviewed on 23-24 April 1997. (This represents an 88% response rate). Interviews were again conducted face-to-face in home. Data were weighted to the demographic profile of the population and to the voting intention of the first wave of the panel.

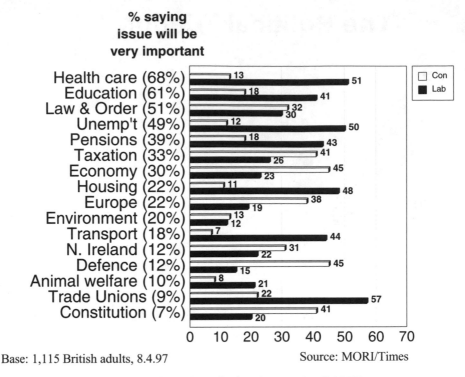

**% saying
issue will be
very important**

Health care (68%)
Education (61%)
Law & Order (51%)
Unemp't (49%)
Pensions (39%)
Taxation (33%)
Economy (30%)
Housing (22%)
Europe (22%)
Environment (20%)
Transport (18%)
N. Ireland (12%)
Defence (12%)
Animal welfare (10%)
Trade Unions (9%)
Constitution (7%)

Con
Lab

Base: 1,115 British adults, 8.4.97   Source: MORI/Times

Figure 13: Best Party by key issues, April 1997

to view with a little scepticism the voters' ability fully to analyse their own motives) are a selection of their answers, verbatim.

It is interesting to note how few of this representative sample of answers make any reference to new issues brought up during the campaign, or even to existing policy issues brought into prominence or cast in a new light. Overwhelmingly it is the personalities or realisation of local tactical necessities, or just the crystallisation of ideas and impressions already in place before the campaign.

Leader Image - Mar 1997

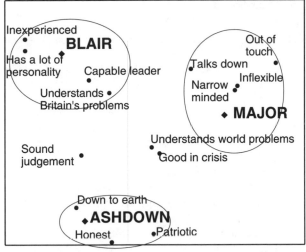

Base: c. 2,000 British public   Source: MORI/Times

Party Image - April 1997

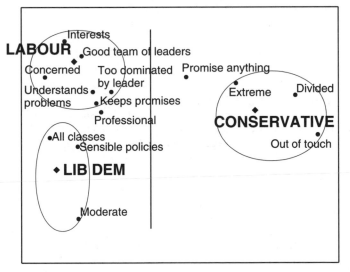

Base: c. 1,100 British public   Source: MORI/Times

Figure 14: Leader and Party Image during the 1997 election

Table 21: Reasons for switching: Verbatim Answers

Q. **When we spoke last you said that you would vote . . . Now you say that. . . . What has made you change your mind? What has attracted you to . . .** (new party)? **What has turned you away from** (party mentioned at wave I)?

'The leader: I think Tony Blair is more charismatic than Major. I can't say I've read a lot about the policies'
— Conservative to Labour, Male 30–34, Aylesbury
'The education: Labour are made for education and with four kids you have to support that'
— Conservative to Labour, Female 25–29, Copeland
'I am voting for a change. There is so much disharmony within the Conservatives'
— Conservative to Labour, Male, 25, Mitcham & Morden
'Basically I don't want to see the Tories get back in . . . I don't believe John Major will stay the leader and if Portillo gets in we are all in trouble'
— Conservative to Lib Dem, Male, 23, Kettering
'Seen some videos from the party. . . . We have been sold to Europe and not told anything about it, we are a satellite state of Germany'
— Conservative to Referendum, Male, 53, Bolton South East
'The more you listen, the more you think they don't know what they're doing'
— Conservative to Undecided, Female, 46, Torbay
'We have an Asian candidate and it's totally geared up for them. Both main parties are Asians'
— Conservative to Undecided, Female, 55–59, Bradford West
'They keep putting all that money from the lottery into old building and old theatres – why can't they put it into hospitals and the Health Service?'
— Conservative to Would not vote, Male, 65–74, Birmingham Edgbaston
'Not too sure what Labour intend to do – they don't give anything away'
— Labour to Conservative, Male, 71, Birmingham Selly Oak
'More reliable. I trust them more. I think their leader is more genuine'
— Labour to Lib Dem, Female, 51, Hove
'More convinced with policies now. Good local MP'
— Labour to Lib Dem, Female, 42, Fife North East
'Still worried about the loony left. I think the Labour Party have been too quiet'
— Labour to Lib Dem, Male, 65, Lewisham West
'I'm going to vote tactically in the hope of keeping the Tories out'
— Labour to Lib Dem, Female, 48, St Ives
'They are not talking enough about the environmental changes'
— Labour to Green, Female, 30, Middlesbrough
'Too much mouth. Full of promises is Mr Blair'
— Labour to Undecided, Male 65–74, Staffordshire Moorlands
'Some things Blair has said have made me think I don't know whether to vote Labour or Conservative'
— Labour to Undecided, Female, 35–44, City of Durham
'Waste of time, they will all change their promises as soon as they get in'
— Labour to Would not vote, Male, 54, Livingston

'Pie in the sky ideas. They don't quite know what they're letting themselves in for'
— Lib Dem to Conservative, Female, 45–49, Aylesbury
'1. Learned more about Lib Dems' European monetary policy. 2. The OECD report. 3. Biggest reason: can't face having a Labour government'
— Lib Dem to Conservative, Female, 38, Daventry
'Liberals have not really got the strength to form a government though I like their policies'
— Lib Dem to Labour, Male, 60–64, Stockton South
'Local Lib Dem has no chance, want to see Conservatives defeated'
— Lib Dem to Labour, Male, 74, Blackpool North & Fleetwood
'Want us to decide if we go into Europe'
— Lib Dem to Referendum, Female, 52, Gordon
'I like the countryside and animals, and do not want to be ruled by Europe and other countries. All other parties talk about Europe'
— Lib Dem to Green, Female, 78, Bolton South East
'I believe in Labour policies and am a staunch socialist. I intended to vote Lib Dem to keep the Tory out but I am increasingly concerned about not supporting Labour. I have supported no other party since 1960'
— Lib Dem to Undecided, Male, 60, St Ives
'Because I don't think the Referendum Party will get in . . . lesser of two evils'
— Referendum to Conservative, Male, 30–34, City of Chester
'They're on about environmental things, and getting young people into work'
— Undecided to Conservative, Male, 22, Erewash
'I eventually always vote for them'
— Undecided to Conservative, Female, 32, Torbay
'Under heavy influence of father, who is Labour'
— Undecided to Labour, Male, 18, Bolton South East
'Try some new blood – I like Tony Blair'
— Undecided to Labour, Female, 54, Liverpool Riverside
'I like most of what they say. Policies on health issues'
— Undecided to Lib Dem, Female, 18, Gordon
'In my opinion it is no longer a wasted vote'
— Undecided to Lib Dem, Male, 55, Torbay
'Better if we had our own Parliament and representative in Europe. Ireland seems to be doing well. Labour's plans are inadequate'
Undecided to Plaid Cymru, Male, 33, Swansea West
'I have never voted before and I feel I ought to now . . . because I don't want Labour to get in'
— Would not vote to Conservative, Male, 30, Birmingham Selly Oak
'Last couple of weeks I have had a warm feeling towards Labour'
— Would not vote to Labour, Female, 31, Mid Bedfordshire
'If I don't vote those votes will go to the Conservatives'
— Would not vote to Undecided, Female, 51, Charnwood

Table 22: Tactical voting 1987–97

Q. **Which of the following comes closest to your reasons for voting for the . . . party?**

	5–6 Jun 1987 %	1–3 Apr 1992 %	Wave I 2–3 Apr 1997 %	Wave II 23–24 Apr 1997 %
It is the party that most represents your views	89	87	82	86
The party you support has little chance of winning in this constituency so you vote for the . . . party to try and keep another party out	8	11	11	10
No opinion	3	2	7	4

Source: MORI/*Sunday Times*/*Independent on Sunday*/*Sunday Mirror*
Base: c. 1,000 British adults 18+

Tactical Voting

A further motivation for voting behaviour which should not be forgotten is tactical voting. The British electoral system imposes on certain voters the knowledge that their favoured party has no chance of winning in the constituency where they are registered, and therefore gives them an incentive to vote for their second choice, or vote for the candidate most likely to defeat their least favoured party, rather than 'wasting' their vote. Historically this has hit the Liberals and now the Liberal Democrats hardest for most of this century, as being the smallest party and in a competitive position in far fewer seats than the Tories or Labour. In 1997, by contrast, there seems little doubt that tactical voting by Labour supporters (or, at any rate, anti-Conservatives) swelled the Liberal Democrat vote considerably where it mattered and was a significant factor in the party's impressive haul of seats.

Was there much more tactical voting than in previous elections? There is little evidence of it in MORI's panel survey, the last wave of which was conducted just over a week before polling; only 10% were admitting that they were voting tactically, not significantly different from the position at the corresponding stage of the 1992 election.

Nor is there much difference if we compare 1992 and 1997's admitted tactical voting by party; the switch of the balance of tactical votes from

Table 23: Tactical voting by party

Q. **Which of the following comes closest to your reasons for voting for the . . . party?**

	1987			1992			1997		
	Con	Lab	Alln	Con	Lab	LD	Con	Lab	LD
	%	%	%	%	%	%	%	%	%
It is the party that most represents your views	91	90	85	91	90	78	88	88	73
The party you support has little chance of winning in this constituency so you vote for the . . . party to try and keep another party out	6	8	13	7	10	19	9	7	21
No opinion	3	2	2	2	*	3	3	5	6

Source: MORI/*Sunday Times/Independent on Sunday/Sunday Mirror*
Base: c. 1,000 British adults 18+

Lib Dem to Labour is just statistically significant, but hardly dramatic; in each case around one Liberal Democratic vote in five was tactical. Again, the bigger contrast is with the substantially lower tactical Alliance vote in 1987, only one in seven of their total.

However, it may be that polling a week before the vote these surveys missed a divergence of behaviour in the final few days[2]. In fact, this would not be implausible. In 1992, following the Sheffield rally which seems to have lowered many voters' esteem for Labour, the Tories launched a concerted campaign aimed at Liberal Democrat voters, portraying a Liberal Democrat vote as being a 'Trojan horse' to put Neil Kinnock in Downing Street, and most commentators agree this had some effect. In 1997, by contrast, the most notable feature of the final weekend was a concerted campaign by the government's opponents to promote tactical voting, most notably by the publication in the *Observer* and *Scotland on Sunday* of a bank of constituency polls (see Table 47 on p. 186 for details) in Tory-held marginals and semi-marginals with the

---

[2] Evidence from the British Election Study, using interviews after the election, and analysis of constituency results, would seem to support this, finding that tactical voting did indeed increase in 1997. See Evans, G., Curtice, J. and Norris, P., 'New Labour, New Tactical Voting?' in Denver, D. et al (eds.), *British Elections and Parties Review*, Volume 8: The 1997 British General Election (London: Frank Cass, 1998), pp 65–79.

Table 24: If the Liberal Democrats could win . . .

Q. **If you thought the Liberal Democrats could win the General Election and form the next government, what effect, if any, would it have on your vote?**

	All %	Con %	Lab %	LD %
It would not change my vote	60	68	60	57
It would make me more inclined to vote Conservative	3	10	1	-
It would make me more inclined to vote Labour	5	1	7	2
It would make me more inclined to vote Lib Dem	23	17	27	34
It would make me less inclined to vote for any party	2	2	1	1
Other	1	*	*	1
Don't know	6	2	5	5

Source: MORI/*Independent on Sunday/Sunday Mirror*
Base: 941 British adults 18+
23–24 April 1997

intention of telling voters how best to vote to dislodge the Tory. On the other hand, the vast majority of these polls came so close to predicting the final constituency result that it doesn't look as if they swung any voters at all.

A related factor is that, as the Liberal Democrats are generally not seen as contenders for government, significant proportions of voters tend to discount them as a voting option. There was evidence that this significantly depressed the Lib Dem share of the vote in 1997: one in six Tory supporters and more than a quarter of those intending to vote Labour said they would have been more likely to vote Liberal Democrat if they thought the party could win.

The 'Outside Influences'

The public and the media coverage

The parties may try to take entire control of the election campaign, but in a modern election it is certain they will not succeed. They can communicate effectively with the voters only via the media, and the media coverage is ultimately in the hands of the editors and proprietors of the newspapers and of the management of the broadcasting stations. Furthermore, it is at this point that opinion polls re-enter the story, for their results are relayed to the public by the media and they make up a substantial part of the election-related news which is not emanating from the party press conferences and statements. Here, too, come the pundits, like the polls claiming to assess the state of the electoral battle and being wheeled out by the media to do so. Let us consider the role of each in turn.

At a Ditchley conference of editors and journalists after the election in 1997, American journalists criticised the British media for trivialising the previous year's American election in their coverage. Some British journalists have in turn expressed outrage at American coverage of the British general election. Reporting of allegations of financial and sexual 'sleaze' dominated the first half of the six-week election in the American media's coverage of the election, and pushed more important news out. But this is not a trait confined to the reporting of other countries' elections. Invariably in modern elections, there comes a point (often not very far into the campaign) when the media become convinced that straight election reporting is beginning to bore their audiences.

The readers, viewers and listeners, for the most part, remain interested in election news, for all the media conviction that they are bored with it. In election after election the media's news editors send reporters out, usually in about the penultimate week of the campaign, to collect vox pops on how bored people are with the election. Sure enough, reporters find people who say they are bored with the election, and myths abound and are reinforced about how boring that election is, and how it is the most boring ever.

In this election however, a week before the election, 16% said they were 'very interested' and a further 42% 'fairly interested' in news about the election, while only 14% were 'not at all interested'; interest was lower than at the end of the shorter 1992 campaign, but only marginally so, and quite a lot higher than in 1987.

As Table 25 shows, the public in this campaign was evenly divided as to whether they thought there was too much coverage of the election in the newspapers, though a majority thought there was at least a little too much coverage on TV; but in both cases, considerably fewer thought there was too much coverage than had done so in 1987 and 1992, though rather more did so than in 1983 (the last election when the gap between the main parties was as wide).

Of course, not everyone is interested in the election, or takes a tolerant view of those that are. One person in five thinks that Party Election Broadcasts should be banned during election campaigns on TV and radio, and 15% of the electorate, that is more than six million people, would ban *all* coverage of the election on TV and radio; 10% , over four million people, would even ban all coverage in the newspapers!

Press coverage of the 1997 General Election

Content

Somewhat over a quarter of the front-page coverage during the 1997 General Election was given over to news about the election in the nation's national daily newspapers, and just under a fifth in the national Sunday newspapers, according to a special analysis carried out by MORI in this election, from newspapers published in the month of April.

The newspapers giving over most space to the election included the *Guardian* and the *Independent*, each of which gave over about half of their

Table 25: Degree of media coverage

Q. **How do you feel about the amount of coverage newspapers have been giving to the election campaign. Have they given . . .?**

	1983 %	1987 %	1992 %	1997 %
Much too much	18	30	34	20
A little too much	18	22	22	21
About the right amount	46	35	32	41
A little too little	3	2	1	2
Much too little	1	1	*	*
No opinion	13	9	10	16
Too much	36	52	56	41
Too little	4	3	1	2

Q. **And how do you feel about the amount of coverage given to the election campaign on television?**

	1983 %	1987 %	1992 %	1997 %
Much too much	24	49	45	29
A little too much	26	22	23	24
About the right amount	40	24	27	37
A little too little	2	2	2	1
Much too little	1	*	*	1
No opinion	7	3	3	8
Too much	50	71	68	63
Too little	3	2	2	2

Q. **And how do you feel about the amount of coverage given to the election campaign on radio?**

	1983 %	1987 %	1992 %	1997 %
Much too much	4	12	13	8
A little too much	4	6	8	4
About the right amount	25	30	32	33
A little too little	3	3	4	3
Much too little	2	2	2	1
No opinion	61	46	41	51
Too much	8	18	21	12
Too little	5	5	6	4

Source: MORI

front-page coverage to election news during the campaign. Among the Sunday newspapers, only the *Observer* gave as much attention to the election, including one fifth of its front-page coverage during the four weeks analysed to the findings of its opinion poll. The only other newspaper giving over ten per cent of its front page to election polls was the *Independent on Sunday*.

News about the election squeezed out other domestic political news, with only about one-twentieth given to non-election political coverage by daily newspapers, and just 2.3% by the Sundays.

Overall, there was much less front-page coverage of the polls in the Sunday papers than in 1992, down from 10.2% to 4.7% on average, and slightly less in the national dailies, down from 3.9% in 1992 to 3.1% in 1997. The biggest change was in the *Mail on Sunday*, which in 1992 had most front-page poll coverage of any paper, 22.3%, but none whatever in 1997 (despite considerable poll coverage inside). The *Observer*, by contrast, doubled its proportion of poll coverage on the front page (mainly by the prominence it gave ICM's bank of constituency polls on the final Sunday), from 9.5% in 1992 to 19.1% in 1997.

Newspaper positioning and bias

In all, there are ten national dailies to choose from, covering the political, social and economic spectrum of opinion and taste. On Sundays, there are nine. Seven in ten adults in Britain read at least one national newspaper regularly, and of those who do almost exactly half read one or other of the leading tabloids, the *Sun* and the *Mirror*. Broadsheet newspapers reach only one British elector in six; while less strident in tone, they still tend to partisan coverage – for example, when the Tories sent out a man dressed in a chicken suit, *The Times* printed the photograph, in colour, on the front page.

The *Sun*, the biggest seller, had backed the Conservatives in the 1992 election. Their headline on election day then was 'IF KINNOCK WINS TODAY, WILL THE LAST PERSON TO LEAVE BRITAIN PLEASE TURN OUT THE LIGHTS', with a picture of the Labour leader Neil Kinnock inside a lightbulb. During the years between the 1992 election and 1997, the voting intentions of *Sun* readers switched from backing the Conservatives

Table 26: Front Page Coverage in national newspapers, April 1997

Newspaper	Election %	Polls %	Other Politics %	Other news %
Guardian	43.6	6.1	4.8	45.5
Independent	41.1	4.9	7.2	46.8
The Times	28.4	4.3	7.7	59.6
Daily Telegraph	29.9	4.7	3.6	61.8
Daily Mail	30.8	4.0	2.3	62.9
The Express	24.2	4.2	7.3	64.3
The Mirror	16.3	0.3	9.0	74.4
Financial Times	15.5	0.8	8.9	74.8
The Sun	13.7	1.1	0.3	84.9
Daily Star	3.7	0.6	0.6	95.1
Average for Dailies	**24.7**	**3.1**	**5.2**	**67.0**
Observer	27.0	19.1	0.0	53.9
Independent on Sunday	18.2	11.7	0.0	70.1
Sunday Times	23.0	3.3	3.1	70.6
Sunday Telegraph	17.4	8.0	2.0	72.6
Mail on Sunday	27.0	0.0	20.0	73.0
Express on Sunday	16.4	0.0	0.0	83.6
Sunday Mirror	0.0	0.0	16.0	84.0
News of the World	1.3	0.0	0.0	98.7
The People	0.0	0.0	0.0	100.0
Average for Sundays	**14.5**	**4.7**	**2.3**	**78.5**

Source: MORI

to backing Labour. So did the backing of the *Sun*. The day after the election was called, they took up four-fifths of the front page with the headline announcing 'THE SUN BACKS BLAIR', and on election day they implored their readers to vote Labour with a picture of Labour leader Tony Blair under the pointing finger of the national lottery logo, and the headline 'IT MUST BE YOU!'.

The *Mirror*'s front page also featured a picture of Tony Blair, with the caption 'YOUR COUNTRY NEEDS HIM', while its sister paper in Scotland, the *Daily Record*, a day or two before the election featured a picture of the late John Smith, Blair's predecessor as Labour leader, complete with black border and an impassioned plea from his widow under the headline 'WIN IT FOR JOHN'. The same day, the *Mirror*'s front page carried a by-lined article by the Labour leader's press secretary, Alastair Campbell.

The so-called 'middle market' is now served by two tabloids, the *Daily Mail* and the *Daily Express*, strong supporters of the Queen, the Church and the Tory Party, and these were hardly less strident in their support of John Major's re-election. On the eve of poll the *Daily Mail*'s front page inset text into a Union Jack with the words: 'There is a terrible danger that the British people, drugged by the seductive mantra "It's time for a change", are stumbling, eyes glazed, into an election that could undo 1,000 years of our nation's history'. Not much question where they stood.

And newspaper readers do know where their papers stand, for the most part. Gone is the day (1979) when, asked the weekend after polling day which party their newspaper supported, a third of the readers of the *Sun* thought that it supported the Conservatives, a third thought that the *Sun* supported Labour, and a third didn't know. (The front page on election day had consisted of a two-word headline, 'VOTE TORY!')

These days they do know, and when asked whether their newspaper supports or opposes the Conservative Party, the Labour Party, and the Liberal Democrats, readers mostly get it right. Table 27 shows the net scores given by readers of the papers, e.g., 75% of *Mirror* readers believe the *Mirror* opposes the Conservative Party and 5% think that it supports it, making a net score of −70%; 79% think that it supports the Labour Party and 4% believe it opposes Labour, for a net score of +75%. To arrive at the net % in the table below, we have averaged the two net scores, and come out with a +72.5 index for the *Mirror*. The negative scores in the table below indicate a net support for the Conservatives, with the *Daily Telegraph* during the week and the *Mail on Sunday* on Sunday being seen by their own readers as the most biased in favour of the Tory Party.

Perceived bias in the Broadcast Media

Unlike the newspapers, the broadcast media – especially TV – have a legal obligation to be neutral. Most viewers agree that they achieve this. When asked 'Thinking about BBC Television/Independent Television coverage, that is ITV and Channel 4, do you think that this is biased towards the Conservatives' point of view, Labour's point of view, or

Table 27: Readers' perceived bias of their own newspapers (net %)

Q. **Do you think the . . . mainly supports or opposes the Conservative Party, or neither particularly supports or opposes it?**
Q. **Do you think the . . . mainly supports or opposes the Labour Party, or neither particularly supports or opposes it?**

	Net favour Con (Support minus oppose)	Net favour Lab (Support minus oppose)	Overall favour Lab (average net score*)
The Mirror	−70	+75	+72.5
Guardian	−57	+63	+60
The Sun	−53	+61	+56.5
Daily Record	−52	+56	+54
Independent	−13	+15	+14
Daily Star	+10	+9	−0.5
Financial Times	+26	−4	−15
The Times	+41	−19	−30
The Express	+63	−51	−57
Daily Mail	+65	−48	−56.5
Daily Telegraph	+73	−51	−62
Sunday Mirror	−59	+65	+62
Observer	−52	+55	+53.5
Independent on Sunday	−30	+33	+31.5
The People	−24	+35	+29.5
News of the World	−23	+28	+25.5
Sunday Times	+41	−26	−33.5
Sunday Telegraph	+61	−45	−53
Express on Sunday	+62	−52	−57
Mail on Sunday	+68	−56	−62

Source: MORI

* Positive is perceived net bias to Labour, negative net perceived bias to Conservatives

some other party's point of view, or do you feel their coverage is unbiased?', somewhat more people think that the BBC is biased than ITV, but not by much. In fact, nearly eight people in ten either say that the broadcast media are unbiased (about 60%) or don't know (20%–25%). About one in eight, 13%, say they think BBC is biased to the Conservatives, and rather fewer, 8%, to Labour, while of Independent Television, the feeling is the reverse, but lower for each, with 7% believing ITV is

Table 28: Perceptions of bias in TV coverage

Q. **Thinking about BBC Television coverage, do you think this is biased towards the Conservatives' point of view, Labour's point of view, or some other party's point of view, or do you feel their coverage is unbiased?**

Q. **And thinking about Independent Television coverage, that is ITV and Channel 4, do you think it is biased towards the Conservatives' point of view, or towards Labour's point of view, or some other party's point of view, or do you feel their coverage is unbiased?**

	23–24 Apr		25–28 Apr	
	BBC	ITV/C4	BBC	ITV/C4
	%	%	%	%
Biased to Conservative	12	5	13	4
Biased to Labour	8	6	8	7
Biased to some other party	1	1	1	1
Unbiased	54	54	58	63
Don't know	25	35	20	25

Source: MORI

biased to Labour, and 4% to the Tories. These figures are down a little since 1992 for the BBC, when 16% thought the BBC biased to the Tories and 9% to Labour, while 7% thought ITV biased to the Tories and 6% to Labour.

Bias can swing voters

From the aggregate analysis of the polls done by MORI during 1997 between the period from the start of January to 16 March, the day before the election was called (when we conducted 13,034 interviews), and the election (during the campaign readership was asked of 13,544 people), there was a 6% swing in voting intention, with a 5% increase in Lib Dem support.

The Labour to Liberal Democrat swing was greatest among readers of quality newspapers, and especially those regularly reading the *Independent* and the *Independent on Sunday* or the *Financial Times*.

Few newspaper readers themselves believe they were swung by the press coverage, even though they recognise its partisan direction. When we asked, a week before the election, which of a number of items on a

Table 29: Net Voting Intention Change during General Election Campaign

	1992 GE (n=1,731) %	1997Q1 n=13,034 %	1997 GE (n=2,304) %	Change during GE %
Conservative	43	29	31	+2
Labour	35	54	44	−10
Lib Dem	18	12	17	+5
Other	4	5	8	+3
Lab lead	−8	25	13	−12
Would not vote	3	9	6	−3
Undecided	5	6	6	0
Refused	3	2	5	+3
Swing since 1992	−	16.5	10.5	−6

list had influenced the way respondents would vote, only 10% of electors say that newspapers have done so. The proportion is similar among Conservative (12%) and Labour (11%) supporters, though much lower among LibDems (6%) – predictably so with no national newspaper endorsing the LibDems. As we have seen, after the election only 6% thought newspaper coverage had 'a great deal' of effect on their final decision. But do the voters really know themselves? The new contribution of the analysis of election media coverage came from several new companies since the 1992 election, which married media monitoring with attitudinal research. The work done by Test Research (the MORI media evaluation company) suggested that the media coverage of the election *did* have an impact on voting patterns.

Of those who read any national daily paper regularly, half read either the *Sun* or the *Mirror*. In the 1992 election, the *Sun* strongly supported the Tories, while the *Mirror* gave only weak support to Neil Kinnock's election; both weighed heavily behind Blair's New Labour Party, as indicated by the table showing readers' perceived bias of their own paper. (See p. 144)

During the 1997 election, Test Research analysed over 4,000 newspaper articles to determine the nature and slant of their coverage. For the first time in an election, Test Research linked this analysis to measures of readership to demonstrate how different social groups were exposed to dramatically different reports on the election. By linking this in turn to

Table 30: Net Voting Intention change by Daily readership 1997

	1997Q1 %	GE %	Change		1997Q1 %	GE %	Change
The Express				**D. Telegraph**			
Con	52	49	−3	Con	57	57	0
Lab	32	29	−3	Lab	27	20	−7
LDem	12	16	+4	LDem	11	17	+6
Other	4	6	+2	Other	5	6	+1
Lab lead	−20	−20	0	Lab lead	−30	−37	−7
Swing			0.0	*Swing*			−3.5
D. Mail				**Fin. Times**			
Con	48	49	+1	Con	43	48	+5
Lab	34	29	−5	Lab	45	29	−16
LDem	13	14	+1	LDem	9	19	+10
Other	5	8	+3	Other	3	4	+1
Lab lead	−14	−20	−6	Lab lead	+2	−19	−21
Swing			−3.0	*Swing*			−10.5
The Mirror				**Guardian**			
Con	12	14	+2	Con	6	8	+2
Lab	79	72	−7	Lab	75	67	−8
LDem	7	11	+4	LDem	14	22	+8
Other	2	3	+1	Other	5	3	−2
Lab lead	+67	+58	−9	Lab lead	+69	59	−10
Swing			−4.5	*Swing*			−5.0
D. Star				**Independent**			
Con	19	17	−2	Con	15	16	+1
Lab	67	66	−1	Lab	67	47	−20
LDem	11	12	+1	LDem	16	30	+14
Other	3	5	+2	Other	2	7	+5
Lab lead	+48	+49	+1	Lab lead	+52	31	−21
Swing			0.5	*Swing*			−10.5
The Sun				**The Times**			
Con	27	30	+3	Con	41	42	+1
Lab	59	52	−7	Lab	38	28	−10
LDem	8	12	+4	LDem	16	25	+9
Other	6	6	0	Other	5	5	0
Lab lead	32	+22	−10	Lab lead	−3	−14	−11
Swing			−5.0	*Swing*			−5.5

Source: MORI Quarterly and Election Aggregates

Base: 13,034 adults (1 Jan – 16 Mar 1997) and 13,544 adults (16 Mar – 1 May 1997)

Table 31: Net Voting Intention change by Sunday readership 1997

	1997Q1 %	GE %	Change		1997Q1 %	GE %	Change
News of The World				**Independent on Sunday**			
Con	25	28	+3	Con	13	14	+1
Lab	61	55	−6	Lab	75	48	−27
LDem	9	11	+2	LDem	10	32	+22
Other	5	6	+1	Other	2	6	+4
Lab lead	+36	+27	−9	Lab lead	+62	+34	−28
Swing			−4.5	*Swing*			−11.0
S. Mirror				**Observer**			
Con	16	18	+2	Con	7	11	+4
Lab	75	67	−8	Lab	76	63	−13
LDem	7	12	+5	LDem	12	22	+10
Other	2	3	+1	Other	5	4	−1
Lab lead	+59	+49	−10	Lab lead	+69	+52	−17
Swing			−5.0	*Swing*			−8.5
The People				**S. Telegraph**			
Con	21	21	0	Con	53	56	+3
Lab	67	62	−5	Lab	29	19	−10
LDem	10	11	+1	LDem	13	17	+4
Other	2	6	+4	Other	5	8	+3
Lab lead	+46	+41	−5	Lab lead	−24	−37	−13
Swing			−2.5	*Swing*			−6.5
S. Express				**S. Times**			
Con	56	53	−3	Con	39	43	+4
Lab	31	27	−4	Lab	42	30	−12
LDem	10	14	+4	LDem	14	21	+7
Other	3	6	+3	Other	5	6	+1
Lab lead	−25	−26	−1	Lab lead	3	−13	−16
Swing			−0.5	*Swing*			−8.0
Mail on S							
Con	47	49	+2				
Lab	35	28	−7				
LDem	13	15	+2				
Other	5	8	+3				
Lab lead	−12	−21	−9				
Swing			−4.5				

Source: MORI Quarterly and Election Aggregates

Base: 13,034 adults (1 Jan − 16 Mar 1997) and 13,544 adults (16 Mar − 1 May 1997)

147

MORI and other opinion poll results, it was possible to show that social groups exposed to the most pro-Tory reporting swung to the Tories, and that those exposed to pro-Labour reports swung the other way.

The media was far from even-handed in its treatment of the main parties, with the *Mirror* and *Sun* blatantly pro-Labour throughout. Of *Mirror* headlines that mentioned the Labour Party, 69% were pro, and none anti, Labour. Most articles in the broadsheets were neutral (81% for Labour and 79% for the Conservatives). However, where the Press did give an opinion, the balance was strongly pro-Labour. Table 32 shows the widespread pro-Labour positioning of much election coverage. Even the staunchly Conservative *Daily Telegraph* was almost as negative about Tory policies as about Labour ones. It is interesting to compare this objective analysis of the newspapers' contents with the readers' own impressions in the table above (p. 144).

On three key policy areas (health, education and Europe), voters across all classes were exposed to more negative than positive coverage of Conservative policies. But because of the stance taken by the main tabloid papers, blue-collar voters were exposed to significantly more positive coverage of Labour. (See figure 15)

On education and health, exposure was predominantly of positive coverage of Labour Party policies. This positive exposure was greatest among the key group of C2 voters, and also considerably greater among DEs than ABC1s.

When it came to each Party's European policy, the balance of exposure was negative among all social groups. However, while the Conservatives' natural supporters (ABs) were exposed to the most negative coverage of this Party's European policies, Labour's target C2 voters were exposed to a considerably lower degree of anti-Labour coverage.

It was on coverage of the Party leaders that the partisanship of some of the Press showed through most clearly. ABs, on balance, would have read slightly more in criticism than in praise of Tony Blair, whilst the C2s and DEs would have seen mainly positive coverage. Everybody would have read more critical than favourable articles about John Major, but the tabloids' stance ensured that working class readers, particularly C2s, would have read even more that was critical than middle-class readers.

Table 32: Partisanship of Press Coverage

Tory Policies 1/4/97–1/5/97	Cuttings	Negative −2 %	−1 %	Neutral 0 %	Positive +1 %	+2 %	Index
Mirror	215	64	16	17	1	2	−139
Sun	110	35	4	43	10	8	−48
Guardian	493	12	15	67	3	2	−32
Independent	500	11	15	67	4	3	−27
Financial Times	279	6	19	70	2	4	−21
The Times	387	4	22	64	7	3	−17
Daily Star	110	21	15	36	14	14	−15
Express	178	12	14	58	8	8	−14
Daily Telegraph	378	9	14	63	7	6	−13
Daily Mail	178	13	9	61	11	6	−12
TOTAL	2828	3	18	62	13	4	−34

Labour Policies	Cuttings	Negative −2 %	−1 %	Neutral 0 %	Positive +1 %	+2 %	Index
Mirror	211	1	2	33	10	53	+112
Sun	195	4	14	33	13	36	+63
Daily Star	147	9	15	51	12	13	+5
Guardian	547	5	11	73	7	5	−4
Independent	587	6	7	75	10	2	−5
The Times	477	6	11	71	11	1	−10
Financial Times	358	5	13	75	5	2	−14
Daily Telegraph	514	8	12	71	6	2	−18
Daily Mail	262	10	23	57	3	7	−26
Express	257	14	15	61	5	5	−28
TOTAL	3555	7	12	60	8	13	+8

Source: MORI/Test Research

We can now compare these differences in election coverage with the different voting behaviour of the groups exposed to it. A comparison of the 1 April MORI poll and the average of MORI's and NOP's final polls on 29 April shows only a small net shift in voting intention across the whole electorate (a swing, in fact, of 2% from Tory to Labour). However, this masked significant variations in swing by social class. What appears to have happened is that the ABs actually swung to the Tories (a swing of 9.5%) but this was balanced by a swing in the opposite direction among other social groups. This becomes particularly significant when

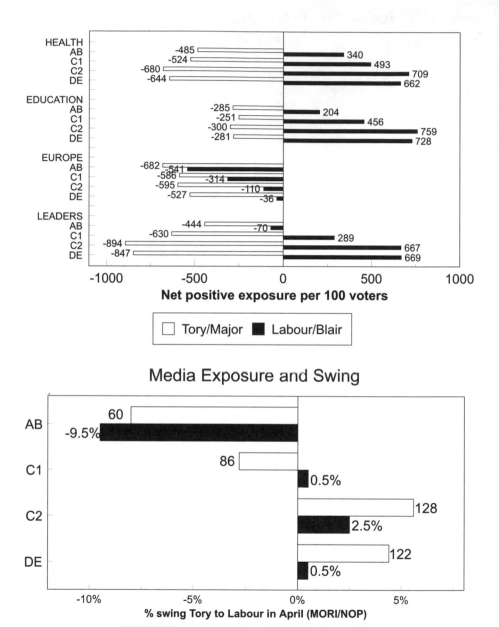

Source: Test Research

Figure 15: The electorate's exposure to positive and negative coverage

placed in the context of variations in media coverage. ABs were exposed to more negative than positive coverage of Labour, whilst other classes (especially C2DEs) saw relatively more positive coverage of Labour. The stance of the *Sun* and the *Mirror* ensured that C2DEs were also exposed to a higher level of anti-Tory coverage than middle class voters were.

The indications are that these variations in media bias contributed to switches in Party support. The chart plots the swing to Labour against an index of the relative bias in media exposure. One can see that the social groups most exposed to pro-Labour coverage swung most strongly to Labour, whilst those least exposed to such coverage (i.e. ABs) actually swung the other way[1]. The findings raise a strong presumption that the print media did, indeed, have significant influence on the voting behaviour of their readers.

The Polls

The conduct and performance of the Polls in 1997

Despite the eagerness of opponents of the polls who would like to argue to the contrary, on the whole, the polls in 1997 'got it right'. The 1997 election has confirmed that the pollsters' diagnoses of the real problems, and the steps consequently taken to overcome them, were largely adequate. The polls were considerably closer to their historically good record.

How good? Well, let's start with the prediction of seats. In this election, I was repeatedly told by broadcasters and pundits that the only thing that their viewers/readers were interested in was who was going to win, and by how many seats. If this is the case (and for some it is, but not so many as these soundbite journalists would have us believe), then let's look at how the polls did, projected from each polling firm's final eve-of-poll General Election findings. (Table 33)

But polls measure votes, not seats. According to the consensus in 1992,

---

[1] Results are based on an analysis of 4,240 articles (388,151 column centimetres) across the 20 national Daily and Sunday newspapers between 1 April-1 May 1997. The MORI/Test Research project was sponsored by Shandwick, the Public Relations Group, and *The Times*.

151

Table 33: The Final Polls – Projected to Labour Overall Majority in Seats

NOP	221
MORI	183
Election result	**179**
Harris	173
Poll average	*159*
Gallup	137
ICM	81

it was the polls' inability to measure the Conservative vote which put them at fault. So let us look at that measurement. Time after time I said the media should keep their eyes on the Conservative share, that in 1992 the Tories got 43% of the vote, and that if they didn't get 43% again they'd lost, and if they didn't get to 39% Labour had won. There were 47 national polls conducted in this election by the five full members of APOPO, the Association of Professional Opinion Polling Organisations (down from 50 and 54 in the shorter 1992 and 1987 elections) – they are listed in full in table 34. Not one poll showed the Tories above 37% (and bar that one ICM finding that seems clearly to have been a rogue, none found them above 34%). The average share in all the polls throughout the campaign was 31% for the Tories, as was the average of the final polls; they got 31.4%.

Sampling theory suggests that with samples of 1,000, there is a 19 out of 20 chance that any result around the 30%/70% level will fall between plus and minus three percent of the average figure, or 95%; there is a two in three chance that it will fall within plus or minus two percent (67%). The average sampling tolerance for samples of c.1,000 is $\pm 3\%$. And there is a fifty-fifty chance that they will fall within plus or minus one percent of the average.

Of the 47 polls reported during the campaign, all but two (96%) had the Tories between 28% and 34%, and 33 of the 47 (70%) had them between 29% and 33%, plus or minus two. Yes, and of the 47 polls, 26 (55%) had the Tories between 30% and 32%!

So it would have been hard for the overall measurement of the Conservative vote, the figure that it was supposedly impossible for us to measure without radical new tricks to smoke out the 'shy Tories', to have been better. Of course, some of the polls were a little more

Table 34: The National Polls During The Campaign

Fieldwork dates	Agency	Client	Publ'n Date	Sample size	Con %	Lab %	LD %	Oth %	Lead ± %	Swing 92–97 ± %
19–21 Mar	Gallup	S. Telegraph*	23 Mar	985	29	54.5	10.5	6	−25.5	−16.75
20–24 Mar	Harris	Independent	28 Mar	1,096	30	54	11	6	−24	−16.0
21–24 Mar	MORI	Times	27 Mar	1,932	29	50	14	7	−21	−14.5
27–31 Mar	Harris	Independent	4 Apr	1,091	28	52	14	6	−24	−16.0
26 Mar–2 Apr	Gallup	D. Telegraph*	4 Apr	1,126	31	52	11	6	−21	−14.5
29–31 Mar	ICM	Guardian*	2 Apr	1,200	32	46	17	5	−14	−11.0
1 Apr	MORI	Times	3 Apr	1,118	28	55	11	6	−27	−17.5
1 Apr–3 Apr	Gallup	C4 News*	9 Apr	1,035	30	54	11	5	−24	−16.0
2–3 Apr	MORI	Ind on S/S Mirror+	6 Apr	1,069	30	55	9	6	−25	−16.5
2–4 Apr	ICM	Observer*+	6 Apr	1,793	33	48	14	5	−15	−11.5
3 Apr	NOP	S. Times	6 Apr	1,575	28	52	12	8	−24	−16.0
4 Apr	NOP	Reuters	7 Apr	1,088	30	51	11	8	−21	−14.5
4–6 Apr	Gallup	D. Telegraph*	7 Apr	1,026	32	53	10	5	−21	−14.5
4–7 Apr	Harris	Independent	11 Apr	1,138	28	52	14	6	−24	−16.0
6–7 Apr	ICM	Guardian*	9 Apr	1,022	34	46	15	5	−12	−10.0
7–9 Apr	Gallup	D. Telegraph*	10 Apr	1,019	30	53	11	6	−23	−15.5
8 Apr	MORI	Times	10 Apr	1,114	34	49	12	5	−15	−11.5
9–11 Apr	ICM	Observer*+	13 Apr	1,002	32	48	15	5	−16	−12.0
9–12 Apr	Gallup	S. Telegraph*	13 Apr	1,043	33	49	12	5	−16	−12.0
11 Apr	NOP	S. Times	13 Apr	1,595	28	48	17	7	−20	−14.0
11–14 Apr	MORI	Eve. Standard	15 Apr	1,778	29	50	15	6	−21	−14.5
11–14 Apr	Harris	Independent	18 Apr	1,136	31	49	13	6	−18	−13.0
12–15 Apr	Gallup	D. Telegraph*	16 Apr	1,025	30	51	12	7	−21	−14.5
13–14 Apr	ICM	Guardian*	16 Apr	1,007	31	45	19	5	−14	−11.0
15 Apr	MORI	Times	17 Apr	1,137	32	49	13	6	−17	−12.5
18–22 Apr	Gallup	C4 News*	23 Apr	1,120	31	50	13	6	−19	−13.5
15–18 Apr	Gallup	D. Telegraph*	19 Apr	1,018	32	50	13	5	−18	−13.0
16–18 Apr	ICM	Observer*+	20 Apr	1,000	32	47	16	5	−15	−11.5
18 Apr	NOP	S. Times	20 Apr	1,595	31	45	17	7	−14	−11.0
17–21 Apr	Harris	Independent	25 Apr	1,177	30	48	15	7	−18	−13.0
18–21 Apr	Gallup	D. Telegraph*	22 Apr	1,294	32	48	12	8	−16	−12.0
20–21 Apr	ICM	Guardian*	23 Apr	1,004	37	42	14	6	−5	−6.5
22 Apr	MORI	Times	24 Apr	1,133	27	48	17	8	−21	−14.5
21–23 Apr	Gallup	D. Telegraph*	24 Apr	1,069	30	50	12	8	−20	−14.0
23–24 Apr	MORI	Ind on S/S Mirror+	27 Apr	941	29	53	12	6	−24	−16.0
23–25 Apr	Gallup	D. Telegraph*	26 Apr	1,012	32	48	14	6	−16	−12.0
23–25 Apr	ICM	Observer*+	27 Apr	1,000	32	47	16	5	−15	−11.5
25 Apr	NOP	S. Times	27 Apr	1,588	29	47	16	9	−18	−13.0
24–28 Apr	Gallup	C4 News*	29 Apr	1,466	31	49	14	6	−18	−13.0
25–27 Apr	Gallup	D. Telegraph*	28 Apr	1,028	30	49	14	6	−19	−13.5
27–29 Apr	Harris	Independent	1 May	1,154	31	48	15	6	−17	−12.5
28–29 Apr	Gallup	D. Telegraph*	30 Apr	1,038	31	51	13	6	−20	−14.0
29 Apr	NOP	Reuters	1 May	1,093	28	50	14	8	−22	−15.0
29–30 Apr	MORI	Times	1 May	2,304	28	48	16	8	−20	−14.0
29–30 Apr	ICM	Guardian*	1 May	1,555	33	43	18	6	−10	−9.0
30 Apr	Gallup	D. Telegraph*	1 May	1,849	33	47	14	6	−14	−11.0
30 Apr	MORI	Eve. Standard+*	1 May	1,501	29	47	19	5	−18	−13.0
1 May	MORI	ITN‡	1 May	15,761	30	46	18	6	−16	−12.0
1 May	NOP	BBC@	1 May	17,073	29	47	18	6	−18	−13.0
1 May	**Election result**				31.4	44.4	17.2	7.0	−13	−10.5

* Telephone survey + Panel survey @ Exit poll ‡ National projection from exit poll in marginal seats

153

fortunate than others in their final measurement, and some critics have tried to suggest that systematic differences between the companies using telephone polling (ICM and Gallup) on the one hand and the rest of us on the other meant that nobody was measuring Tory share correctly and that two errors were simply cancelling out. The table showing each company's average results over the whole campaign demonstrates that this is not the case.

While the polls measured Conservative share effectively, they collectively over-estimated the Labour share at the expense of the Lib Dems, probably because they failed to detect the full scale of last minute tactical switching. But the error was not a very substantial one and, significantly, is not related to the errors which occurred in 1992. There is no uncured malaise hanging over the polls.

So overall not perfect, it is true, and not quite as successful as occasionally in the past, but, we believe, entirely adequate. It is unhelpful for commentators to ignore the inherent limitations of sample surveys, as many critics do. These include timing, sampling, semantics and sponsors' limitations of budget and space. The polls in 1997 used varying question wordings and methodology, different sampling and data collection methods, different timing of their interviews and different weighting, and some 'adjusted' their data while some did not, yet they got their estimates commendably close both to each other and to the actual result.

The historic record of the opinion polls

Thus 1997 fits into the context of the generally good record of the British polls over the years. In 1983, all six were within sampling tolerance, given sample size, three within plus or minus one percent. In 1987, all six were within plus or minus one and a half percent, on average for the share of each party. 1997 was not quite that good, but certainly good enough to prove the point.

Over the fifteen British General Elections since the polls have been around they have performed, on average, about as well as would be expected, most within sampling tolerance, given their sample size, and not allowing for any design error or the fact that they are tested against

Table 35: The final opinion polls in 1997

Pollster	MORI	Harris	NOP	ICM	Gallup	MORI	Poll of	Final
Client	Times	Indy	Reuters	Guardian	D Tel	E Std	polls	Result
Fieldwork	29–30	27–29	29	30	29/30	30		1st
Party	%	%	%	%	%	%	%	%
Con	28	31	28	33	33	29	**31**	**31.4**
Lab	48	48	50	43	47	47	**47**	**44.4**
LDem	16	15	14	18	14	19	**15**	**17.2**
Others	8	6	8	6	6	5	**7**	**7.0**
Ave error	2.3	1.8	3.3	1.2	2.1	2.2	**1.3**	-

Exit polls

Pollster	MORI	NOP	Final
Client	ITN	BBC	Result
Fieldwork	1 May	1 May	1st
Party	%	%	%
Con	30	29	**31.4**
Lab	46	47	**44.4**
LDem	18	18	**17.2**
Others	6	6	**7.0**
Ave error	1.2*	1.7	-

Source: APOPO (Association of Professional Opinion Polling Organisations)

*: N.B. The MORI/ITN exit poll was carried out only in marginal constituencies; the figures given here were a national projection from the exit poll figures, and the error arises mainly from the psephological projection rather than the accuracy of the polling. (The average error in measuring the vote in the 100 marginals polled was 0.5.%)

Table 36: Average results found by the different polling companies during the campaign, 1997

| | Conservative | Labour | LibDems | Other | Con lead |
	%	%	%	%	%
ICM	33	46	16	5	−13
Gallup	31	50	13	6	−19
Harris	30	50	14	6	−20
MORI	30	50	14	6	−20
NOP	29	49	14	8	−20

their *forecast*, not their *measurement*. The margin of error on the gap should be approximately double that of share, according to sampling

Table 37: Regional and Other Non-National Polls 1997

Fieldword dates	Agency	Client	Publ' Date	Sample size	Con %	Lab %	LD %	Nat %	Oth ±%	Lead ±%	C-Lab Swing 92–97
SCOTLAND											
11–14 Mar	ICM*	Scotsman	20 Mar	1,000	17	47	10	23	3	–30	8.5
20–24 Mar	Sys 3	Herald	26 Mar	1,006	17	52	9	20	2	–35	11.0
27–30 Mar	Sys 3	Herald	2 Apr	1,200	12	53	9	26	0	–41	14.0
29–31 Mar	ICM*	Scotsman	2 Apr	1,000	20	47	9	22	2	–27	7.0
2 Apr	NOP	S Times Scot	6 Apr	844	18	49	6	25	2	–31	9.0
5–6 Apr	Sys 3	Herald	9 Apr	1,081	14	51	10	23	2	–37	12.0
11–13 Apr	ICM*	Scotsman	15 Apr	1,000	19	42	15	23	1	–23	5.0
12–14 Apr	Sys 3	Herald	16 Apr	1,080	13	52	9	24	2	–39	13.0
17 Apr	NOP	S Times Scot	20 Apr	950	15	47	8	28	2	–32	9.5
18–20 Apr	ICM	Scotsman	22 Apr	1,000	18	47	11	21	3	–29	8.0
19–20 Apr	Sys 3	Herald	23 Apr	1,080	15	47	12	24	2	–32	9.5
24 Apr	NOP	S Times Scot	27 Apr	1,000	14	49	12	24	1	–35	11.0
25–27 Apr	ICM*	Scotsman	29 Apr	1,000	18	46	13	21	2	–28	7.5
26–27 Apr	Sys 3	Herald	30 Apr	1,084	14	50	9	26	1	–36	11.5
1 May	**RESULT**				**18**	**45**	**13**	**22**	**2**	**–27**	**7.0**
WALES											
20–21 Mar	MRW	Western Mail	28 Mar	1,000	15	67	7	8	3	–52	15.5
4–8 Apr	NOP	HTV Wales	10 Apr	1,095	20	59	9	10	2	–39	9.0
24–25 Apr	MRW	Western Mail	1 May	1,000	19	61	10	9	2	–42	10.5
1 May	**RESULT**				**20**	**55**	**12**	**10**	**3**	**–35**	**7.0**
GREATER LONDON											
1–2 Apr	MORI*	Eve. Std.	3 Apr	1,087	27	59	10	–	4	–32	20.0
1 May	**RESULT**				**31**	**49**	**14**	**–**	**5**	**–18**	**13.0**
SIX SELECTED MARGINAL SEATS: ITV 500 PANEL											
8 Apr	MORI*	ITN	8 Apr	463	30	53	12	*	5	–23	n/a
10 Apr	MORI*	ITN	10 Apr	458¶	31	52	12	2	3	–21	n/a
22 Apr	MORI*	ITN	22 Apr	516¶	31	49	13	2	5	–18	n/a
29 Apr	MORI*	ITN	29 Apr	502¶	26	51	18	2	3	–25	n/a
1 May	**RESULT**				**31**	**53**	**12**	**1**	**3**	**–22**	

* Telephone survey. All MORI's telephone surveys were conducted by MORI On-Line Telephone Surveys.

¶ Second or subsequent wave of a panel (with or without boosters of new respondents)

Table 38: The Record of the Polls 1945–97

Year	Mean error in lead %	Average error in party share %	Number of polls
1945	3.5	1.5	1
1950	3.6	1.2	2
1951	5.3	2.2	3
1955	0.3	0.9	2
1959	1.1	0.7	4
1964	1.2	1.7	4
1966	3.9	1.4	4
1970	6.6	2.2	5
1974 Feb	2.4	1.6	6
1974 Oct	4.5	1.4	4
1979	1.7	1.0	4
1983	4.5	1.4	6
1987	3.7	1.4	6
1992	8.7	2.7	5
1997	4.4	2.1	5
AVERAGE	3.8	1.8	61

theory, and indeed it is, according to the empirical evidence of 61 election forecasts over 52 years.

Another way to look at it is by average error of the collective polls in each election over the years. This demonstrates that while there have been occasional elections where the polls have erred in one direction or the other, there has not been any persistent bias in any direction. (This, of course, is in direct contradiction of those, especially our Tory critics, who during the 1997 election tried to suggest that the polls always underestimate Conservative strength, thus taking up the traditional Liberal Party claim.)

But (as can be seen from the tables), something did go awry in 1992. The five major pollsters, Gallup, Harris, ICM, MORI and NOP averaged a 1.3% Labour lead, the final result was a 7.6% lead for the Conservatives. The polls backed the wrong winner, by a wider margin than can be accounted for by sampling error, and were widely criticised for their inability to perform to expectation. The campaign polls had been showing a pretty steady picture also, steady across company and generally over time. They certainly weren't out of line with the final polls – indeed, on average they found a bigger Labour lead. Whatever problems

Table 39: The Polls, 1945–97 – no consistent bias

	Conservatives %	Labour %	Liberal Democrats %
1945	+2	−2	+1
1950	+1	−3	+1
1951	+2	−4	+1
1955	+1	+1	−1
1959	0	+1	0
1964	+1	+1	−1
1966	−1	+3	−1
1970	−2	+4	−1
1974 Feb	0	−2	+2
1974 Oct	−2	+2	0
1979	0	+1	0
1983	+2	−2	0
1987	−1	+2	−1
1992	−5	+4	+1
1997	0	+3	−1
Average	**−0.13**	**+0.60**	**0.00**

affected the final polls affected the earlier campaign polls as well. The campaign tracking polls were broadly in line with the two national panel studies being published at the same time, and the results of all these face-to-face polls were matched by the small number of telephone polls which were conducted.

Commentary on the 1992 election polls was patchy, some of it solidly researched and thoughtful, but also some of it inaccurate, misleading or misguided. Unfortunately, it is the more sensational, critical or speculative conclusion that tends to stick in the public, and indeed the journalistic, mind. A mythology has built up around the 1992 election, and its implications for polling. It is because too many people, including both the BBC and the former Prime Minister, John Major and his advisers, believed these myths, that so many politicians and pundits ended up with egg on their faces in the 1997 election. The way in which the polls have been misreported and misunderstood has lessons not only for pollsters and those who report their work, but perhaps more generally for those who seek to achieve public knowledge and understanding of statistical, and indeed any technical, subject matter.

What went wrong in 1992? The media pundits have their say

Much space in the newspapers was given over after the 1992 election to 'POLLSTERS ADMIT ELECTION MISTAKES' (30 April 1992) and 'THE INVISIBLE VOTERS WHO FOOLED THE POLLSTERS' (1 May 1992) in the *Independent*, as well as to the various letter writers' expressions of their own prejudices. They came up with plenty of theories; but, with a very few perceptive exceptions, they were a first demonstration of what was to become more obvious during 1997, that the media neither understand polls nor care particularly about their failure to do so. Their suggestions, from pundits, psephologists and letter writers alike, in *The Times*, *The Daily Telegraph*, the *Guardian*, the *Independent*, the *Financial Times* and elsewhere, are set out – and for the most part easily refuted – in the next couple of pages.

Just a day or two after the election, letter writers and critics alike were united in dismissing 'any late swing lame excuses' from the pollsters.

One of the most popular knee-jerk reactions to the polls' failure was to blame **sample size**. It is manifestly apparent that sample size is not the key to quality of the findings. The ICM poll in the third week of the 1992 campaign had a sample of over 10,000 in 330 sampling points taken over nearly a week, yet was almost identical in its voting intention to the findings of a 'smaller' poll conducted over the same period.

The fact that the final polls of the campaign, all taken the day or two before polling day, were so consistent makes it clear that neither sampling size nor sampling variation were responsible for the magnitude of the difference between the final polls and the actual result. While any one poll with those sample sizes might have been so inaccurate by chance, the probability of five independent polls all being equally inaccurate, and in the same direction, is indescribably small.

Another letter writer claimed government by fraud, reporting that in 1987 the Conservatives had enfranchised **millions of expatriate Britons**, giving them the right to a postal vote, which of course the polls would have missed. Unfortunately for this theory, only 34,454 of these expatriates were actually registered to vote, an average of just 53 per constituency.

Others suggested it was all the fault of the hated **'poll tax'**. Millions of people, many young and mostly Labour supporters, it was suggested, were dropping off the electoral register to hide from the Community Charge. If pollsters' samples reflected the population, instead of the unrepresentative electoral register, of course they would over-estimate the Labour vote. An intelligent suggestion, but also wrong. In fact most of the pollsters excluded respondents who said they were not on the electoral register, and in any case their quota samples were based on a survey which used the electoral register rather than the general population as its sampling frame. But even had the pollsters been totally unaware of the problem, the numbers involved are just not big enough to explain even a significant fraction of the error.

A more popular theory expounded by numerous letter writers and pundits was that millions of Britons were lying to interviewers; one academic critic, Ivor Crewe, even titled his paper on the polls in implied agreement, '**A Nation of Liars**' (quoting a post-election column by Robert Harris[2]). But in fact detailed investigation has found no evidence to suggest that this was the case. Indeed, it would involve not just lying, but lying intelligently and consistently, for the three panel studies which repeatedly interviewed the same respondents had comparable results before during and after the election, as did the separate British Election Panel Study (which found too many rather than too few claiming to be Tory). In the campaign tracking studies which asked a bank of other questions as well as voting intention, there was no evidence of inconsistency between the electoral and other attitudinal questions. In fact, as it turned out, it was possible to explain the whole of the error in the polls even on the assumption that every single respondent told the truth; this vision of the mendacious British public was another myth.

So what really went wrong? A committee of inquiry, set up by the Market Research Society, took two years to investigate and reported[3] in the summer of 1994.

There are three principal ways in which a quota poll might in theory go wrong and fail to predict the outcome of the election. First, the size

---

[2] *Sunday Times*, 12 April 1992.
[3] *The Opinion Polls and the 1992 British General Election: A Report to the Market Research Society* (London: Market Research Society, 1994.)

of the different quota and/or weighting cells in the survey design might not match the profile of the relevant population: the pollsters might set out to interview too many council tenants, or they might try to interview a sample representative of all adults when the relevant population, those registered to vote, was significantly different.

Secondly, even if the basic survey design is correct, the samples within each cell might not be properly representative of the relevant sector of the population: those most easily available for interview or those prepared to be interviewed might be unusual, skewing the sample, and as with any sample survey there is the possibility of statistical sampling variation.

Thirdly, even if a representative sample is interviewed, their answers might be misleading: they might lie, they might change their minds between the survey and the moment of voting, or those who refuse to reveal their intentions may be disproportionately supporters of one party.

The MRS report concluded that there were three principal reasons for the failure of the final polls in the 1992 to forecast the result accurately, which correspond to these three theoretical possibilities. Late swing (including 'churning', that is 'don't knows' deciding to vote and those who had named a party failing to vote, as well as 'switching' between the parties) certainly played a role, accounting for around a third of the error, perhaps more. The population profiles used for weighting and quotas were flawed, being skewed towards naturally Labour-voting groups, which of necessity contributed part of the bias in the overall samples. (Data from the 1991 Census was not yet available at the time of the 1992 election, and in its absence it turned out that all the polling companies relied heavily on the same alternative data source, which later proved to have been misleading.) Finally, it seems likely that unrepresentativeness of the samples interviewed within each cell played an important part, and that this was caused by differential reluctance on the part of Conservatives to be interviewed. But the enquiry also concluded that these errors should be avoidable, and the quota sampling as such was not the cause of the 1992 error.

I was one of the members of the MRS Inquiry team (which also included academics and market researchers not involved in polling), and fully agreed with its conclusions. I was able to further develop my thoughts in a paper to an Ordinary Discussion Meeting of the Royal

Statistical Society on 14 June 1995, later published in the Journal of the Royal Statistical Society[4]. This discussed in depth some of the suggested explanations for the inaccuracy of the polls in 1992, and drawing on this, as well as on the MRS report and on results of our own experimentation with methodological variations, we began to plan MORI's strategy for the 1997 election.

What was the solution in 1997?

Achieving representative samples

Each of the four companies conducting regular polls[5] had to decide how to deal with the three apparent sources of error in 1992, and each of the four came to different conclusions.

One solution being pressed on us from the very start came not from any of the practical pollsters who had been engaged in the 1992 election (or who were to be in 1997), but by academic critics[6]. They, essentially, disagreed with the conclusions of the MRS Inquiry, and argued that changes in the nature of the British electorate have meant that their opinions can no longer be measured accurately by quota polls. It is a conclusion with which we disagreed, and which 1997 gave us our first real chance to disprove.

Our critics avowed that one factor in particular – failure to achieve representative samples of the population within each quota or weighting cell – was overwhelmingly the most significant source of error, and that this arose not from differential refusal by Tories but from an availability bias. Their theory was that those who our interviewers could most easily

---

[4] Worcester, R., 'Political Polling: 95% Expertise and 5% Luck', *Journal of the Royal Statistical Society, Series A*, 159, part 1 (1996).

[5] Harris was not polling regularly between the elections; their methods during the election period were closest to NOP's. For details and discussion of NOP's methodology, see Moon, N., *Opinion polls: History, theory and practice* (Manchester: Manchester University Press, 1999).

[6] Jowell, R., Hedges, B., Lynn, P., Farrant, G., and Heath, A., 'The 1992 British General Election: The Failure of the Polls', *Public Opinion Quarterly*, LVII, pp 238–63, and Lynn, P., and Jowell, R., 'How Might Opinion Polls be Improved?: The Case for Probability Sampling', *Journal of the Royal Statistical Society*, Series A, 159. Part 1 (1996).

Table 40: Historical Record of Random and Quota Samples in Britain

Average error on percentage lead in final polls (Number of polls conducted):

	1970	Feb 1974	Oct 1974	1975 Ref'm	1979	Mean error 1970–9
Random	7.3 (3)	3.7 (2)	8.0 (2)	10.0 (1)	1.6 (1)	**6.3**
Quota	5.4 (2)	1.7 (4)	3.5 (4)	3.9 (5)	1.7 (4)	**3.0**

contact were systematically (and unavoidably) different in their opinions from those they could not. They dismiss the possibility that late swing and differential turnout in all its forms played more than a minor role; they do not consider at all design faults in the quotas and weighting which could have been easily corrected if recognised. Given this analysis, their solution was that all the polls should revert to face-to-face probability sampling.

Jowell et al base their claims that quota samples suffered from an availability bias on an analysis of the 1992 British Election Study, a cross-section survey using random sampling methods. It is unnecessary to rehearse in detail the weaknesses of their analysis, which were set out in the 1994 MRS report. In any case, if there were a problem, a similar availability bias would apply to a random poll with a restricted time-scale. Similarly, if quota polls have a problem with differential refusal to participate (as the MRS enquiry suggested happened in 1992) this also applies in equal measure to random polls.

It is simply not true to say, as is frequently asserted, that random polls are 'the more reliable method', especially for election polling. In fact, in the best single empirical test of random against quota samples in Britain (the 1975 referendum), the random poll performed considerably worse than quota polls, three of which were within 1% of the outcome while the random sample was 5% out, well beyond sampling tolerance. The historical record of random face-to-face polls in Britain was far worse than that of quota samples in those elections where both methods were used.

None of the polling companies decided to revert to probability sampling with face-to-face interviewing. The argument in favour (which, apart from Jowell et al, apparently appealed to the BBC) partly depends on a misunderstanding of our objections to random sampling for election polls, perhaps because they equate 'quick' with 'cheap' or 'low quality'. We want our polls to be quick, but not for that reason.

The timing element means that random samples are especially weak for predictive eve-of-poll surveys. The possibility of a late swing – generally agreed to have been a major factor in the polls' error in 1970, when mainly random methods were used, and also found to be a significant contributory factor in 1992 and certainly present in 1997, even with faster quota polling – puts a high premium on minimising the period between start of fieldwork and polling day.

An election poll is necessarily carried out in a short period of time – its entire purpose is to derive a snapshot of opinion at a particular moment. The principal difficulty with random polls is not, as the BBC guidelines suggest, that there is a bigger gap between fieldwork and publication, but that the fieldwork itself takes longer – not only is much of the data out-of-date, but it does not refer to any particular point in time. In a fast-moving election campaign this could be highly misleading. (Jowell and his colleagues are connected with the British Election Study, the survey designed for academic study of the election which – because it is not intended to lead to immediate publication of the results – can be conducted at a much more leisurely pace than an ordinary poll, and seem unreceptive to arguments that an election poll cannot be run in the same way.)

The time-consuming element of a random poll is contacting and getting responses from the pre-generated list of respondents; the shorter time that is available for fieldwork, the lower proportion of the intended sample can be interviewed and the less reliable the results will be – not simply through a low sample size but because those who are difficult to contact are likely to be systematically similar and a bias is inevitably introduced – more so than a quota poll, which tries to control this factor by the way it divides up the population into quotas.

None of the pollsters adopted the Jowell argument in full, but we all gave careful consideration to the question of how to avoid unrepresentative samples. Here there were essentially four options:

1. We could **change the sampling method** altogether, dropping quota sampling: both ICM and Gallup chose this option, though instead of

switching to the face-to-face random sampling that had been tried unsuccessfully in the earlier days of British polling, both instead switched to interviewing by telephone, with a more or less random selection of the telephone numbers to be called. (In the final analysis, it is the telephone number rather than the respondent that they randomly select. Gallup's method, which uses random digit dialling and then selects the household member to be interviewed by a birthday rule is rather purer than ICM's 'quasi-random method', which is directory-based and makes greater use of quotas in selection of respondents, but neither is pure equal probability sampling – they cannot make allowance for the unequal numbers of potential respondents who can be contacted on any given telephone number. Also, although the time constraints which handicap random face-to-face surveys do not apply to the same extent to the 'random' telephone sampling, which makes it much easier to make multiple attempts at an interview within a practical time-scale, they are still forced to accept a contact rate much lower than the ideal.) Both quota and quasi-random telephone methods performed satisfactorily in 1997, though no doubt there will be further fine-tuning to methodology in the future – as, indeed, is always the case.

2. We could **redesign the details of the quota sampling** method, while retaining its principles. This was the mainstay of MORI's response, and NOP also adopted more limited methodological changes. MORI took the view that, although the *details* of the quota sampling in 1992 were one of the contributory factors towards the error, the basic method was sound and suggested problems such as availability bias, interviewer bias, anti-rural bias and even differential refusal bias could be overcome by more carefully designed quotas and weighting. Consequently we concentrated on ensuring the reliability of the demographic data used and fine-tuning the details of the sampling and weighting, in the belief that we could thereby achieve representative samples.

3. We could accept that the raw data was not, or might not be, absolutely representative, and compensate for its imperfections by **weighting**. To some extent this approach is already inherent in any quota sampling, and virtually all quota polls are designed to be subject

at least to demographic weighting. However, demographic weighting had failed to correct the error in 1992. Both ICM and NOP decided, in addition to their normal demographic weighting, that they would weight their surveys by declared past vote, a decision which MORI rejected.

ICM's adjustments are based on the Spiral of Silence theory first developed in Germany by Elisabeth Noelle-Neumann[7], which I introduced to Nick Sparrow in the first place, during one of the meetings of the MRS Inquiry team. Few are more admiring of her than I, having worked with the *grande dame* of our industry for nearly thirty years and continuing to serve with her as one of the founding co-editors of *the International Journal of Public Opinion Research* (the third being Professor Seymour Martin Lipset). I treasure my signed copies of her books which she has sent to me over the years, and have studied them with interest. I am proud to have succeeded her as a president of the World Association of Public Opinion Research, and as the recipient of the WAPOR Dinerman Award, and have tried to replicate the effect of her 'Spiral of Silence' here in Great Britain for some two decades – but without, I confess, much success (as did Bob Wybrow of Gallup). The application of mathematical formulae based upon people's recall of their past voting behaviour has in past elections here been misleading and derived wrong conclusions rather than improved the forecasts of British measures of likely electoral behaviour.

When Professor Noelle-Neumann wrote to me during this election, and offered to put the resources of herself and her Institute's methodologist at our disposal to adjust our data, I willingly sent it to her. When she came back she strongly urged me to use adjustments based on her theories in my final forecast. In the end I did not, and relied on attitudinal data contained within the surveys' results to make any adjustments as I had in earlier elections, and in the end, made little adjustment, and none based on her theory. This was largely on

---

[7] See especially Noelle-Neumann, E., 'Public Opinion and the Classical Tradition: A Re-evaluation', *Public Opinion Quarterly*, 43, 143–56, and *Spiral of Silence: Public Opinion – Social Skin*, (Chicago, Ill. and London: University of Chicago Press, 1984), *Die Schweigespirale: öffentliche Meinung – unsere soziale Haut*, (Munich: R Piper & Co Verlag, 1980).

the basis that had I done so in past elections, prior to 1992, in every instance MORI would have had a worse, not better, forecast of the outcome than we in fact did. Respondents' report of their past voting behaviour is, we know, in Britain a faulty guide to the representativeness of a sample, though it is one of many measures related to current voting intentions which can sometimes be used as a surrogate in the case of refusals.

Of course, unless a poll forecast is perfect, it is always possible that by luck an adjustment may make it better; equally, it may make it worse unless it is founded on solid evidence of a cause of error and the means of correcting it. The adjustments introduced by the other companies after 1992 were mainly a reaction to the perception of a 'spiral of silence' and the legendary shy Tories; in the event, we find little evidence that this problem still existed in 1997. As we learned from MORI de Mexico's experience in 1994, adjusting the data against a phantom problem can be a risky business. ICM's final poll demonstrated that their adjustment mechanism was not the panacea that its director would like to think for ensuring a perfect measurement of the Labour lead. The adjusted ICM lead was 10 points (43%–33%), creditably close to the actual lead of 13; but then the unadjusted lead was 16 (46%–30%), exactly as accurate (or inaccurate). As several critics had suggested beforehand, the ICM adjustment was overcompensating, although fortuitously they were able to point to a one-point improvement in the LibDems and others – not what the adjustment was really intended to achieve – which marginally improved their overall score and allowed them to claim justification.

4. Finally, we could have left the polls uncorrected, but compensated for their imperfections in the 'predictions' we made from them, with a pre-conceived fixed adjustment – this would have the minimalist solution, and none of the companies chose to go down this perilous road.

Data sources for weighting and quotas

The question of design error was much more straightforward, and the companies were in general agreement, following the recommendations of the MRS Enquiry to seek better and more diverse sources of information for weighting and quota targets. (The sources used by MORI are enumerated below, p. 176).

Avoiding misleading answers

The third question was how to get the most useful answers from our respondents, and how to interpret them. We were confident that, as the MRS Inquiry had found, there were not significant numbers of respondents lying to us. But we needed to avoid their answers being misleading in other ways, by their changing their minds before polling day or by differential likelihood of their actually turning out to vote; we also needed to avoid being misled if those respondents who refused to tell us how they would vote were disproportionately supporters of one party.

Some of these corrections are obvious, and indeed have been used in the past. For example, we would always make corrections for turnout, reporting the voting intentions of those 'certain to vote' if they differed from the intentions of all adults. For this purpose, we have always found that a simple scale question on likelihood of voting suffices, and it proved entirely adequate in 1997. (In our final *Times* poll, 71% told us they were certain to vote, and the eventual official turnout was 71.4%.)

Another option is to compensate for late swing by polling later. MORI's final published figures were based not on the raw results of our face-to-face polls, but on last-minute re-interviewing a sub-sample of respondents from our earlier polls by telephone, giving us a measure of the late swing. This is method with a pedigree, which had almost saved the pollsters from disaster in 1970, and it is clear that in 1997 it allowed us to get nearer to the final result than we could otherwise have done.

A more radical possibility was to change the questions altogether. ICM did this most dramatically, completely redesigning their voting intention question.

By far the most striking and consistent company difference in the 1997 polls was ICM's consistently higher reading of the LibDem share, with a correspondingly lower Labour share and hence lower Labour lead over Conservative. This had nothing to do with ICM's much vaunted 'adjustment' of their data, contrary to some press analysis, which generally

Table 41: The final hours

Poll Client	MORI Times (initial findings)	MORI Times (with phone recall)	MORI E Std (phone recall)	VOTE GE '97
Fieldwork	29.4	30.4 early p.m.	30.4 late p.m.	1.5
n=	2,304	2,304 (of which 385 recalled)	1,501	Actual
	%	%	%	%
Con	27	28	29	31.4
Lab	51	48	47	44.4
LibDem	15	16	19	17.2
Other	7	8	5	7.0
Lead	−24	−20	−18	13.0

had no effect on LibDem share. (The difference between ICM's average adjusted and unadjusted LibDem share was 0.1%.) It seems plain that it was in fact caused by the question wording: ICM's distinctive question wording names the main parties to the respondent before asking how he or she will vote. ('*The Conservatives, Labour, the Liberal Democrats and other parties would fight an immediate general election in your constituency. Please tell me which party you think you would actually vote for in the polling station.*') Unlike the other pollsters, ICM were reminding respondents of the possibility of voting LibDem, and it has long been recognised that using such a preamble is liable to push up the LibDem share in any poll.

MORI prefers not to use such a tactic, for two reasons. The first is simply past experience – experiments with this sort of question wording at the time of the SDP breakaway convinced us that there is an unacceptably high risk of distorting the data. Nevertheless, it must be admitted that this did not occur in 1997 – viewed naively, the ICM polls were a better indicator than the other campaign polls of the eventual LibDem share. But our second objection is more a philosophical one – what are the polls trying to measure? We are committed to the ideal that any poll (except the final predictive poll, which is a special case) should attempt to be an accurate snapshot of the actual voting intention of the population at the moment when it is taken. Viewed on these terms, we are quite confident that our polls gave a better measure of LibDem strength; there really were only 12%–13% intending to vote for the LibDems early in the campaign.

For it is my view, unlike some of the other pollsters and psephologists, that what the British public expect of the polls is the systematic and objective measurement of British public opinion, what they tell us the public does, knows and thinks, not what we think they might be thinking under different conditions than pertain at that moment[8]. As I have said often, 'polls don't ever forecast – but pollsters sometimes do'. I am also mindful of the wise words of the Code of Conduct of the Market Research Society: 'When presenting results, members shall endeavour to make a clear distinction between the results themselves and their own interpretation of the data and recommendations.'[9]

Thus I have during my career as a pollster faithfully and to the best of my ability tried to report to my clients in the media, and through the media to the public, what I have found by asking a representative sample of the adult population what they think, using as even and unbiased questions as I know how to ask. (The only exception to this is, I readily confess, on the eve of an election, when what clearly is expected of me is my best guess as to what the outcome will be – then I will, as I have been doing since the British General Election of 1970, apply whatever adjustment factors I have at my disposal, including reported registration, certainty of voting, caring who wins, effect on the voter and their family, etc., to help me to determine what I think the outcome will be, and then, based on regional database information and after boundary change, the received wisdom of its effect, the likely split in terms of seats in the House of Commons.)

We accept, as we had imagined ICM would argue, that the LibDems normally start a campaign at a level that is unrealistically low and will almost inevitably pick up support as their profile increases. But our job is not to guess what will happen, nor what we expect to happen, or what ought to happen, but simply what actually is already happening. We

---

[8] Worcester, R., 'Why do we do what we do? A Review of what it is we think we do, reflections on why we do it, and whether or not it does any good', *International Journal of Public Opinion Research*, Volume 9, Number 1, Spring 1997, p. 2–16.

[9] Section C. 11, Code of Conduct, *1996 Market Research Society Yearbook*, p. 73.

would therefore feel that ICM's campaign polls are, in short, neither a real measurement nor a real prediction (for, of course, they make no claim to predict future reaction to the course of the campaign), but a vague compromise between the two.

Surprisingly, Nick Sparrow of ICM apparently believes that his question wording measures real rather than potential support. He argued :

'All ten published ICM polls in the campaign put the Liberals within sampling error of their actual performance . . . [T]he rise in Liberal support seen in many recent elections may not be a result of their campaigning prowess but a function of the pollsters' question wording. In any event, a rise from an average 12.1 per cent in late March to 17.2 per cent on election day (a 43 per cent increase) looks to me too spectacular to be true.'[10]

I entirely disagree (and indeed predicted precisely such an increase long before the election). The ICM polls picked up not only those who were intending to vote Liberal Democrat, but also those who would switch to such an intention if prompted to do so. This is in effect a measure of public reaction under laboratory conditions – the respondents in ICM's polls were no longer representative of the British public, precisely because they had been subjected to the prompting of the ICM preamble – and, of course, this applies not only to the intended effect on the voting intention question, but also to any questions that ICM go on to ask afterwards.

Another option that we had to consider was whether we should 'impute' answers for some respondents – that is, calculate how they were likely to vote on the basis of their answers to other questions, rather than relying on the voting intention question. Both ICM and Gallup used imputation to predict the voting behaviour of the 'don't knows' and refused-to-says.

In fact, we can see in retrospect that MORI's quota samples performed in 1997 even better than is apparent from our published figures; had we imputed a voting intention (on the basis of declared past vote) to the respondents who refused to tell us how they would vote, which unfortunately we decided not to do, we would have achieved a near-

---

[10] Sparrow, N., 'How the pollsters got it wrong in 1997', *Guardian*, 11 June 1997.

Table 42: MORI's final poll 1997 – best projection with hindsight

	Eve Std Published figures %	Eve Std including refusers by reported '92 vote %	Result %
Conservative	29	31	**31.4**
Labour	47	45	**44.4**
Liberal Democrat	19	19	**17.2**
Others	6	6	**7.0**
Average error	2.2	0.95	

perfect final prediction. Of course, it is a great deal easier after the event to find the interpretation of the data that brings it nearest to the true election result, and 1997 was the first opportunity to try out in a general election the theories we had formed since 1992. When we added the refusers into the *Evening Standard* figures – that is the 5% of the sample who said they were certain to vote, but wouldn't say how they would vote – using their *declared* 1992 vote[11] as an indicator of how they would vote this time, the voting intention figures come even closer to the final result. Oh well, we shall know that for next time.

This would have made it comfortably the best of the poll projections of share (as we would have expected it to be, being also the latest to interview).

'Adjusted polls'

Because the reasons for and implications of the changes made by each of the different companies were not well understood, there was a great deal of rather ill-informed debate on the subject of 'adjusted' polls. This term came to be applied rather loosely in the period of experimentation following the 1992 election to any extra manipulation of voting intention figures on top of the standard 'raw' figures. But it was misleading – pollsters did not even in 1992 publish 'raw' figures in the sense of being

---

[11] We consider declared past vote to be an unreliable indicator of actual past vote, but it may be a powerful indicator of current voting intention.

entirely unmanipulated – even then they were at the least demographi-cally weighted. MORI subsequently became the standard-bearer for 'unadjusted' polls; but MORI had already incorporated its adjustment, which was a reform of its quota sampling method, and which had acted on the 'raw' figures before they ever reached the office. Gallup, in the end, was doing much the same: although its published figures were subject to an 'adjustment', its effect was invariably tiny, and the significant change was the adoption of telephone sampling. NOP, by contrast, made little change to its sampling method, but relied on the weighting in its 'adjustment' to bring the figures into line. Hence it was a nonsense to talk about comparing the polls' unadjusted figures (and here we must admit that MORI may have been partly responsible for unintentionally engendering the misunderstanding): it simply was not a comparison of like with like. MORI's figures were intended to be used unadjusted, NOP's were not.

A major culprit in propagating this confusion, unfortunately, was Nick Sparrow, head of ICM. 'I think there is a good chance of unadjusted polls being more wrong in '97 than '92.', he told the *Guardian*[12]. This was simply nonsense, as the final polls proved. The only unadjusted polls being published were MORI's, but they were throughout the campaign broadly in line with the adjusted polls of NOP, Harris and Gallup, and indeed, as far as the measurement of Conservative share goes, generally in line with ICM until the penultimate *Guardian* poll (which is in retrospect even more clearly than at the time a rogue). Furthermore, the adjusted figures and the unadjusted figures from the same companies were frequently not significantly different. David Butler commented on this the following weekend: '. . . adjustments are not at the heart of the current problem [the differences between ICM and the other companies' polls]. In ICM's own poll the unadjusted Labour lead is only 1 per cent higher than the published adjusted figure.'[13] One letter-writer to the *Guardian* went further, noting that 'It has been clear for some time that your adjusted and unadjusted figures have been converging. . . . This

---

[12] MacAskill, E., 'Tories' turning point? Or still trailing points?', *Guardian*, 22 April 1997.

[13] Butler, D., 'Sudden blip in the polls gives Tories a small straw to clutch', *Financial Times Weekend*, 26/27 April 1997.

convergence serves to undermine the theory behind the ICM adjustment – the so-called 'spiral of silence' effect.'[14]

For our part, we feel the 1997 results in general justified us in our decision not to 'adjust' our polls. We will continue to rely on the simple virtues of sound sampling and letting our respondents speak for themselves without having their replies massaged. We will continue to make minor adjustments *in the eve-of-poll prediction only* to reflect factors such as turnout, refusals and the weather, based on the assessment of the particular circumstances of that election as revealed by all the data available to us, and not by some dogmatically rigid formula based on abstract theory or guesswork.

What did MORI change and why? The details

We can leave the other companies to explain or justify the full details of their own changes, but it seems sensible to set out systematically exactly what the MORI strategy was, and why we adopted it. MORI retained face-to-face quota sampling, but made major modifications to the details. The changes made were three-fold, and applied both to our main, stand-alone series of election polls for *The Times*, and to our regular Omnibus surveys (which provided the sample for our final telephone panel projection in the *Evening Standard*).

Most importantly, we moved to **using much smaller, randomly selected sampling points**, to reduce discretion given to interviewers in selection of respondents, giving us much greater control over the nature and location of the sample and lessening the scope for unconscious interviewer bias. Instead of the constituency sampling points used in 1992, the *Times* surveys used the postcodes corresponding to single census enumeration districts (EDs) consisting typically of a couple of hundred addresses, and the Omnibus used clusters of about five EDs[15]. Quotas were set separately for each sampling point.

---

[14] Noble I., Letter to the Editor, *Guardian*, 24 April 1997.

[15] The selection of the *Times* sampling points was on a simple stratified random basis, making the *Times* surveys to all intents and purposes random location samples. For the Omnibus a more complex, two-stage, process was used, with an initial selection of 175 constituencies so as to

This gives us much greater control over whom our interviewers interview: using constituency sampling points gave the interviewers a lot of discretion within the scope of their quotas. This decision followed considerable experimentation on the MORI Omnibus, which convinced us that smaller sampling points significantly improved our samples:

- We have very tight control over the nature of the sample. The random selection of EDs is made on the basis of stratification by MOSAIC type. (MOSAIC is a sophisticated lifestyle classification developed by CCN Marketing). This enables us to ensure that all the different types of neighbourhood and local environment are proportionately represented in our samples, as well as more conventional demographic measures. This takes a lot of the pressure off the quota, because much more of the process of selection of respondents is controlled from the office before it reaches the stage where the interviewers are given discretion within their quotas.
- It eliminates most of the scope for unconscious bias in interviewers' selection of respondents. (For example, rural voters would normally be under-represented – in a rural constituency, interviewers would tend to fill their quotas in the towns. Journalists sometimes characterise this effect as avoiding houses with long driveways or inner-city tower blocks; setting quotas in specific EDs ensures that this sort of bias can be eliminated from MORI's samples.)
- All interviewing on our political surveys is now in-home. (This was not a change that was necessary in itself, but is a consequence of the switch to ED sampling.)

Secondly, **extra variables were added to both quotas and weighting**, to improve their discriminatory power. In addition to the extra control we gain by using ED quotas, we have replaced social class with household tenure (which controls much the same characteristics but on which more detailed and reliable data is available), and added a quota

---

maximise the national and regional representativeness of the selection as judged by a number of political and demographic variables, then within each constituency a random selection of a single ED, followed by random selection of further adjacent EDs until the target population was reached, with the resulting cluster tested for correlation of its demographic profile with that of the constituency, with insufficiently representative clusters rejected and redrawn.

control for household access to a car, which is an economic behaviour variable which seems to be much more closely related to vote than the traditional social class divisions. We also controlled the time of day of interviews.

Additional variables, more closely correlated with voting behaviour, have also been added to our weighting matrices, which are now much more complex than in 1992[16]. These include:

- Household access to a car. (If the 1992 election surveys had been weighted by car ownership on the available data, that alone would have corrected almost the whole of the error not attributable to late swing.)
- Self-employment. There is a great deal of evidence to suggest that the self-employed vote differently from employees who are otherwise demographically similar.
- Unemployment is now controlled at regional level.

Finally, **data for our quotas and weighting have been comprehensively reviewed**, updated and are now drawn from diverse and reliable sources, including the Labour Force Survey, the General Household Survey, the Family Expenditure Survey, the National Readership Survey and the 1991 Census (updated by the Registrar-General's midyear estimates of population).

In fact, although we call our sample a quota sample, it is very close to the technique known as random location sampling. In this context, it is worth noting the impressive findings from the Orton paper presented to the Cathie Marsh Memorial Seminar organised by the RSS and SRA 8 November 1994, in which he concluded:

'I have no doubt that random probability sampling, assuming a high response rate, is the best possible technical approach, but I do not think that that makes it 'perfect' nor mandatory. We recognise and accept imperfection in most of the tools available to us – most notably, the questions we ask – why is it so difficult to accept that alternative sampling methodologies can still play a valid and useful role?

---

[16] The final weighting design used rim-weighting to combine seven separate matrices of target weights.

'A well-designed, well-controlled random location sample can offer design advantages which are well-nigh impossible in random probability designs, and massive cost and time savings which may be used to increase sample sizes and apply intelligent design features such as intentional skews.'

In 1997, MORI conducted three 'final' polls:-

- One face-to-face survey for *The Times* in people's homes on the Tuesday before polling day with a sample of 2,304 adults, ringing back 385 'won't says', 'undecideds' and 'might change' respondents on the following day, Wednesday, to measure any change in their voting intentions. This poll led to *The Times*' headline on its election-day front page: 'MORI points to 180-plus majority.
- A second, panel, survey with 1,501 electors via MORI/On-Line Telephone Surveys on the Wednesday for the London *Evening Standard*, recalling people interviewed face-to-face earlier in the election. This was our final pre-election prediction, and led to the headline 'Last poll puts Blair on brink of landslide', with its pundit, Peter Kellner, forecasting a 129 seat majority.
- A final 'Exit Poll' for ITV of over 15,000 voters as they left polling stations in 100 Conservative-held marginal constituencies on Thursday, and led to my own estimate of a 161 seat Labour majority, and ITN's of 159.

For the record, MORI's 'Last Word' was based on our Exit Poll for ITN, from 14,888 interviews up to 9:15 p.m., made at 9:35 p.m. which forecast a 12% swing in the key marginal seats, and the exit poll's prediction of the change in the share of the vote in the 100 constituencies where we interviewed was almost spot on (actual change in brackets): Conservatives −12.9% (−12.0%), Labour +10.7% (+10.6%), Liberal Democrats −0.6% (−1.5%). Projected nationally, this implied a share of Conservatives 30% (31.4%), Labour 46% (44.4%), Liberal Democrats 18% (17.2%) and Others 6% (7.0%), but in fact the marginal constituencies swung more than the country as a whole, and so the national projection, which was not of course what the poll was designed for, was less accurate.

The purpose of the exit poll was to produce a seat prediction. Using the 'MORI Swingo Model' developed by Dr Mortimore, I translated

Table 43: Seats projections from ITN/MORI Exit Poll through the day

Phone-in cut-off	Con	Lab	LibDem	Other (GB)	Lab maj.
10 a.m.	182	408	43	8	157
12 noon	183	407	43	8	155
3 p.m.	180	411	42	8	163
5 p.m.	180	410	43	8	161
7 p.m.	170	420	43	8	181
8.15 p.m.	178	412	43	8	165
9.15 p.m.	**180**	**410**	**43**	**8**	**161**
10 p.m.	182	408	43	8	157
RESULT	**165**	**419**	**46**	**10**	**179**

Source: MORI. *Projections by MORI Swingo model with 'handset' assumptions in some seats*

the data into a seats forecast: Conservative 180 [actual 165], Labour 410 [419], Liberal Democrats 43 [46], Others 8 [10] for an overall majority of 161 [179]. Not bad, though with so accurate a reading of the share in the seats where we polled we might have hoped to be even closer, but that was beyond our control. The fact is that the exit poll was conducted in, and was designed to predict the results in, marginal seats. But Labour's landslide was so big that all the marginal seats fell *en bloc*, and the size of the Labour majority depended on how many 'safe' Tory seats they could capture. In the event Labour did even better in these seats just outside the 'official' definition of 'marginals' than in the marginals themselves, so we slightly underestimated the majority.

The exit poll, incidentally, shows how remarkably steady the voting figures were through the day. In fact, if we had shut up shop at ten in the morning, handed over the figures to ITN and gone home, we would have had exactly the same results as we finally reached twelve laborious hours and 14,000 further interviews later. But of course we didn't know that at the time!

I toyed for a few seconds with adjusting the forecast to account for postal and proxy votes from data collected through the campaign, and for the legendary 'shy Tories'. The postal adjustment would have reduced the Tory-Labour swing by 0.15%, making a very slight improvement in the marginals measurement. The shy Tories, by our reckoning, would have accounted for a further 0.85% swing. But this adjustment would have overshot the mark, leaving us exactly as accurate as the unadjusted

Table 44: Interest in the election

Q. **How interested would you say you are in each of the following?**

	1992	1997	Change 1992–7
(% 'very' or 'fairly' interested)	%	%	± %
News about the election	60	52	−8
What the opinion polls say about the election	40	33	−7
Party election broadcasts	36	32	−4
Politicians' speeches	43	40	−3
(% 'not at all interested')	%	%	± %
News about the election	14	22	+8
What the opinion polls say about the election	25	28	+3
Party election broadcasts	32	36	+4
Politicians' speeches	28	30	+2

Source: MORI

data (and, as it happens, with a considerably worse seat projection, although the national vote forecast of Conservative 31%, Labour 45%, Liberal Democrats 18% would have been better). So where were those shy Tories?

Do opinion polls affect voting behaviour?

Many of those who are hostile to opinion polls, whether or not they believe what the polls are saying, base that hostility on the belief that reading the results of polls has an effect on electors' voting behaviour. In fact I would agree, though I believe the effect to be a very modest one; but I do not see why (assuming the polls are achieving a satisfactory degree of accuracy) such an effect should be considered pernicious. In a democracy, voters are surely entitled to the best information available, and it should be entirely a matter for them which factors they choose to allow to influence their votes.

Just over six people in ten, 63%, say they were aware of any national opinion polls in this election, down sharply from 89% at the last election, when there were more polls over a shorter period, with certainly more

Table 45: Public Awareness of the Polls

Q. **Have you seen or heard any national opinion polls in the past week giving the position of the parties?**

	%
Yes	63
No	37

Q. (To all who have seen/heard any national opinion polls in the past week) **Thinking about the last nationally conducted opinion poll you remember seeing, which party was in the lead?**

Q. **And which party was second?**

	(Base: 627)	
	Lead	Second
	%	%
Conservative	3	90
Labour	94	3
Liberal Democrat	*	2
Other	0	1
Don't know	3	4

Source: MORI
25–28 April 1997
Base: 997 British adults 18+

Q. **From what you can remember, what did the opinion polls, published on the day of the election, predict the results would be?**

	%
Was not aware of the polls/Don't know	17
Aware:	
A large majority for Labour (Majority of more than 100 MPs)/Landslide for Labour	54
A medium-sized majority for Labour (Majority of 51–100 MPs)	14
A small majority for Labour (Majority of up to 50 MPs)	3
No overall majority for either party	*
A small majority for the Conservatives (Majority of up to 50 MPs)	*
A medium-sized majority for the Conservatives (Majority of 51–100 MPs)	0
A large majority for the Conservatives (Majority of more than 100 MPs)	0
Majority for Labour (don't know what size)	3
Majority for Conservatives (don't know what size)	*
Can't remember	9

Source: MORI
7–8 May 1997
Base: 1,192 British adults 18+ interviewed by telephone

Table 46: Banning of Election Coverage

Q. **During an election campaign, do you think there should or should not be a ban on . . .?**

(% 'should be a ban')	1983 %	1987 %	1992 %	1997 %
Party political broadcasts of the election on TV and radio	14	25	24	20
Publication of opinion polls	22	25	24	16
All coverage of the election on TV and radio	13	24	21	15
All coverage of the election in newspapers	9	16	13	10

Source: MORI

coverage on the BBC than in this election. Many more men, 73%, than women, 54%, were aware of having heard poll findings in the previous week (18–25 April) including two-thirds of those 45 and over, and three-quarters of middle-class respondents but only just over half, 55%, of working-class electors. Nearly all, 94%, of those aware of having seen any polls recalled that the Labour Party was in the lead.

The public seem to want to continue to hear poll findings, and remain interested in what the polls are saying, despite the persistent sniping from the media and the spin doctors; while interest in the polls was less in 1997 than in 1992, the fall was in line with the more general drop in interest in election coverage.

A week after the election, five in six people said they recalled what opinion polls were saying, and over half recalled them as saying it would be a Labour landslide.

Banning polls during elections gets scant support. Only 16 per cent of the public believe that polls should be banned during elections, while more than three people in four do not, down sharply from the last election. Who are those who would ban the publication of opinion polls (other than the politicians of course, and perhaps John Birt)? Those opposing a ban (78%) are more likely to be men, younger (82% of under 35, 77% of 35 and over) and more likely to be middle-class (82%) than working class (75%). We should note that this figure compares with one person in five who would ban Party Election Broadcasts, 15 per cent who would ban all coverage of the election on radio and television, and one in ten who would ban coverage of the election in newspapers!

But then when asked who they trust to tell the truth, over half, 55 per cent, said they trust pollsters; only 12 per cent trust Government Ministers (somewhat fewer than the 15 percent who say they trust journalists). Perhaps this puts into perspective former Prime Minister John Major's unjustified pre-election slur that the MORI poll in *The Times* was 'complete rubbish' and that the Tories' private polls showed the election much closer.

To understand what an election would be like if there were no neutral and objective polling figures to counter the politicians' wilder claims, one need only look at 1997, when the Conservatives clearly believed that there was sufficient scepticism about the polls for their contrary message to be taken seriously. Major persisted with his claims that 'the difference out on the doorstep with what we are seeing in the opinion polls is very striking indeed – very striking. This election is there to be won, of that I have not a shred of doubt and I believe that we are going to win it. . . . The polls are rubbish.' Bob Wybrow of Gallup responded: 'A leader has to put on a brave face and given that we were wrong about him in '92, he has a slight edge but the position is different this time.' He also compared Mr Major to the Labour leader, Michael Foot, in the 1983 election: 'Foot was saying "no, no, the polls have got it wrong. I have been at meetings up and down the country" and we all know what happened in 1983.'[17]

In Central Office, Danny Finkelstein and Andrew Cooper were making similar noises, aided by the one published poll that, out of line with all the others, seemed to lend some support to their case. 'I think Nick Sparrow's figures [the 5% ICM lead] are correct,' said Finkelstein. 'Labour know that over the last week we have been gaining ground and that our prospects have been transformed. Bob Worcester says we are facing the biggest swing against us this century, that Conservative MPs with 18,000 majorities will be swept away; well, if he thinks that he's wildly out', and 'I am absolutely stone cold certain Bob Worcester will be looking ridiculous on the Friday after polling day.'[18]

---

[17] MacAskill, E., 'Tories' turning point? Or still trailing points?', *Guardian*, 22 April 1997.
[18] Quoted in Jones, N., *Campaign 1997: How the General Election was Won and Lost* (London: Indigo, 1997), pp 236–7.

Of course, Major probably did not believe this himself. After the election his chief of communications, Charles Lewington, said that on 15 April 'John Major confided to a trusted campaign aide: "You know we can't win it" . . . The Prime Minister didn't need to read the bleak findings of our private polls to know that the cause was lost. He was a seasoned campaigner and smelt defeat in the spring air.' That was the day on which, according to Lewington, 'we at Central Office learnt it was all over.' There was bad news from the constituencies, and

'The second blow came from the pollsters. The news from ICM was that our best hope – a hung Parliament – was now impossible. The word from the research department was of a "spectacular" defeat. . . . On the ground and in the polls we were being blown away.'[19]

Peter Kellner put the case for paying more attention to the polls than the politicians: 'Labour and Conservative politicians are trying hard, both on and off the record, to persuade anyone who will listen that the race is closer than the polls are saying. Labour is trying to guard against complacency, while the Tories are seeking to revive morale. Both stances are understandable, but neither has anything to do with the truth . . . Don't let the spin doctors persuade you otherwise, even – perhaps especially – when the spin doctors of both main parties are in agreement.'[20]

The Stock Exchange and the polls

One battle I lost in this election, as I do in every election, was with the Stock Exchange, one place where the opinion poll findings certainly matter. I wrote early on to the Chairman of the Stock Exchange to warn of the habit of some in the City to use opinion polls, real or fictitious, to ramp share prices, exchange rates, etc., during the campaign. Dismissed by 'some . . . in the City . . . attributed it [my warning] to publicity seeking on Mr Worcester's part.' John Willcock wrote the story up in the

---

[19] Lewington, C., '"You know we can't win . . . how do you think history will judge me?"', *Sunday Telegraph*, 8 June 1997

[20] Kellner, P., 'Landslide: The word neither side wants to hear', *Evening Standard*, 22 April 1997.

Independent on 8 April[21]. On the morning of 22 April rumours about the following day's *Guardian* poll began circulating in the City, as we were told by a number of callers, who wanted reassurance that the 'sharp swing to the Conservatives' stories were untrue. We didn't comment, but learned later that ICM had not yet had the findings of their 5% Labour lead shocker until later in the day, after the rumours had started circulating. ICM did the private polling for the Conservative Party, and that morning's *Daily Mail* had carried a rather confused account[22] of a Central Office 'leak' that the private polls showed a single figure lead. Was this the inspiration? Who knows? What we do know is that the next day rumours circulated in the City that a MORI poll was coming out in *The Times* the following day which would confirm the ICM lead. We were not aware of any such finding, as we had not then had that poll's results, nor had anyone else. When we did, it didn't, and the complacent guardians of the City's reputation, the Stock Exchange, were guilty again, for the fifth election in a row, of ignoring clear warnings of money and stock market manipulation going on under their noses, for which their answer is to do nothing except pooh-pooh the warnings they were given in good faith.

Peter Kellner, commenting in the *Evening Standard*, observed, 'It happens at least once in every General Election campaign: and someone, somewhere makes a lot of money out of it. "It" is a City rumour that an opinion poll will show a sharp change in the fortunes of the parties. Yesterday morning, sterling was steady at DM2.79, and the FT–100 share index virtually unchanged on its overnight level of 4329. Then word spread that a new ICM poll would show Labour's lead sharply down . . . Suddenly the pound perked up and so did the stock market. By yesterday afternoon the FTSE index had climbed 17 points while the pound was up 1½ pfennigs against the Deutschmark. Somebody somewhere will have done extremely well out of those movements; that somebody will have been the source of the rumour. For when the rumour started circulating, ICM itself did not have the figures. The rumour-monger had simply made a plausible guess.'[23]

---

[21] Willcock, J., 'Opinion poll chief warns about false election leaks', *Independent*, 8 April 1997.

[22] 'Poll gap slashed say Tories', *Daily Mail*, 22 April 1997.

[23] Kellner, P., 'Pollster's wobble that pays off nicely for City', *Evening Standard*, 23 April 1997.

Nor was this the only incident during the 1997 election. On election day itself, a rumour apparently swept the City that leaked early returns (at about 10.30 a.m.) from one of the exit polls showed a 3% to 5% Tory lead. Not true. There was no leak, and neither our exit poll for ITN nor NOP's for the BBC showed anything but a Labour landslide at any point of the day – but it moved markets. If these false rumours had been about, say, a forthcoming company report or take-over bid, would the City's regulators have been so disgracefully relaxed about it?

Constituency polls

One respect in which we might reasonably expect to find a noticeable effect on voting behaviour by the polls is in the case of constituency polls, which may offer specific local indications on tactical voting and the like. Indeed, this was the avowed aim of the *Observer* which on the final Sunday of the campaign published a series of constituency polls commissioned from ICM. (In the same exercise, *Scotland on Sunday* sponsored three in Scotland.) In fact, there seems little evidence of any tactical swings in the vast majority of cases – the poll figures are creditably close in each case to the final constituency result, a tribute to the efficiency of the polls but of course suggesting no movement in the light of the published results. Table 47 shows all the constituency polls published in the national press during the campaign.

Media (Mis)Reporting of Opinion Polls

But however efficiently the pollsters poll, we are still dependent on presenting our poll results to the public through the filter of the media. Though there are many skilled and honourable exceptions, too many journalists and editors (and one Director-General) failed to do us justice in 1997. Some insisted on investing individual polls with far more significance than they could reliably bear. Others took the unchanging view that the polls were rubbish, and attacked them, downgraded them, or simply tried to ignore them.

185

Table 47: Constituency polls 1997

Fieldwork dates	Agency	Client	Publ'n Date	Sample size	Con %	Lab %	LD %	Nat %	Oth %	Lead ± %	C-Lab Swing 92–97 ± %
ABERDEEN SOUTH											
21–26 Apr	ICM*	Observer	27 Apr	c.700	27	35	23	13	2	−8	10.5
1 May	**RESULT**				**26**	**35**	**28**	**10**	**1**	**−9**	**11.0**
BECKENHAM											
2–4 Apr	ICM*	Observer	6 Apr	707	42	38	17	–	3	+4	17.5
1 May	**RESULT**				**42**	**33**	**18**	**–**	**7**	**+9**	**15.0**
BRAINTREE											
21–26 Apr	ICM*	Observer	27 Apr	c.700	40	43	10	–	7	−3	13.0
1 May	**RESULT**				**40**	**43**	**12**	**–**	**5**	**−3**	**13.0**
BRIDGWATER											
21–26 Apr	ICM*	Observer	27 Apr	c.700	33	30	32	–	5	(+3)	(11.0)
1 May	**RESULT**				**37**	**25**	**34**	**–**	**5**	**(+12)**	**(6.5)**
BRISTOL WEST											
21–26 Apr	ICM*	Observer	27 Apr	c.700	31	39	24	–	6	−8	15.0
1 May	**RESULT**				**33**	**35**	**28**	**–**	**4**	**−2**	**12.0**
COLCHESTER											
21–26 Apr	ICM*	Observer	27 Apr	c.700	32	32	31	–	5	0	9.0
1 May	**RESULT**				**31**	**31**	**34**	**–**	**4**	**(0)**	**(9.0)**
EASTWOOD											
2–4 Apr	ICM*	Observer	6 Apr	701	30	42	10	13	4	−12	17.5
1 May	**RESULT**				**34**	**40**	**12**	**13**	**2**	**−6**	**14.5**
EDINBURGH PENTLANDS											
21–26 Apr	ICM*	Scotland on Sun	27 Apr	c.700	34	42	7	15	2	−8	8.5
1 May	**RESULT**				**32**	**43**	**10**	**13**	**2**	**−11**	**10.0**
ENFIELD SOUTHGATE											
21–26 Apr	ICM*	Observer	27 Apr	c.700	45	41	11	–	3	+4	14
1 May	**RESULT**				**41**	**44**	**11**	**–**	**4**	**−3**	**17.5**
FOLKESTONE & HYTHE											
21–26 Apr	ICM*	Observer	27 Apr	c.700	39	25	26	–	10	+14	13.0
1 May	**RESULT**				**39**	**25**	**27**	**–**	**9**	**+12**	**12.0**
GALLOWAY & UPPER NITHSDALE											
21–26 Apr	ICM*	Scotland on Sun	27 Apr	c.700	29	23	6	40	2	(+6)	(11.5)
1 May	**RESULT**				**31**	**16**	**6**	**44**	**3**	**(+15)**	**(7.0)**
GLOUCESTER											
8 Apr	MORI*	The Sun	14 Apr	672	33	52	13	–	3	−19	14.0
22–24 Apr	MORI*	The Sun	28 Apr	501¶	35	46	14	–	5	−11	10.0
1 May	**RESULT**				**36**	**50**	**11**	**–**	**4**	**−14**	**11.5**

HASTINGS & RYE

Dates	Pollster	Publication	Date	Sample	C	L	LD	Nat	Other	Lead	Swing
21–26 Apr	ICM*	Observer	27 Apr	c.700	28	34	29	–	9	–6	19.0
1 May	RESULT				29	34	28	–	9	–5	18.5

KETTERING

Dates	Pollster	Publication	Date	Sample	C	L	LD	Nat	Other	Lead	Swing
21–26 Apr	ICM*	Observer	27 Apr	c.700	42	43	12	–	3	–1	11.0
1 May	RESULT				42	43	11	–	3	–1	11.0

LEEDS NORTH EAST

Dates	Pollster	Publication	Date	Sample	C	L	LD	Nat	Other	Lead	Swing
1–3 Apr	ICM*	Guardian	7 Apr	503	32	54	11	–	2	–22	15.5
1 May	RESULT				34	49	14	–	3	–15	12.0

LOUGHBOROUGH

Dates	Pollster	Publication	Date	Sample	C	L	LD	Nat	Other	Lead	Swing
19–21 Mar	MORI*	Mail on Sunday	23 Mar	602	33	57	7	–	1	–24	15.5
1 May	RESULT				38	49	12	–	2	–11	9.0

LUDLOW

Dates	Pollster	Publication	Date	Sample	C	L	LD	Nat	Other	Lead	Swing
21–26 Apr	ICM*	Observer	27 Apr	c.700	45	29	21	–	5	+16	7.5
1 May	RESULT				42	25	30	–	3	+12	9.5

NORFOLK SOUTH WEST

Dates	Pollster	Publication	Date	Sample	C	L	LD	Nat	Other	Lead	Swing
21–26 Apr	ICM*	Observer	27 Apr	c.700	39	41	15	–	5	–2	15.0
1 May	RESULT				42	38	14	–	6	+4	12.0

ST ALBANS

Dates	Pollster	Publication	Date	Sample	C	L	LD	Nat	Other	Lead	Swing
21–26 Apr	ICM*	Observer	27 Apr	c.700	32	43	23	–	2	–11	16.5
1 May	RESULT				33	42	21	–	4	–9	15.5

STEVENAGE

Dates	Pollster	Publication	Date	Sample	C	L	LD	Nat	Other	Lead	Swing
1–3 Apr	ICM*	Guardian	7 Apr	500	29	56	12	–	2	–27	16.0
1 May	RESULT				33	55	9	–	3	–22	13.5

STIRLING

Dates	Pollster	Publication	Date	Sample	C	L	LD	Nat	Other	Lead	Swing
21–26 Apr	ICM*	Scotland on Sun	27 Apr	c.700	29	50	6	15	–	–21	10.5
1 May	RESULT				32	48	6	14	*	–16	8.0

TATTON

Dates	Pollster	Publication	Date	Sample	C	L	LD	Nat	Other	Lead	Swing
2–4 Apr	ICM*	Observer	6 Apr	706	40	38	19	–	3	+2	20.5
7 Apr	ICM*	Eve Std	7 Apr	296¶	29	–	–	–	71		–
9 Apr	MORI*	The Sun	11 Apr	525	40	–	–	–	60		–
17–18 Apr	ICM*	Observer	20 Apr	410	39	–	–	–	61		–
1 May	RESULT				37	–	–	–	63		–

TAUNTON

Dates	Pollster	Publication	Date	Sample	C	L	LD	Nat	Other	Lead	Swing
21–26 Apr	ICM*	Observer	27 Apr	c.700	39	19	38	–	4	(+20)	(6.5)
1 May	RESULT				39	14	43	–	5	(+25)	(9.0)

WIRRAL SOUTH

Dates	Pollster	Publication	Date	Sample	C	L	LD	Nat	Other	Lead	Swing
19–20 Apr	MORI*	The Sun	25 Apr	700¶	36	54	8	–	2	–18	17.0
1 May	RESULT				36	51	10	–	3	–15	15.5

* Telephone survey. All MORI's telephone surveys were conducted by MORI On-Line Telephone Surveys.

¶ Second or subsequent wave of a panel (with or without boosters of new respondents)

Those who report poll results have a responsibility to their readers and viewers and to their own profession of journalism as well as to the pollsters who carried out the survey. This includes accuracy in reporting the findings, completeness in ensuring that the information that is reported is not so divorced from other information that it is misleading, that the basic information of the precise question wording, sample size, fieldwork dates, etc., are reported to give the reader confidence that the poll was carried out according to proper procedures, and, to the journalists' ability, that the poll results are related to other known information about the subject of the survey's findings. They should also be quick in my view to clarify misleading 'leaks' from their clients when truth becomes stretched.

Journalists should not 'hype' their findings. Polls are not accurate to fractions of 1%, nor do they translate directly into seats to be won without increasing the margin of error. And they don't predict the future.

When I could, unhampered by the two-sentence soundbite imposed by too much of the television coverage, I likened the taking of the public mood to the weather forecasters, saying 'Suppose that I were to send 100 interviewers out on Wednesday with a thermometer each, asking them to stand at the highest point in their assigned constituency, and at precisely noon read out the temperature, and phone in the result. We collated their reports in the office, and released our findings. Then suppose I were to do the same the following day. Would you expect the reading to be exactly the same? Then why do you expect me to be able to forecast the election with precision, when public opinion is more mercurial than the weather?' Still, they expect us to read the runes, gaze into the crystal ball, read the tea leaves and the palms, and report the future. The wonder is that we get it right as often as we do.

After the 1979 election, Ivor Crewe propounded[24] three propositions about the way the polls are reported in Britain:

1. However static public opinion actually is, the polls enable the media to give an impression of flux, change and excitement. The more polls there are, the more true this is.

---

[24] Crewe, I., 'Improving but could do better', in Worcester, R. and Harrop, M., *Political Communications: The British General Election of 1979* (London: Macmillan, 1982).

2. However clear the outcome and trend, polls allow the media to hedge its bets. The more polls there are, the easier it is to hedge bets.
3. However improbable a poll finding is, the media will always publish (broadcast) it. The more improbable a poll finding, the more likely the media will give it prominence.

To this I added[25] a corollary:

'However close the polls get to the actual results, the academic psephologists will pick at their performance. The more polls there are, the more likely there will be something to pick at.'

All of these were proved true to a depressing extent in 1997.

Which poll stirred the most attention in this election? On 23 April the ICM poll published in the Guardian showed only a 5% Labour lead. It was headlined by the *Express* ('Labour's Lead in Freefall – Stunning new poll backs Major's claim that Tories are closing the gap'), the *Daily Mail* ('Labour Lead Crashes in the Polls') and even in the *Daily Telegraph* which buried its own Gallup poll with the headline 'Labour lead collapses in new poll' and featured in pride of place the poll of its rival. The writers of the *Telegraph* 'splash' even reported that

'The ICM findings are in line with the Tories' own polling and with reports from the constituencies, where candidates report that Europe is featuring on the doorsteps.'[26]

Well, they would, wouldn't they, as ICM did the Tories' private polling and canvassers always overestimate their own party's support. For all of that, it was quickly proved a 'rogue', showing it can happen to anyone, and that one shouldn't be too quick either to defend or confirm it without other data.

We should emphasise that these problems are mostly with the secondary reporting of polls, and that we work closely with our clients to ensure that the initial reports are as accurate as possible. There are some myths

---

[25] Worcester, R., Introduction to *British Public Opinion: The British General Election of 1987*, (London: MORI, 1983).

[26] Jones, G. and Shrimsley, R., 'Labour lead collapses in new poll', *Daily Telegraph*, 23 April 1997.

and misconceptions about this. Ken Gofton, writing a 'Soap Box' column in *Marketing* Magazine on 1 May[27], peddled several of them:

> 'I remember, in the 80s, talking to market research company AGB in its pre-Maxwell days, when it used to do a lot of work for the *Sun*. In shocked tones, they told me the paper had requested a quick poll on an issue of the day – 'and this is what the headline will say'.

Perhaps that was the case once. We now do the polls for the *Sun*, and working with its political editor, Trevor Kavanagh, I can state categorically that we have never, ever, been told what the headline will be, what question wording should be, or in any way felt manipulated whatsoever.

> 'You can be sure that when new findings are delivered to politicians, they're accompanied by a full debrief by a qualified researcher on what they really mean. You can also bet that isn't the case in the heated atmosphere of the newsroom. Or, if it is, newspapers and TV stations don't have the time or inclination to go into all the boring qualifications . . .'

Quite the contrary. It certainly doesn't always happen with the parties' private polls. (In 1983, when Sir Christopher Lawson was the 'marketing director' of the Tory Party, the findings were delivered to Keith Britto, the back-room analyst, who gave them to Chris, who gave the report to the Party Chairman, who may or may not have given them suitably 'analysed' to the Leader. They were 'filtered' in subsequent elections as well, in both main parties.) On the other hand Peter Riddell of *The Times* trudges over to our offices faithfully for each and every poll, and a group of analysts gather together to go over the findings together with 'all the boring qualifications'; following the conference, Peter's copy is faxed over to us and gone through in word-by-word detail, and any qualifications or afterthoughts then dealt with on the telephone. We work directly (and very happily) with the *Times'* graphics department, and check their artistic interpretations of our crude graphic suggestions. When the poll is published, all the 'boring bits' are there in the technical note at the end of the column, the sample size, the fieldwork dates, the 'won't votes', 'won't says' and 'undecideds'. Where you probably won't see any of this, unfortunately, or indeed much real understanding of the

---

[27] Gofton, K., 'Opinion polling is like politics – an inexact science', *Marketing*, 1 May 1997.

poll at all, is in the secondary reports of the polls in the other media, often written by news staff rather than poll specialists. This is where the inaccurate reporting, the hyped reporting, the downright biased reporting and, in 1997, the openly hostile reporting, is mostly to be found.

From the outset I warned people generally and the media especially[28] against concentrating on the lead or gap, rather than the share. To little avail. Even the *Times*' sub-editors who wrote the headlines over Peter Riddell's excellent, checked and double-checked, copy sometimes burdened it with headlines screaming 'Gap Slashed'. This overwrote the findings of the poll and undercut my own efforts and those of my colleagues to prevent even experienced and otherwise careful pundits falling into the trap of continuing to place emphasis on comparing lead, rather then share – which is what polls do measure, no matter how inconvenient it is for pundits and headline writers.

One clear victory for reason was the excellent presentation of the polls twice weekly on the BBC's *Nine O'Clock News* by Peter Snow. Nobody is more enthusiastic and nobody works harder to listen to reason about the presentation of opinion polls during election, and no one has made them the object of such intense study among broadcast journalists. In this election, hemmed in by BBC Guidelines (see below) and the BBC's edict against his beloved but overused 'poll of polls', he did what I had been pleading with him to do in earlier elections – report the findings of each poll, bracket them, and then draw a line-of-best-fit through the middle. This the miracle of TV in colour, moving pictures, can do better than any other medium, and it was quite illuminating to see how he presented it on his regular slots on Wednesday and Saturday each week.

Media disbelief of the polls: the Aftermath of 1992

'The error in the polls at the 1992 General Election said more about the British people than the polls', said a perceptive American academic to me after the last election. After a run of five elections with a record of never being more than one per cent away from the share for each party

---

[28] Worcester, R., 'Rescuing Pollsters from their Bad Press', *UK Press Gazette*, 7 March 1997.

on the day, MORI was four per cent out on the Tory share, and five per cent out on Labour, in 1992. The other polls were comparable, with little to choose between them, all forecasting a hung Parliament. The Exit Polls fared better, with a four percent and five percent lead for the Tories, but the BBC figures were never released on TV on the night, being withheld for some weeks, and although ITN broadcast a vote share prediction early on the night, once, all details of the poll were subsequently withheld for months. For that period, as a result of faulty seat forecasts, the pollsters were taunted with 'The polls forecast a Labour victory, and the Exit Polls did no better'. This was even defended in an article by Curtice and Payne, who patiently explained that the better figures came not from a poll done to forecast the result, but another poll they just happened to have conducted on the day but not analysed until months afterwards.[29]

For this, we endured five years of censorship by the BBC, literally hundreds of press, radio and television interviews which began 'The polls got it horribly wrong at the last election . . .' and wise words after the event from (mostly well-meaning) academic and other 'experts', who usually used 'debacle' to describe the pollsters' error while ducking their own culpability in the way the exit poll data was converted into seats forecasts, just a few of whom were scathing about methodology or questioning techniques and one or two even suggested mendacity on our part.

In the November 1996 issue of *British Public Opinion Newsletter*, I noted[30] that

> 'Several myths about the '92 election still pertain and are repeated by some pundits and political journalists, despite the findings from the exhaustive analysis done by the Market Research Society's Inquiry',

and went on to list them. Almost all were, nevertheless, subsequently repeated in the coverage of the 1997 election: -

---

[29] Curtice, J., and Payne, C., 'Forecasting the 1992 election: the BBC experience', in Crewe, I., and Gosschalk, B., *Political Communications: the General Election Campaign of 1992*, (Cambridge: Cambridge University Press, 1995).

[30] Worcester, R., 'Letter to Our Readers: Rogues Gallery?', *British Public Opinion Newsletter*, Volume XIX, No 9 (November 1996).

- *Myth 1: The polls forecast a Labour win.* They didn't, any of them. All the pollsters forecast a hung Parliament instead of the 21-seat Conservative victory.

Early in April 1997, writing in the *Evening Standard*, Peter Kellner noted

> 'In recent days, [John Major] has scorned the opinion polls. Many Conservative voters, he says, refuse to admit their allegiance to the pollsters. In a Channel Four interview he pointed to the last election. "The polls,", he said, "put us eight points behind, with just four days to go; yet look at what happened on the day. We won by eight points."'

Kellner put him straight:

> 'No poll ever showed Labour eight points ahead . . . MORI conducted two local polls during the Wirral South by-election. Neither made any adjustment for "shy Tories". The first poll put the Tories on 36 per cent, the second on 35 per cent. On the day the Tories won 34 per cent. No evidence there that a "spiral of silence" is causing the polls to underestimate Tory support.'[31]

- *Myth 2: They missed by a mile* – a gap of nine per cent in the average of the polls against the Torie's lead over Labour, when the margin of error is plus or minus three per cent. As I have said so many times, watch the share for each party, especially the Government's, not the gap, and the margin of error for the gap is twice that for the share. In fact, if one person in two hundred who voted in 1992 for the Conservatives had voted for the second party, it would have been a hung Parliament.
- *Myth 3: In-street interviewing caused the problem* – the Inquiry team found that there was no difference whatsoever between the results of those polls carried out in the street, in the home, or a combination of the two.
- *Myth 4: Quota sampling was to blame* – There was no difference whatsoever between the findings of the polls carried out face-to-face using a quota sample and those carried out randomly by telephone.

  The myth of the inherent superiority of random sampling is one for which the academic community must take the blame. It has been

---

[31] Kellner, P., 'The four million reasons for Tories to despair', *Evening Standard*, 1 April 1997.

widely accepted as true – for example in the BBC's poll guidelines – yet the historical record belies the case. In fact, in the best empirical test of random against quota samples in Britain (the 1975 referendum), the random poll performed considerably worse than quota polls, three of which were within 1% of the outcome while the random sample was 5% out, well beyond sampling tolerance.

• *Myth 5: People lied to the pollsters, ashamed to admit they were going to vote Tory* – The Inquiry team found no evidence for this whatsoever, yet this myth continues to be repeated *ad nauseam*. One journalist to back up his assertion claimed 'I always lie to pollsters', yet when challenged admitted that he, like most people, had never been interviewed.

Though were some honourable exceptions, few of the sceptics took any real interest in the pains that the pollsters had taken to ensure that the errors of 1992 were not repeated. Their attitude was exemplified by what I believe to be the worst article in any election in memory, published a week before the 1997 election. Error-ridden and misguided, it was written by a one-time pollster, Conrad Jameson, described as the 'retired managing director of a market research firm', and appeared in the *Independent* on 24 April under the heading 'Polling: It's Broke, But How Do We Fix It?'

'Inadequate methods and unreliable respondents are challenging pollsters, says Conrad Jameson,' was the sub-head. The article contained howler after howler. The second paragraph demonstrated that he did not even know how to calculate swing. Using emotive and lurid language, he seemed to be suggesting changes:

> 'Its gaskets blown, its tyres flat, the clapped-out opinion poll needs an upgraded replacement, featuring long, cross-examining questionnaires, panels for tracking opinion over time and experiments to find out which issues and personalities really do flip voting intentions.'

What did he think we were doing? Had he asked we could have shown him just that – the analysis he seemed to think didn't exist is the basis of this book. Total fiction replaced reason, colourful similes took the place of factually-based argument, ignorance of methodology and techniques passed off as understanding and knowledge, even the name of the

Independent's own pollster got wrong. His most serious, and unproven, allegation is that

'All of us, lay and professional alike, know the answer [as to why the polls were inaccurate in 1992]: Poll respondents were lying'.

They weren't this time – nor is there any evidence that they were in 1992. He went on:

'Pollsters are don't knows, too, in that they don't know which way the "don't knows" will flip. That, no doubt, is why "don't know" scores are so rarely published.'

But they are published, they are, every month, year in and year out in Peter Riddell's write-up of our monthly poll in *The Times* and every week during the election; the *Daily Telegraph* is normally just as punctilious in presenting its Gallup poll data. All he needed to have done was look. This was a supposedly-quality broadsheet newspaper's most substantial contribution to its readers' understanding of the polls in 1997, narrowly beating a do-it-yourself poll carried out by the paper's own journalists, and not worth the paper it was printed on.

The most frustrating aspect of the reporting of the polls in 1997 was the attitude of the BBC. As I wrote before the election campaign began:

'The BBC censor political poll findings. They say they don't, but their journalists and editors complain privately that they do, and the evidence is there, from the *Today* programme to *What the Papers Say* to the news broadcasts. They've thrown the baby out with the bathwater, and ignore the only systematic and objective measure of British public opinion and replace it with vox pops, phone-in ('voodoo') polls, interviews with party spokesmen and their own spin.'[32]

The BBC's blinkered approach of caution and ghettoising poll reports would be analogous to blaming Michael Fish for getting the October 1987 hurricane wrong and then virtually banning all weather forecasts from being broadcast until there was another hurricane, and Fish forecast it correctly. This has been partly dictated by the *Producer's Guidelines* on

---

[32] Worcester, R., 'Letter to our Readers', *British Public Opinion Newsletter*, Volume XX, number 2 (March 1997).

polls, adopted as an over-reaction to the 1992 election. Many of the cautions in the BBC's guidelines on how to report polls are useful reminders of good practice. Nevertheless, there are also serious errors and implications of some alarming underlying attitudes. The point should be made, of course, that the guidelines and the attitudes they enforce are the work of the BBC's management, not of its political journalists. Many of those who report the polls work hard, and successfully, to understand them and their significance. But they are then denied full freedom to convey this to their audience.

Most importantly, the guidelines show little understanding of why polls are news. They seem to imply an underlying attitude that public opinion is only important if politicians react to it. This must be wrong. The UK is a democracy and the BBC is a public service broadcaster. If the BBC is seen to be dismissive of the importance of the opinions of the British public (for which read licence-payers, voters or the BBC's audience, as appropriate), it will be in trouble. Opinion polls are simply the best, and only effective, means of measuring those opinions at regular intervals.

This observation applies to public opinion polls in general, but is equally true of voting intention polls in particular. The purpose of opinion polls asking a hypothetical voting intention question is wider than simple prediction of a future result (which is why we continue to poll regularly between elections). Asking about a 'general election tomorrow' is not intended to *predict* anything unless there *is* a general election tomorrow: it is a measure of the mood of the nation here and now. The fact that only 33% say they would vote Tory tomorrow is no less a fact because they will not get the chance tomorrow, or because it does not predict what will happen in two years' time. The comparison of today's findings with the results of similar questions asked over the last half-century offers, at the very least, a more objective assessment of the political realities than relying on the gut feelings of journalists and columnists as to which way the wind is blowing. This was never more true than in the election campaign just concluded.

These facts are certainly not irrelevant to the politics of the next general election. Arguing that voting intention polls should not be published now because they do not predict the result of the next election is analogous to saying that current football league tables should not be published because they do not predict who will win the championship at the end of the season. The news value of polls is not restricted to their being 'a driving force behind debate'. They measure tangible fact – even if, occasionally, marginally inaccurately, still infinitely more accurately than their surrogate, the political pundit's guess (often influenced by his/ her knowledge of current poll results, or worse, three or four vox pops, or worst of all, the phone-in poll). 'The political discussion they engender' is a legitimate but definitely subsidiary part of their significance – what they actually say, or rather the public opinions that they are measuring, are important in themselves, not as predictions but as indicative of the current situation.

For example, if in the 1992 election the Sheffield rally made people less likely to vote Labour, that would be a relevant fact about Sheffield and in reporting the rally, whether or not those figures are 'predictive' (which they would plainly not be with eight days of the campaign to run) and whether or not the parties themselves pick it up and discuss it. Why should the politicians have a monopoly on filtering the news? That is the political journalist's and certainly the BBC's job, and they accept it willingly enough (too willingly?) in every other part of their election campaign coverage. Is the BBC really saying that if all the politicians ignore a piece of bad news, that is justification for the BBC letting it fade quietly away?

As the guidelines note, 'politicians seize on apparent evidence of shifts in opinion to encourage their own supporters or taunt their opponents'; to base reporting of a poll on the criterion of whether 'reaction to it is so significant as genuinely to merit a headline' is playing into the manipulators' hands. The 1997 election gave a perfect illustration of this. When ICM's rogue 5% lead was published, it was in the interests of both parties to treat it as plausible, even though it wasn't and both parties knew it. Labour wanted to guard against complacency, the Tories to convince their own troops that there was still a battle worth fighting. That day's Gallup and the following morning's MORI figures, which contradicted ICM by indicating little had moved, were much less welcome to the parties. Did the BBC really think their journalistic duty was to report the 'reaction' to ICM, and not the deafening silence that followed MORI and Gallup?

A policy of not leading bulletins with a poll is also an utterly artificial constraint. This seems in practice to be interpreted that you cannot lead with a British poll, but a poll from anywhere else in the world is OK – as the BBC has subsequently in both the French and Irish elections. This is absurd. It might also be considered absurd that of all the infinite number of leads, only opinion polls (carried out in Britain) are singled out for this ban. Further, this leads to excessive caution on the part of editors, who turned down reporters' requests to commission polls on the grounds that 'we don't commission polls any more', when the subject was the effect of a rail strike, nothing whatsoever to do with voting intention. One BBC current affairs editor wanted me to get a poll commissioned so he could report it. When I asked why he didn't commission it himself, he said getting approval wasn't worth the hassle. I have had senior presenters of main news and current affairs programmes express to me privately the absurdity of going throughout a six-week election campaign and not being allowed to report poll results, and another saying that when he did, admittedly before the election, lead into a question to a Government Minister with a preface 'In light of the poll finding that . . .' only to receive a note afterwards that 'We do not introduce poll results when putting a question to . . .'. It also led in the past to unequal treatment – giving full details of polls co-sponsored by the BBC and one national newspaper while ignoring polls published by others.

How did the BBC policy pan out in 1997? The decision made initially in the 1997 general election was to banish poll reporting on television altogether except for a carefully circumscribed 'limited edition' version by the *Newsnight* team on the *Nine O'Clock News* twice weekly, and to the limited audience *World Tonight* on BBC Radio 4. I was told on the Monday when I protested that I was 'banging my head against a brick wall, and that it would do no good', but was somewhat relieved on the Wednesday to be told that this decision had been modified, and that polls from the APOPO firms would be allowed to be broadcast, but only in specified slots in selected programmes, and as part of interviews with politicians when appropriate. This meant that among other things they were virtually never reported during the day on Radio 4 as news, nor discussed except by the tautly circumscribed head of political research

Bill Bush, at the end of the *Today* Programme at about 8:45 am each morning when the 'chattering classes' had gone off to the press conferences, to their studios and press rooms and were getting on with the day. Even then he never seemed to report the polls straight, but always with the stream of clichés 'if we can believe the polls', 'if the polls can be trusted', 'the polls, for what they're worth', etc. Towards the end of the campaign however, some journalistic integrity seemed to force its way through, and final poll findings found their way even into news broadcasts, if briefly, never the lead, and couched carefully with more health warnings than were given to either politician's lies about their private poll results or pundits' opinionated guesses about what was happening on the ground.

Another comment in the BBC guidelines that we should mention, since it outrages one of the most important principles of our work, is 'It is for the programme and department to decide whether to use a commissioned poll'. This is a potentially dangerous doctrine. While pollsters would certainly not wish to interfere in any way with editorial independence, equally there should be no question of the BBC supposing that it may suppress inconvenient or even supposedly implausible poll results. (In the case of genuinely uninteresting poll results there may be no point in publishing them except as a matter of form, but that is a different matter – the guidelines are explicitly talking about 'sensitive cases'). In that case, the pollsters should be, and in our case are by reference to our standard terms and conditions of contract, free to release the data to other media, other interested parties and to the ESRC Archives, once an editorial decision against publishing/broadcasting a poll's results is made.

While it is certainly true that polls 'suggest' or 'indicate' rather than 'prove' anything, this should not be used as an excuse to equate polls with other 'indications' (straw polls, sales of coloured cheeses or chocolate lollipops, or even journalists' own guesses at which way the wind is blowing); there is a danger that the opening section of the guidelines will lead to this temptation. Polls cannot prove anything because they are subject to statistical margins of error and the possibility of other distortions, but they remain the most scientific and reliable tool for estimating public opinion. Their limitations should be recognised but not exaggerated.

One topic on which we agree with the BBC Guidelines is Polls of Polls. These are, indeed, as the guidelines suggest, generally a bad idea. By combining polls with different fieldwork dates they may be at best misleading and at worst purporting to measure something non-existent – the state of public opinion at some non-existent moment in time. The particular difficulty of a poll of polls is that it exaggerates the effect of any rogue polls. This is particularly true of 'rolling polls of polls', since a rogue poll that has entered the average remains there for a number of days, distorting a series of poll of poll results, and then by dropping out of the average causes an apparent change in opinion as the average moves back towards the correct position. (The same goes for the Gallup rolling poll carried by the *Daily Telegraph* in the 1997 election.)

Importantly, of course, a poll of polls is more out-of-date than the most recent snapshot poll, and this may be important in a fast-moving election campaign. It would be best for the BBC not merely to stop compiling polls of polls, but to avoid as far as possible all reporting of separate polls as averages, which continues to be done despite the ban. All that has changed is that they are no longer described as 'poll of polls', but 'we have averaged the latest polls . . .'. The way Peter Snow reported the polls in the 1997 election, showing each poll, shading their spread, and then showing the line of best fit was, in my view, excellent, and should be commended. On another current affairs programme however when I tried to get them to report polls in the same way, I was blocked from doing so because of their interpretation of the BBC's revised guidelines issued especially for this election.

The media need to revise their expectations of what polls are and what they can do. It is not enough merely to mention margins of error in the introduction to a report on a poll if the report then goes on to treat the figures as if they were accurate to fractions of one per cent. Nor should the BBC or anybody else take the attitude that because polls cannot be accurate to fractions of one per cent they are therefore useless.

This is particularly the case with exit polls. The BBC's embarrassment over its 1992 exit poll seems to have been in large measure the cause of the new guidelines and of the BBC's excessive suspicion of the polls in 1997. The error in the share of the vote in the exit polls in 1992, though larger than the pollsters would have liked, was considerably smaller than the error in the campaign polls and in any case showed a clear and significant lead for the Conservative party. Most of the error in the BBC's exit poll 'prediction' arose not from failures in the polling but from failures in the psephology – the design of the poll to enable it to predict numbers of seats won.

- The margin of error allowed on the seat prediction in the BBC exit poll was far smaller than was realistic: it needs to allow not only for the normal sampling variation margin of error in measuring the overall vote, but for variance in swing between constituencies which would affect the translation of votes into seats.
- The BBC exit poll was heavily dependent on the assessment of the likely results in 'special seats' where the exit poll itself was not expected to be able to provide a meaningful prediction, e.g. seats where there had been an intervening by-election. Most of these assessments were inaccurate, and a considerable proportion of the error in the prediction poll was attributable to this factor rather than to inaccuracy in the polling.
- The BBC put all its eggs in one basket by relying upon its marginals (prediction) poll for seat projection. It made no allowance for use of figures from its national (analysis) poll, and indeed arranged matters so that these were not available at an early stage – in fact, somewhat fortuitously, these figures would have given a very accurate indication of the share of seats. Furthermore, the importance of the error in the prediction exit poll was magnified by the way in which it was tied into the on-going computer projection on a regional basis, so that even after many results had been declared and it was clear that the exit poll was unreliable, it was still being used to predict the results of seats in many parts of the country.

None of these mistakes were the fault of the pollsters. Nevertheless, there followed a policy of not commissioning exit polls. But the only means of experimentation available to test methodologies for national exit polling is to carry out a national exit poll, and national electoral contests are few and far between – the only concrete effect of the broadcasting organisations' failure to commission a national exit poll in the 1994 European elections was to ensure that they went into the 1997 general election as badly off as before, with no chance to test any new methods or procedures. On the other hand, we were commissioned to conduct such an exit poll (in London) by the Electoral Reform Society and were able to apply lessons learned there to our work for ITN. We also had the benefit of the consultancy of Dr Robert Waller, who had in 1992 been part of the Harris exit poll team. One can only hope that the BBC's decision to commission an exit poll in 1997 – from the same pollsters as in 1992, NOP – and its comparative success in predicting the result, will herald a more realistic attitude.

In any case, it makes a nonsense of a BBC determination not to commission exit polls if they are then as eager to get hold of and broadcast the results of other organisations' exit polls as was the case in the European elections. MORI was put under considerable pressure from various levels of the BBC to release the result of its European exit poll for the Electoral Reform Society, which was not designed for the purpose of predicting the vote. In the event, this exit poll achieved a high degree of accuracy.

Since the 1997 election here, we have had British polls ignored, while every Guideline has been broken in the case of first the French election and then the Irish election, where BBC radio and television news broadcasts led with, quoted, discussed and debated tracking polls and then exit polls in both elections, unlike a month or so earlier when British polls were systematically kept from the listening and viewing British voter/licence-fee payer.

'Voodoo polls'

A further problem the polls face is the risk of being discredited by the way that, too often, the media confounds them with unscientific straw polls, takes the parties' assertions about their private polls as seriously as the published polls where everything is above board and clear to see, or (a comparatively new menace in 1997) tries to contradict them by reporting the findings of focus groups (which is not what focus groups are for and which they are not equipped to do.)

Everyone connected with the market research industry knows, and for that matter every other intelligent person will realise after a moment's thought, that 'voodoo' polls – phone-in and write-in polls – are worthless as a measure of public opinion. The limitations of self-selecting samples should be obvious, whether they be organised phone-ins run by a newspaper or TV programme, the spread of views expressed by the callers on a broadcast radio phone-in, or the selection of letters written to MPs. Voodoo polls are representative of nobody: they measure only the opinions of self-selecting samples of the audience which saw the invitation to vote in the first place, and are 'weighted' only by the determination and energy of participants attempting to register multiple votes.

Yet voodoo polls seem to be becoming more prevalent. They are the beloved tool of certain radio and TV programmes and newspapers as a form of audience participation (and sometimes in the latter case also as an underhand revenue raiser, since they can generate a substantial profit by using premium-rate phone lines). But, instead of remembering that they ought to be 'just a bit of fun', and treating them accordingly, reporters too often treat the results as if they were serious measures of public opinion. This, naturally, encourages interested parties and pressure groups to manipulate them, by trying to 'rig' the results and indeed sometimes setting up their own voodoo polls with the intention of producing a different result from properly conducted representative surveys.

Of course, voodoo polls, both formal and informal, have been with us for a long time. Two examples from the past illustrate how worthless they are. The first, Tony Benn in his argument in the House of Commons against Britain's participation in the Falklands War. Brandishing a handful of letters that supported him (and those who did would of course be those who wrote – a self-selecting sample), he avowed 'Public opinion is swinging massively against the War!' Our poll a few days later in *The Economist* showed 83% of the British public favoured sending the task force to the Falklands. (Very little has changed in this respect. On 11 February 1998 an unnamed Tory MP was quoted in the *Independent*, disbelieving to the previous day's ICM/*Guardian* poll showing support for bombing Iraq: 'I was on a phone-in show at the weekend and nearly everyone was against it.')

203

A second example from the past was Desmond, writing a letter to the *ening Standard*, pleased that 'his side' won in the LBC phone-in poll, *ing* 'voted' 157 times himself.

It might be argued that when these voodoo polls are simply run as an entertaining marketing exercise, with no attempt to portray them as valid measures of public opinion, they are harmless enough. The phone-in poll run by the Glasgow *Herald* over a number of days in 1998 to recommend a new national anthem for Scotland might be cited as an example: the journalists got many days of entertaining copy, their readers had the chance to 'vote' on something that many of them cared about and some writer will benefit from the *Herald*'s prize after the call for a new anthem to be composed beat all the familiar contenders. Nobody is trying to present it as a valid and binding referendum of Scottish public opinion. (Just as well, as there was nothing to stop readers phoning-in from England!)

More cynical was the fax-in poll on the future of Europe by 'Fax Polling Associates'. These enterprising entrepreneurs sent out hundreds of thousands of 'The Referendum on Europe' forms, 'Last chance to vote!', and asked mugs to fax them back to vote to 'stay in' or 'get out' of 'Europe?' to what turned out to be a premium phone line, at a cost to the sender of £1 per minute at all times. They claimed they got back some 15% of the hundreds of thousands they got back, so must have pocketed a pretty penny[33].

But the real trouble is these polls tend to be picked up and reported as 'a poll says . . .', with no warning to the unsuspecting reader that they have no validity. This can be especially worrying when the subject is a serious one and a poll result liable to contribute to debate and decision making. National news bulletins were recently led by reports that 'a poll in *Doctor* magazine' had found that a quarter of all British doctors had been sexually harassed by their patients. It was only later that it emerged that the poll was a voodoo poll of *Doctor* readers and not worth the paper it was written on[34].

Can it be argued that voodoo polls, in spite of their inherent faults,

---

[33] *Independent on Sunday*, 13 April 1997.
[34] Hammond, P., 'Sexual Harassment? It's all in a day's doctoring', *Independent*, 13 January 1998.

Table 48: 1997 Election Marketing Voodoo Polls

	Con %	Lab %	LDem %	Green %	Loony %
Tesco 'Electoral Roll' (cheese) poll	23	25	23	17	13
Bass Beerometer (Marquis of Granby)	28	37	35	n/a	n/a
Thorntons (chocolate leaders' heads)	38	31	13	n/a	17
General Election Result	**31**	**44**	**17**	**1**	**0**

come reasonably near to making an accurate measurement of opinion anyway? Of course not. As with the serious opinion polls, a general election is the only easily verifiable empirical test of a voodoo poll's accuracy, so let us consider the voodoo polls in the 1997 election.

The marketing wheezes that crawl out of the woodwork at each election do not have an impressive record, as the table of reported results of the three receiving the most press coverage in 1997 illustrates.

Of course, these are not meant to be taken seriously. (As far as their electoral effect goes, the *Guardian* diary claimed to have put the wind up Tesco's by warning them that if they did not stock equal numbers of each party's cheese roll they would be in breach of the Representation of the People Act − a pity this is probably untrue.).

Clearly more dangerous are constituency polls carried in the local paper. On 25 March 1997, the *Guardian* reported 'a telephone poll by the *Worcester Evening News*', putting Labour on 73% support in the key marginal and the Conservatives on just 22%. This ludicrous poll was, in fact, a phone-in voodoo poll. Labour actually secured 50% of the vote and the Conservatives 36%. (By comparison, the average difference between poll findings and the final election vote share of the three main parties and SNP in the 28 constituency polls carried out across the country during the election by ICM and MORI was 2.4%.)

Another offender was the *Daily Record*, which led their election day round-up of the polls with their own phone-in poll: 'A massive 64 per cent of readers backed Labour in a Daily Record poll', with the figures in a prominent panel. (This was the same *Daily Record* which earlier in the election, presumably by an innocent mistake, managed to report[35] a

---

[35] 'Election Bites', *Daily Record*, 27 March 1997.

non-existent 'opinion poll in the *Scotsman* today', giving the figures from the ICM/*Scotsman* poll of the previous week. Forgot to look at the date on the press release, perhaps?)

It is not difficult to see why voodoo polls are so inadequate: they are totally open to cynical manipulation, and even if unmanipulated cannot reasonably be expected to be representative of any relevant audience. Respondents can only be drawn from those who see the invitation to phone in – and that in itself of course can be manipulated by pressure groups, ensuring that their own supporters are aware of the poll and of the numbers to telephone. Furthermore, there is usually no bar to multiple voting from a single telephone line, let alone multiple voting by a single individual from different telephone lines. The same applies with, if anything, more force to postal voodoo polls.

Naturally enough, interested parties frequently avail themselves of this opportunity. The former Labour Chief Whip Michael Cocks admitted a couple of years ago 'When I was Chief Whip, I would occasionally sit colleagues down with instructions to make repeated telephone calls to telephone poll numbers to distort the result'[36], and the other parties are no more innocent. Who can forget the fiasco of the 1996 BBC Radio 4 *Today* programme Personality of the Year poll? Tony Blair disqualified at the nominations stage on the suspicion of Labour Party supporters rigging the voting, but John Major qualifying for the shortlist and subsequently winning (beating Lisa Potts, the primary school teacher who protected her class against a madman wielding a machete, into second place). Even the BBC had to shamefacedly admit that there had also been some multiple voting in favour of Mr Major, but not in their opinion enough to affect the result. Similar distortions happened throughout the history of the annual *Today* poll – Mrs Thatcher was a frequent winner.

The BBC, unfortunately, is a slow learner. Indeed, the 1996 *Today* poll was the BBC's second lesson of that kind in as many months. In November, to celebrate the Corporation's 60th birthday, they threw open the schedules to 'Auntie's All Time Greats', showing the programmes winning a phone-in poll in each of eleven categories; press

---

[36] *Independent*, 18 March 1996.

reports suggested[37] that the unexpected victory of *Dr Who* as Favourite Popular Drama, defeating *EastEnders* and *Casualty*, was orchestrated by well-organised Dr Who fan clubs. At the end of 1998, the same was happening again, with pranksters reportedly orchestrating a campaign to ensure that David Beckham won the BBC Sports Personality of the Year Award with e-mail votes from the City[38].

Even without multiple voting, orchestrated voting to ensure that a particular minority punches above its weight can be equally distorting. An international example arose during 1997 when *Time* magazine requested nominations for its Man of the Century feature. Reports vary on whether it was even intended to be a voodoo poll – the request was only for nominations, not votes – but it was reported as using voodoo methodology by the Turkish media, and a campaign followed during which *Time* was bombarded by several *million* votes for Kemal Ataturk. The amusing upshot, later reported, was that the Greek media, fearing an Ataturk victory, quickly organised a counter-campaign which swept Winston Churchill into the lead[39].

At the time of the Carlton TV Monarchy 'debate' and phone-in at the start of 1997, MORI made an attempt to measure the extent of multiple voting, including a question about participation in the 'poll' as part of our nationally representative Omnibus survey a few days later. We found that 13% of those who said they had voted in the phone-in poll claimed to have voted three times or more. One of the multiple voters was certainly the columnist Ann Leslie, a guest on the show, who demonstrated the ludicrous nature of the exercise by ostentatiously connecting while sitting on stage, using the repeat button of her mobile phone. Carlton received 2.6 million calls, which almost every newspaper reported naively as being participation by 2.6 million voters; our figures suggest as few as 1.5 million may have actually participated.

Most dangerous of all is deliberate use of voodoo polls and voodoo poll results in public debate on issues where the perception of the state of public opinion can be expected to have an effect on government

---

[37] *Guardian*, 4 November 1996.

[38] Goodbody, J., 'Vote Beckham, say leg-pullers', *The Times*, 3 December 1998.

[39] Sapsted, D., 'Greeks make Churchill politician of the century', *Daily Telegraph*, 1 May 1998.

policy and perhaps even on the public's own views. Such use may sometimes be merely innocent ignorance, but on some occasions it is clearly more cynical.

Two recent issues have provided examples of organised pressure groups actively attempting to influence the results of voodoo polls and subsequently attempting to portray the results as being representative of public opinion. In late 1996, during the passage of bills through Parliament to restrict gun ownership following the Dunblane massacre, Prince Philip criticised the proposed ban as an over-reaction, adding some unfortunate remarks to the effect that a cricket bat in the wrong hands was as dangerous as a handgun. Shortly afterwards the pro-gun lobby produced 'poll figures' which purported to show that the majority of the public agreed with Prince Philip, and these improbable figures were reported uncritically by several reputable newspapers. The 'polls', of course, were voodoo polls. All serious surveys both before and after Prince Philip's intervention found huge majorities in favour of the handgun ban.

In 1997, the issue was Michael Foster's Private Member's Bill to ban hunting with dogs. The organisers of a TV debate on the subject, which was to conclude with a voodoo poll of viewers, came to have suspicions that not only had pro-hunting groups publicised the poll in advance to their adherents, urging them to vote, but that the supposedly secret numbers to be used for the poll had been leaked. Consequently, the numbers were switched at the last moment before the programme went on the air. Cue much publicised anguish among hunt supporters unable to prevent the pre-programmed telephone systems in their empty offices registering endless votes for the wrong side throughout the evening. On the basis of another 'poll', the hunters assailed Michael Foster himself, hiring motorised billboards to put across their message that the majority of his constituents opposed his bill, a protest which drew national media coverage. The figures were based on a voodoo poll for a local paper – in fact the same *Worcester Evening News* whose election poll had told Mr Foster he was going to win 73% of the vote, so he would probably not have lost much sleep over it, even if he did not already have the reassurance of a properly conducted MORI poll showing that 72% of Worcester electors were in favour of the bill.

For an example combining voodoo polling and misuse of focus groups, we can turn to the Scottish National Party. 'Salmond Favourite To Be First Minister – Survey', was the headline on a party press release in February 1999, trumpeting a Teletext 'poll' which seemed to show Alex Salmond preferred to Donald Dewar as Scotland's first minister by 82% to 18%. But as it happened we knew, from a properly conducted System Three survey of a representative sample of Scots, for the *Herald*, that at the time the Teletext poll was taken Donald Dewar actually had a 50%–37% lead over Mr Salmond. The press release had the cheek not only to call the *Herald* poll in support by mentioning that it had found a rise in SNP support (while carefully not mentioning that it also totally contradicted the Teletext voodoo poll), but it also added 'While the Teletext is not a scientific poll, it does reflect focus group research which also awarded victory in the [*Scotsman*] debate to Alex Salmond'. Sadly the SNP are by no means the only party capable of this sort of manipulation.

None of these examples had any real impact. But they all shared an intent to spread propaganda for a point of view through the media, on the basis of figures which the perpetrators must have known were at the best unreliable and at the worst untrue. In extreme cases this behaviour becomes a deliberate con, often by groups that that dare not commission a representative poll because they dare not face the truth of public opinion. Politicians are frequent users of such tricks, especially by their quoting of canvass returns; some pressure groups, sadly, behave similarly. Used in this way, especially if used in an attempt to counter or deny the results of a reputably conducted sample survey, a voodoo poll is nothing short of dishonest.

The voodoo poll, unfortunately, seems to be spreading. Its baleful influence may soon stretch as far as the pound in your pocket, or at any rate the euro in your pocket: the Italian government has reportedly used a TV phone-in voodoo poll as the public consultation exercise in selecting the designs to appear on the Italian version of the euro coins. Even those in the media who recognise the worthlessness of such polls fall into the trap of taking them seriously: a recent *Times* editorial on one such poll commented that 'The survey . . . is hardly scientific. . . . the sample was self-selecting and would be dismissed by any reputable pollster', but then went on immediately to say 'But like many such surveys, it still makes gripping reading' – and commented at some length on the figures. Such surveys are only gripping reading in the sense that John Grisham is gripping reading. They are fiction, not worthy of serious news reporting. And, in an election at least, when there is a genuine possibility that they will be mistaken for serious polls and may even influence voters on that assumption, it is far better that they should not be reported at all.

Equally alarming during the 1997 election was the *News of the World*'s do-it-yourself poll in Basildon[40], which some commentators naturally assumed was by MORI since we had conducted that paper's poll the previous week. On a base of '1,000 locals quizzed', the sub-headline blazoned '52% will back New Labour' – but this turned out to refer to the figures *before* repercentaging, with the don't knows running second on which basis they reported 'the Conservatives trailed in a poor third' – a classic reporting blunder which no polling company would be likely to let their clients make with their data. The figures should have read Labour 71%, Conservative 20%! *Private Eye* later carried a leaked report of the *News of the World*'s methodology:

> 'The *Screws [News of the World]* did not commission a professional poll to get these "stunning" results: it sent local hack Vanessa Large and some news agency bods to question voters. But it proved difficult for them to find 1,000 people who would talk as local blue rinses did their best to dodge the seedy hacks.
>
> 'Eventually they found an audience who didn't object to answering questions – a stream of people leaving Towngate Theatre. It was only after dozens of them had responded that Large noticed how all were Labour supporters . . . not surprising as they were leaving the local Constituency Labour Party's weekly meeting.
>
> 'So the hacks did what all hacks do in an emergency: they went to a pub where they conducted an extremely scientific and in-depth poll, reaching the conclusion that Basildon would probably vote Labour.'[41]

More amusing, though potentially dangerous as its prominent headline was the only political coverage on the front page, was the *Mirror* story on

---

[40] Black, E., 'True Blue Basildon Turns on the Tories', *News of the World*, 6 April 1997.
[41] 'Street of Shame', *Private Eye*, 18 April 1997.

11 April. Headed 'New Poll Sensation: Labour "Bloody Miles Ahead"',
it stated:

> 'A shock *Mirror* poll has sensationally revealed that Labour are "very likely"
> to win the election by a massive landslide. The poll, conducted by a quick
> show of hands yesterday round the *Mirror* newsroom, confirmed that
> absolutely nobody gives John Major and his hopeless Tory cronies a cat in
> hell's chance.'[42]

Misuse of focus groups

Not much better than voodoo polling is the misuse of focus groups as a
source for quantitative data. There is nothing wrong in principle with
focus groups, which as we have noted are a valuable research tool for
exploring issues in depth and for developing quantitative questionnaires.
The media could certainly make interesting and constructive use of them
in reporting an election; the *Guardian* (ICM) and to a lesser extent the
Sunday Times (NOP) did so. But they are not a substitute for opinion
polls, as the *Financial Times* tried to make them in 1997[43], and certainly
not capable of contradicting the polls, as the *Independent*'s reporting tried
to suggest[44]. Lucy Kellaway (writing in the *Financial Times*) hit the nail
on the head when she wrote 'One of the silliest aspects of this remarkably
silly election campaign has been the great enthusiasm for the focus
group.'[45]

It was however the self-same *Financial Times* which commissioned and
gave extensive space to reports of focus groups run by an advertising
agency. In one memorable article they percentaged the responses of 79
people who were representative of nothing other than they had been
willing to take part in these focus groups, reporting not even the group
findings but telephone re-interviews of their 'panel' packaged as 'a new

---

[42] 'New Poll Sensation: Labour "Bloody Miles Ahead"', *The Mirror*, 11 April 1997.
[43] e.g. Blitz, J., 'Europe provides Major with glimmer of a silver lining', *Financial Times*, 18 March 1997
[44] Bevins, A., 'Out there, it's not over yet', *Independent*, 21 April 1997.
[45] Kellaway, L., 'The long and short of executive pay', *Financial Times*, 28 April 1997.

survey of the mood of "floating" voters in marginal constituencies'[46]. Laura Marks, chair of the Association of Qualitative Research Practitioners, who is an eminently sensible woman, wise in the use of focus groups to discern the 'whys' of what people are thinking, and alert to their misuse (as utilised by the *Financial Times* and other newspapers and broadcast media) to attempt to forecast voting behaviour, pointed out their limitations on BBC Radio 4's *Today* programme. Kellaway observed:

> 'The appeal of focus groups is that they are cheap and immediate. But not only are the samples so small that they don't mean a thing, they do not even reflect the views of the members of the groups . . . They can be useful if what is wanted is new ideas . . .'[47]

Of course, much greater users of focus groups are the parties themselves, for whom – if properly used – they can be of considerable value in campaign planning.

'Leaked' private polls

The 'leaking' of private polls, which political journalists reported extensively during the 1997 general election with little attempt made by the media to ascertain their veracity, is another even more pernicious form of political manipulation and spin-doctoring. This arose in 1997 to a greater degree than at any previous election that I can remember, leaking both of findings from 'private' polls and from focus groups done by and for the political parties. In previous elections there has been the occasional leak, or spin from party spokesmen claiming that results from their own 'private' polls were somehow different from the results of public polling done often by the same organisation. The Code of Conduct of the APOPO Group, which comprises all of the major polling organisations, calls for Members to clarify any misleading references to polls they have conducted when leaked by party spokesmen. At one

---

[46] Blitz, J., 'Floating voters drift Labour's way', *Financial Times*, 11 April 1997.
[47] Kellaway, L., 'The long and short of executive pay', *Financial Times*, 28 April 1997.

juncture in this campaign I raised a question with Nick Moon of NOP, whose private polls had allegedly been leaked, as to the veracity of what had been said. He replied that he had raised the issue with the Labour Party, and they had denied any knowledge of such leaking. Yet names were quoted to me by journalists, telling 'porkies' to my knowledge. Didn't happen in Percy Clarke's day when I did the Labour Party's private polling, I can tell you, for he would advise me of any planned leak, and would dutifully post on the board in the Lobby the fieldwork dates, sample size and specific question wording of the findings that had been leaked. I should add that the then Labour Party's General Secretary, the late Ron Hayward, expressed some regret when MORI entered public polling in 1975, saying that from that date on he could no longer lie about what the Party's private polls were saying.

I was amused after Labour's denial that anyone had leaked any of their private polling to read in Colin Brown's article in the *Independent* that 'Mr Mandelson said Labour believes there are between 10 and 15 per cent of "don't knows" still to be won over — half the amount the Tories estimate could decide the outcome of the election . . . Labour claimed that Mr Blair's personal lead over Mr Major has increased by 22 per cent since the election began . . . Labour claims it has a 12 per cent lead on "standing up for Britain's interests abroad", with a 19 per cent lead on improving living standards at home. Its polling shows that Labour is winning over younger women.'[48]

ICM's Nick Sparrow directed the private polling for the Tory Party, and what his polls for the Conservatives were saying first reached a peak of speculation on 31 January, when they were brought into play by the Prime Minister himself, According to Peter Riddell in *The Times* the following day, Mr Major 'broke a cardinal rule of politicians: never claim that your secret opinion polls tell a better story than published polls unless you are prepared to back that with the facts.'

Riddell's column said the Prime Minister 'provided no evidence for his assertions. Conservative Central Office staff later refused to disclose any details, claiming that they were private.' Riddell went on to say 'It would be surprising if what the private Tory polls showed was different

---

[48] Brown, C., 'Labour gets bullish as party polling spells victory', *Independent*, 28 April 1997.

... there is no reason to doubt current polls pointing to a Tory share of about 30 per cent ... Mr. Major was whistling in the wind. Worse, he was making precisely the mistake he himself criticises in others of selectively using polls when it suits him.'[49]

Later, towards the end of the campaign, John Curtice noted on 21 April that 'John Major ... in yesterday's *Sunday Telegraph* declared that he found the opinion polls 'baffling', that they bore 'no relationship either to the feel out there or to the detailed canvass returns from constituencies' ... Michael Foot made similar claims while leading Labour to its heaviest defeat in 1983 ... Mr Major appears to be looking through blue-tinted spectacles, just as Michael Foot observed the 1983 campaign through rose-tinted ones. Surrounded as they are for most of the time by the party faithful, party leaders are perhaps the least reliable witnesses of all as to the "feel" of a campaign.'[50]

David Butler, writing on the same day, agreed: 'It is a good rule never to believe anything that the parties say publicly about their canvass returns – or their private polls. One should even disbelieve what they say privately and in good faith; the capacity for self-deception grows as the campaign advances'.[51]

The Pundits

If there were no opinion polls, disinterested attempts at election prediction would be entirely in the hands of the pundits. During each election, the news media seek out those who have some claim to be able to read the runes and are willing to attend radio and television studios, write articles for the press and otherwise pronounce on what the election is all about, what the impact will be of political events, and try to foretell the future. Not content to report the past, the media seek those who by their academic training or position can somehow read tea leaves, gaze into crystal balls, ascertain Tarot cards' meaning or otherwise peer into

---

[49] Riddell, P., 'Major's poll claims do not fit the facts', *The Times*, 1 February 1997.

[50] Curtice, J. 'Blue-tinted view of opinion polls that could lead to the fate of Foot', *The Scotsman*, 21 April 1997.

[51] Butler, D., 'Still far off the 38% they need', *Financial Times*, 21 April 1997.

Table 49: Average Estimates of Reuters' 'Panel of Experts'

Survey dates	3 Oct %	30 Oct %	2 Dec %	8 Jan %	3 Feb %	5 Mar %	2 Apr	9 Apr %	16 Apr %	23 Apr %	30 Apr %	GE %	Diff-erence %
Conservative	37	37	37	36	36	36	35	35	35	35	34	**31.4**	+2.6
Labour	42	42	42	42	43	43	44	45	44	44	44	**44.4**	−0.4
Lib Dem	17	17	16	16	16	16	15	15	15	16	16	**17.2**	−1.2
Others	5	5	5	5	5	5	6	6	6	6	6	**7.0**	−1.0
Labour lead	+5	+5	+5	+6	+7	+7	+9	+10	+9	+9	+10	**+13**	−3.0
Lab majority	36	37	34	41	46	56	77	83	79	82	92	**179**	−87

Source: Reuters

the public's mind to see what the electorate will do come that day certain when the electorate will decide which party will take power over the lives of Her Majesty's subjects for the next four or five years.

Dr David Butler, the doyen of the academic psephologists who has covered every election since 1945, argues 'Experts are no more likely to make accurate predictions than anyone else, they just make them for more sophisticated reasons.'[52] Butler also noted in an article in the *Financial Times* on 1 April in a footnote: 'thirty days left and every national poll gives Labour a lead of 20 per cent or more. That is a 14 per cent swing from 1992 and, applied nationally, indicates a clear majority of about 200 seats for Labour. No one has yet had the courage to predict that.'[53]. Nor did they.

Reuters set up a panel of twenty 'Experts' across a broad spectrum of political scientists, psephologists, political historians and pundits to track the election, so in a way this became an experiment in the Delphi Technique, in that following each of 11 recalls on the panel they distributed the findings so that each panellist could see how their estimates of the election outcome compared with others on the panel, and adjust, or not, their own answers accordingly.

The Reuters Expert Panel was first polled on 3 October 1996, and collectively forecast the outcome as being likely to be a Labour majority of 36 seats, on a 37% Conservative, 42% Labour, 17% Liberal Democrats,

---

[52] Richards, H. 'Whether or not forecasters', *Times Higher Education Supplement*, 27 March 1997.
[53] Butler, D. , 'Marginal results from intensive campaigning', *Financial Times*, 1 April 1997.

5% Other parties share of vote. Table 49 shows how this changed over time, and how it compared with the eventual outcome. As can be seen, the panel overestimated the Conservatives' share by 2.6%, underestimated Labour's only marginally, understated the Liberal Democrats' comeback, and underestimated the collective vote of the other parties. On balance, not bad on share, but woefully wrong, by some 87 seats, on turning their share estimates into seats in the House of Commons.

Individually, panellists were all over the place, from David Carlton's hung parliament, to 'unattributed's 153, but none of the panel were close to the eventual 179 seat majority. Sadly, John Curtice had presciently forecast an overall Labour majority of 185 seats right up to the wire, consistently expecting a Labour landslide (believing the polls?), but at the last minute havered, and dropped his forecast to 131, to end up in fourth place behind the unattributed 153 (actually David Butler), Paul Whiteley's 145, and John Benyon's 143.

Just two of this panel of experts guessed Labour would do so much better than average in its marginal seats, and predicted a majority significantly higher than their share predictions would have given on uniform swing: John Curtice (who had explained how his analysis of ICM's poll data led him to expect this on 12 April[54]) and John Benyon both predicted a majority about thirty seats higher than uniform swing – in the event Labour's majority was around fifty higher than uniform swing would have predicted.

To paraphrase a post-election article criticising the polls by the *Economist*'s Political Editor, David Lipsey, who was not one of the panel,

'The Reuters' Panel of "Experts" predicted Labour's landslide more accurately than politicians, gamblers and most commentators. But that is saying little. In fact, the "experts" were inaccurate to a degree that, in a closer election, could have led them to predict the wrong result.

'The only pre-election bull's eye on the Labour lead was Whiteley's. But this was thanks to two errors (on the Labour and Tory share of the vote, respectively) that cancelled each other out, both being equally wide of the mark. This is a good example of one of many reasons that commentators

---

[54] Curtice, J., 'Geography of poll swings maps out a landslide for Labour', *Guardian*, 12 April 1997.

Table 50: Final Forecasts of Reuters' 'Panel of Experts' (30 April 1997)

	C %	Lab %	LD %	Oth %	Lead %	Majority (seats)
Unattributable*	30	46	16	8	16	153
Election result	**31.4**	**44.4**	**17.2**	**7**	**13**	**179**
John Benyon (Leicester Univ)	32.5	45	17.5	5	12.5	143
Paul Whiteley (Sheffield Univ)	33	46	16	5	13	145
Bob Worcester (MORI)	33	45	17	5	12	101
Ivor Crewe (Essex Univ)	33	45.5	15.5	6	12.5	119
Ben Pimlott (Birkbeck College)	33	45	16	6	12	101
Justin Fisher (London Guildhall Univ)	34	45	15	6	11	91
Peter Kellner (Independent analyst)	34	45	15	6	11	121
John Curtice (Strathclyde Univ)	34	45	15	6	11	131
Panel average	**34.2**	**44.4**	**15.7**	**5.8**	**10.3**	**92**
Sydney Elliot (Queen's Univ, Belfast)	34	44	17	5	10	67
Dominic Wring (Nott'm Trent Univ)	34	44	15	7	10	93
Colin Rallings (Plymouth Univ)	34	43	16	7	9	81
Unattributable	34	43	17	6	9	71
Michael Thrasher (Plymouth Univ)	34.5	43.5	16	6	9	65
Neil Carter (York Univ)	35	44	16	5	9	71
David Denver (Lancaster Univ)	35	44	15	6	9	71
Eric Shaw (Stirling Univ)	35	44	16	5	9	73
Unattributable	35	46	13	6	11	81
David Sanders (Essex Univ)	37	43	17	3	6	55
David Carlton (Warwick Univ)	39	41	15	5	2	0

* This 'unattributed' was revealed by himself after the election as David Butler (Nuffield College)

Source: Reuters

and poll pickers, politicians and pundits, and especially headline writers and caption writers should watch the share, not the gap. It not only doubles the margin of error of the polls misleadingly, it confuses the public.

'This election also shows that you cannot simply rely on "experts" to read the polls and their own water and extrapolate from these to the number of seats. Most of the Reuters' "experts" underestimated the Conservatives' vote, while collectively getting Labour's spot on. Their error was compounded by collectively and individually failing to spot the Liberal Democrats' resurgence and the strength of the combined other parties in this election.'

With some of the Reuters panel, it is not clear how they reached their conclusions. Others, however, were writing regular columns. Those who trusted the polls tended to do substantially better than those who did not.

Peter Kellner was one whose reasoning was open for all to see, in a regular pollwatch column in the London *Evening Standard* that ran for months up to the election. He generally considered the polls to be reliable, although he thought that some over-estimated the Labour lead. His final poll article in the *Observer* predicted 'Labour on course for three-figure majority'[55]. Kellner continued in the *Evening Standard* to predict a Labour landslide, with his own estimate of a 121-seat overall majority before the final polls were published[56], which he upped to 129 on election day[57].

Kellner also wrote up the MORI poll conducted among voters in London for the *Evening Standard* in the first week of April. It proved remarkably predictive:

'If Labour were indeed to achieve this, the political landscape of the capital would be utterly transformed . . . Michael Portillo would be unavailable to stand as the Right's standard-bearer in an early leadership election. His seat in Southgate would fall . . . The Tories would lose 33 seats, leaving them with just eight in the capital.'[58]

They ended up with eleven.

Ben Pimlott was another who upped his final prediction after the Reuters figures were collated. He told the *Daily Telegraph*:

'The temptation is to follow what everyone else is saying. I was saying 101 but I think that's more likely to be too low than too high. I'll say 121.'[59]

[55] Kellner, P., 'Labour on course for three-figure majority', *Observer*, 27 April 1997.
[56] Kellner, P., 'Whatever the polls' history, it's still Labour by over 100', *Evening Standard*, 28 April 1997.
[57] Kellner, P., 'Labour with 129 majority', *Evening Standard*, 1 May 1997.
[58] Kellner, P., 'Labour massing at the gates of the Tory citadels in London', *Evening Standard*, 4 April 1997.
[59] 'Were the experts right?', *Daily Telegraph*, 2 May 1997.

And John Curtice, writing in *Scotland on Sunday*, in his 'What the Polls Say' column, was headlined 'Forsyth, Lang and Rifkind heading for defeat'.[60] And my own 'last gasp' was given in a speech to the Carlton Club's political committee on 30 April, when I said that 'It could be as much as 120'.

The one Reuters' 'Expert' whose predictions stood out from the rest was a lecturer in politics at the University of Warwick, Dr David Carlton, who week in and week out avowed that the best result that Labour could hope for was a hung Parliament, and kept his forecast of the seat result at a steady zero overall majority in the weekly Reuters report. As if that weren't enough, he wrote articles in the *Sunday Telegraph*[61] and was quoted in the *Spectator* by Sarah Bloomfield as saying that a hung result was likely.

The final weekend of the election saw the *Sunday Telegraph* feature the hapless Carlton's repeated forecast under the headline 'Get ready for a hung parliament: Don't believe what the opinion polls are reporting.'[62] His continuing bravado in the face of the united opposition of all the other score of Reuters' 'Experts', the opinion polls, and most commentators other than Bruce Anderson and Woodrow Wyatt was based on his analysis of 'how real voters have behaved on past occasions', pointing out that '. . . if history is any guide, low turnout is detrimental to Labour'. History wasn't any guide. The turnout in 1997 was the lowest since the war, and yet was Labour's greatest victory ever. His final paragraph concluded '. . . a Labour landslide is quite unlikely. Much more probable is a close result, perhaps even a hung parliament.'

Undeterred after all that, Carlton was in the *Spectator* again a fortnight after the election, arguing from 'real voters' the same faulty analysis line, and pleading that he be allowed to continue political punditing.[63] Having forecast a hung Parliament with a nil seat lead, he criticised one pollster for his forecast of a Labour victory of 101. He described the forecast of the Reuters panel as a 'mere 92–seat overall majority for Labour — a massive 87 seats below the actual result' while neglecting to mention that

---

[60] Curtice, J., 'Forsyth, Lang and Rifkind heading for defeat', *Scotland on Sunday*, 27 April 1997.

[61] Carlton, D., 'Voters doubts begin to turn tide for Tories', *Sunday Telegraph*, 13 April 1997.

[62] Carlton, D., 'Get ready for a hung parliament', *Sunday Telegraph*, 27 April 1997.

[63] Carlton, D., 'On getting it wrong', *The Spectator*, 10 May 1997.

his own forecast was 179 seats below the actual result, double the average of the panel. He also compounded his foolishness by stating that the 92-seat overall majority for Labour was 'roughly what a majority of opinion polls were then predicting': the headline in *The Times* the morning of the election was 'MORI points to 180+ majority' and Tony King reported in the *Daily Telegraph* of 29 April, 'An average of the polls over the weekend also suggests a majority of nearly 200.'[64]

Professor David Sanders has, in the past, relied upon economic determinism, producing statistical models of voting behaviour from economic indicators such as the Economic Optimism Index (EOI). In 1987, the r^2 co-efficient of correlation between MORI's EOI and the Conservatives' lead over Labour was no less than 0.90, that is, 90% of the variation in the electorate's voting intention in the six months leading up to the election could be explained by the 'feel-good factor', leading to Sanders' accurate prediction six months in advance of the election that the Tories would win and by how much. In 1992 however, it was only 6%, and in 1997 as we have seen, less than 2%. His economic formulae didn't help him this time, his own dismal showing only outdone by Carlton's.

Like David Sanders, Colin Rallings and Michael Thrasher, of the *Local Government Chronicle* elections centre at Plymouth University, allowed their predictions to be influenced by their belief on the basis of past history that what the polls were implying was effectively impossible (but which turned out on 1 May to be perfectly possible). Under a headline they would probably not have preferred, 'Don't bank on a Labour landslide', they wrote

'What if, as the Tories' gloomy party political broadcast began last week, the polls are right? A 12% swing away from the Tories . . . would put Tony Blair in with a majority of more than 150. Labour would win in places like Braintree, where Tony Newton, leader of the House, is defending . . . , and in Thanet South – Jonathan Aitken's seat – which has returned Tories at every general election since 1918 . . . Labour is more likely to get a comfortable majority than a landslide . . . There is something very familiar and misleading about polls which show health and education

---

[64] King, A., 'Brutal truth facing the Tories', *Daily Telegraph*, 29 April 1997.

– issues on which Labour scores well – to be of greatest concern to voters. In the polling station, these count for little.'[65]

Later in the election, on 25 April, based on votes cast in local government elections (which they reminded readers and viewers so often were a better guide than opinion polls to the outcome in 1992), Rallings and Thrasher reported that 'Our computer projection from these results suggests that Labour support was equivalent to a national share of 44% with the Conservatives on 31% and the Liberal Democrats on 20%', which would have been remarkably accurate had they believed it. Instead they adjusted their published prediction to Labour 43.5%, Conservative 34.5%, Liberal Democrat 16%, and forecast a 65-seat majority for Labour[66], and their final Reuters predictions a couple of days later were both close to this.

Still, most of the Reuters' 'Experts' were more expert than some of the paid commentators such as Stewart Steven, who wrote with a self-important certainty in the *Mail on Sunday* in December that the polls suggest that the next election is going to be a shoo-in for Labour, but they're wrong. 'People lie something rotten when they speak to the pollsters', he asserted, saying that the country is in a cautious mood, and that although we want more spent on the public services, we are 'all too aware these days that if we spend too much, it is our pocket which will suffer'. In this respect, he concluded, 'Mr. Major is surely a safer bet than Mr. Blair'.[67] Later he admitted that what one pollster had to say was 'nevertheless compelling', but that he contended still that 'I have nothing against opinion polls, I just don't take them as seriously . . .'[68] Perhaps now he will, and his readers will take him less seriously than they might have before.

Or the *Daily Mail*'s Simon Heffer, 'the pundit the politicians dread' as the *Mail* bills him, no doubt to his embarrassment: 'One reason why I

---

[65] Rallings, C. and Thrasher, M., 'Don't bank on a Labour landslide', *Sunday Times*, 13 April 1997.

[66] Rallings, C. and Thrasher, M., 'Poll gurus predict Labour to win with 65-seat majority', *Local Government Chronicle*, 25 April 1997.

[67] Steven, S., 'Why the polls could be wildly wrong', *Mail on Sunday*, reported in *The Week*, 7 December 1996.

[68] Steven, S., 'Sorry Michael – but the fat lady has cast her vote', *Mail on Sunday*, 13 April 1997.

have never subscribed to the Labour landslide school of thought is a firm belief that many people are lying to the opinion polls.'[69] I wonder what he thinks now; though we shall no doubt be told, for one thing is certain – even an error more colossal than that of the pollsters in the 1992 election, multiplied by a factor of ten, will not stop the pundits from punditing.

Chief among the sceptics, of course, was John Major, at least in public, claiming to rely variously on canvassing returns, on his party's own private polls (which, of course, he wouldn't publish), and his own instincts as an experienced candidate.

Major's public position had little credibility. On 1 April, writing in the *Evening Standard*, Peter Kellner counted heads, and pointed out that the task of the Tories over the month until election day was to gain back the four million lost votes that were represented by the difference between the 30 per cent share, where they then stood, and the 43 per cent that it would take the Conservatives to return to their 1992 level and where they needed to be to win the 1997 election. (They won back only less than a tenth of them during the final month of the campaign.) He went on to comment on John Major's scorning of the polls. 'In recent days, [John Major] has scorned the opinion polls. Many Conservative voters, he says, refuse to admit their allegiance to the pollsters. In a Channel Four interview he pointed to the last election. "The polls,", he said, "put us eight points behind, with just four days to go; yet look at what happened on the day. We won by eight points.'"

Kellner put him straight: 'No poll ever showed Labour eight points ahead . . . MORI conducted two local polls during the Wirral South by-election. Neither made any adjustment for "shy Tories". The first poll put the Tories on 36 per cent, the second on 35 per cent. On the day the Tories won 34 per cent. No evidence there that a "spiral of silence" is causing the polls to underestimate Tory support.'[70]

The Tories, though, stubbornly clung to the belief that the spiral of silence was still there. At Central Office, Andrew Cooper stated 'We're

---

[69] Heffer, S., 'Battle for those missing millions', *Daily Mail*, 5 April 1997.

[70] Kellner, P., 'The four million reasons for Tories to despair', *Evening Standard*, 1 April 1997.

convinced the spiral of silence is much greater than in the 1992 election and that many of the people who are disinclined to give their views to pollsters and canvassers are more likely to vote Conservative than anything else. If Bob Worcester goes on predicting a landslide for Labour right up to polling day, he'll lose in spades.'[71] On 23 April, the Prime Minister again expressed his scorn for the polls: 'I've never commented on polls [sic] whatever they may be. By and large they are of no real use in determining what people are going to do on election day.'[72] Other Tories were making similar noises: Scottish party chairman Annabel Goldie was quoted at the start of April: 'Our support is always underestimated in opinion polls. . . . Our campaign is just getting started and come polling day I am confident we will increase our share of the vote and win more seats.'[73] (Their share in Scotland actually fell eight points, and they lost all eleven seats they were defending.)

Martin Kettle, writing in the *Guardian* on 8 April, had already pointed out the flaws in Major's argument. He noted that 'Every politician, aide, strategist and almost every commentator is certain that the polls will be proved wrong in three weeks' time. They are convinced that the result will be much narrower. In forecasting this, every one of them makes a huge discount. But this discount is wholly impressionistic, is based entirely on hunch and is made in defiance of every piece of polling evidence . . . On the basis of the averaged polls, the result of the election would show Labour with 444 seats (they got 419), the Conservatives 167 (165), the Liberal Democrats 22 (46) and the others 24 (29) . . . Ah, say the professional politicians, but these are all broad-brush national polls. Once you get down to the constituency level, . . . To which the answer is simply to look at the constituency polls, and in doing so remember that in the recent by-election in Wirral South those constituency polls were spectacularly accurate in predicting Labour's big win. . . . It will certainly be an irony if the British people have more confidence in Labour than Labour has ever had in the British people.'[74]

---

71 Quoted in Jones, N., *Campaign 1997: How the General Election was Won and Lost* (London: Indigo, 1997), pp 236–7.
72 Curtice, J., 'Making sense of the polls' position', *Guardian*, 24 April 1997.
73 Dinwoodie, R., 'Scandal takes its toll on the Tories', Glasgow *Herald*, 2 April 1997.
74 Kettle, M. 'What if the polls have got it right?', *Guardian*, 8 April 1997.

Andrew Adonis in *The Observer*[75] reported that ' "We haven't believed the polls for years", says one Tory candidate of long experience, "I'm not saying that we aren't behind, but it is still recoverable. On the doorstep, at least a third haven't made up their minds; press them, and two out of three are ex-Tories. The Tories can win this election without taking a single vote from people who tell pollsters they are voting Labour." ' Adonis commented '. . . if disbelief in the polls, plus the absence of a viable alternative strategy, keeps panic at bay before the election, the despair and bloodletting will be all the greater after 1 May.' So it happened, and so it is happening. Will the Tories now realise that they cannot ignore or disregard public opinion? The leader in the *Guardian* a fortnight after polling day was entitled 'A party that still won't listen'[76]. After the 1983 election, remember that it took 14 long years to make Labour electable again, mainly because they too wouldn't listen.

Of course, the disingenuous nonsense that was spoken by politicians on both sides is understandable if not justifiable as a campaigning tactic, even if in the long term the cure is worse than the disease. Less easily excused are the newspaper pundits who took their cues from Major. Bruce Anderson argued:

'I could not detect any sign of a Labour landslide . . . A majority of the voters would prefer to see Mr Major as prime minister . . . I did not, however, come across many former Tory voters who had repudiated their allegiance . . . A Tory victory is still possible, though unlikely. But an overall Labour majority seems equally unlikely. At the time of writing, I do not believe that Mr Blair is on course to win the 57 seats he would need for an outright win.'[77]

and he subsequently elaborated:

'A hung parliament with the Tories the largest party on 315. Labour 304 and Liberal Democrats 12.'[78]

Even further from the mark was the late Woodrow Wyatt:

---

[75] Adonis, A., 'Don't drop that invisible vase, Tony', *Observer*, 13 April 1997.
[76] 'A party that still won't listen', *Guardian*, 14 May 1997.
[77] Anderson, B., 'The election will be decided by the undecided', *Spectator*, 26 April 1997.
[78] 'Were the experts right?', *Daily Telegraph*, 2 May 1997.

'I believe that John Major, who has fought brilliantly, is on course for a majority of around 30–40.'[79]

Another share to seat translation exercise was conducted by the (Glasgow) *Herald*'s academic analyst Malcolm Dickson who on 10 April translated the poll's averages into seats, with 'Labour would have around 440 [actual result 419] with the Conservatives trailing on 170 [165]'[80]. Not bad for averaging 'a basket of polls' three weeks before the vote. At the end of the campaign, however, Dickson (who is a lecturer at Strathclyde but was not in my lecture there the previous day so far as I know) wrote on 30 April 'Labour could achieve a huge swing in safe seats but a smaller swing in the marginals and thus not produce as resounding a victory as the polls might be suggesting.'[81] Perfectly plausible, but in fact exactly the opposite of what actually happened.

Also trusting his polls was Tony King, who suggested that he too thought that 'Turnout on election day could be the lowest since the 1939–1945 War.'[82] So it was, to the embarrassment of ITN/Harris's David Cowling who took a page in the *New Statesman*[83] on 4 April to say that he did not expect a low turnout: there seemed to him to be sparse evidence and he said 'I think 1 May will be a popular day indeed.' He so convinced his Editor, Ian Hargreaves, that Ian bet me a bottle of champagne that the turnout wouldn't be the lowest since the War. It was, he lost, and it went down nicely, thank you Ian. Cowling went on the adage that 'flying by instinct, while preparing for a crash', his own guess was that there would be a Labour majority of about 50 seats'.[84] And then on his final guess, he reduced his estimate, admitting that he would be 'even more perverse and state that I think it will be a majority of 47. As the man once said: "Publish and be damned." '[85]

---

[79] Wyatt, W., 'Don't be duped by the polls', *The Times*, 29 April 1997.

[80] Dickson, M., 'Opinion pollsters face waiting game from one in three voters', Glasgow *Herald*, 10 April 1997.

[81] Dickson, M., 'Crucial questions still unanswered', Glasgow *Herald*, 30 April 1997.

[82] King, A., 'Only two-thirds of electors say they will definitely go to polls', *Daily Telegraph*, 8 April 1997.

[83] Cowling, D., 'A turnout with attitude', *New Statesman*, 4 April 1997.

[84] Cowling, D., 'I can't believe the numbers', *New Statesman*, 11 April 1997.

[85] Cowling, D., 'Swings in the extremities', *New Statesman*, 25 April 1997. An unfortunate omen,

King was less prescient in his *Daily Telegraph* analysis two days before the election: 'The Tories . . . may not lose quite as comprehensively as the polls now suggest. A considerable number of individual Tory MPs, fearing for their seats, may be pleasantly surprised when the time comes.'[86]

Even Hugo Young, the *Guardian*'s pundit, 'There will be no electoral melt-down for the Conservatives on May 1. It's hard to imagine them emerging with fewer than 200 seats in the next Parliament.'[87]

By contrast, my perspicacious client at the *Independent on Sunday*, the Editor, Rosie Boycott, headlined her newspaper the Sunday before polling day 'Labour landslide', making her colleagues (and her pollster) exceedingly nervous at the time.

In fantasy land, literally and literarily, was *The Times*' Philip Howard, whose well-known scepticism of polls and pollsters spilled over into Tolkienery. 'Both hobbits and pollsters are sometimes silly. Both set out to dazzle outsiders with cod scholarship. Both hobbits and opinion polls are branches of fantasy. Both are popular because they are escapes from being grown-ups in the real world.'[88]

Meanwhile, other editors opened their columns to the stargazers. The *Express* noted that

> 'A Tory victory is written in the stars, according to the leading Asian astrologer Vasudeva. He predicts a Tory win by between 12 and 15 seats. He says Tony Blair is doomed due to the poor positioning of something called the planet Rahu.'[89]

Oh well, closer than Woodrow Wyatt! In the *Evening Standard*, Shelley von Strunckel was given a whole page of to avoid committing herself to any numerical predictions whatsoever, but giving the general impression that a hung Parliament should be expected. 'People are not always honest when polled,' she opined. 'John Major's greatest challenge is not political,

---

as 'the man' credited with saying it is the same Duke of Wellington who was the last Tory leader to achieve a worse election result than John Major.

[86] King, A., 'Brutal truth facing the Tories', *Daily Telegraph*, 29 April 1997.

[87] Young, H., 'Tories bloom in their new-found freedom', *Guardian*, 16 April 1997.

[88] Howard, P., 'Rogue or telephone or greasy – polls can be hobbit forming,' *The Times*, 11 April 1997.

[89] *The Express*, 26 April 1997.

it is overcoming the shadow caused by the moon in his birthchart. . . . Now Blair's in for it – on election day, Saturn is next to Blair's Venus. . . . The results are likely to be as inconclusive as the stars. Which means Labour loses its huge poll lead, Tories gain points, and both the Liberal Democrats and the Referendum Party get more votes than expected.' All this under the headline 'Forget polls, the result is in the stars'.[90]

The election of 1997 was a textbook example of why objective public opinion polling is necessary to the understanding and predicting of elections and voting behaviour. The pundits who ignored the polls, faced with an unprecedented situation and having nothing to fall back on but their own experience, which in this case simply didn't apply, were all at sea. Historians may be lucky in predicting the future, but only if it happens to resemble the past; such pundits are the fairer target for Philip Howard's tag of 'cod scholarship'. If there are any ineluctable laws of political behaviour in Britain, nobody has yet discovered them. But polls by contrast, always accepting their imperfections, are dependent not on extrapolating from the past but on measuring the present. In the absence of such measurements, we might as well all rely on the planet Rahu.

---

[90] von Strunkel, S., 'Forget polls, the result is in the stars', London *Evening Standard*, 28 April 1997.

How many and who actually swung during the campaign?

According to the evidence, the 1997 British General Election campaign, the 'tactics' if you will, as opposed to the election itself, was won by the Liberal Democrats. Second were the Conservatives, and third, Labour.

At the beginning of the campaign, aggregating over 13,000 interviews taken by MORI in the first quarter of 1997, Labour had a 25 point lead over the Tories, and the Liberal Democrats stood at just 12 per cent. On election day, some thirty one million people, in, as predicted, the lowest turnout since the War, gave Labour a 13 per cent lead, with the Tories up two, but the Liberal Democrats gaining five, to 17 per cent, with other parties up two points to seven.

The evidence of our panel survey for the *Evening Standard*, with 1,501 electors interviewed in the first weeks of the campaign and then re-interviewed on the eve-of-poll, shows that the underlying net movement was much more even than this suggests – as the diagram on p. 213 shows, projecting the percentage figures onto the full electorate suggests 11.6 million switched during the campaign – and this doesn't include those who switched briefly but had returned to their original allegiance by the time we re-interviewed them, those who stayed 'don't knows' but changed categories within that group (e.g. undecided electors who at the second wave had decided positively not to vote), or the continuing swing to the Tories on the final day after we stopped interviewing.

The shift of votes week by week

The Tories began the election on 29%, struggled up to 31% and then, briefly 32%, to fall back to 31% on the day. The table below shows clearly what happened during the campaign, and tracks the slight rise in

Table 51: Week by Week Poll of Polls

Fieldwork period:	Con %	Lab %	LDem %	Other %	Lead	Swing
Week starting 17 March 1997	29	53	12	6	−24	−16
Week starting 24 March 1997	30	50	14	6	−20	−14
Week starting 31 March 1997	30	53	12	6	−22	−15
Week starting 7 April 1997	31	49	14	6	−18	−13
Week starting 14 April 1997	31	48	15	6	−17	−12.5
Week starting 21 April 1997	31	48	14	7	−17	−12.5
Week starting 28 April 1997	30	48	16	6	−18	−13
RESULT 1 MAY 1997	**31.4**	**44**	**17.2**	**7.0**	**−13.0**	**−10.5**

the Tory share once sleaze and chickens were set aside for serious politics, and then how they fell back as the focus of their message was lost on the electorate and as Labour trod carefully, some said too carefully, and as the Liberal Democrats benefited from their exposure and the efforts of their Leader, Paddy Ashdown, who seemed to appear everywhere. During the campaign, the Liberal Democrats put on 3.5 points in Gallup, four points in Harris, five points in MORI, two points in NOP and one point in ICM, from the starting poll to the final one for each organisation.

These shifts seem to have accelerated in the final hours. For one thing, both the Harris exit poll for ITN in 1992, and NOP's exit poll for the BBC in 1997 found 11% of voters saying that they had changed their mind about whom to vote for in the 24 hours before voting (and so, by definition, after they would have been interviewed by eve-of-poll opinion polls, two of which carried out their fieldwork more than 24 hours before the polling stations were opened).

From panel studies we can tell how many people changed their mind as to whether to vote or not and if they do vote, which party they will vote for. The best measure that we have comes from the eve of poll telephone recall conducted for the *Evening Standard* on people interviewed initially face-to-face the opening weeks of the election. (See the diagram on p. 231). This shows that 28% of the electorate, some 11.5 million people, actually gave different answers at the end than they did at the beginning of the campaign. This actually underestimates the 'churn' for there will be within this sample many people who will have

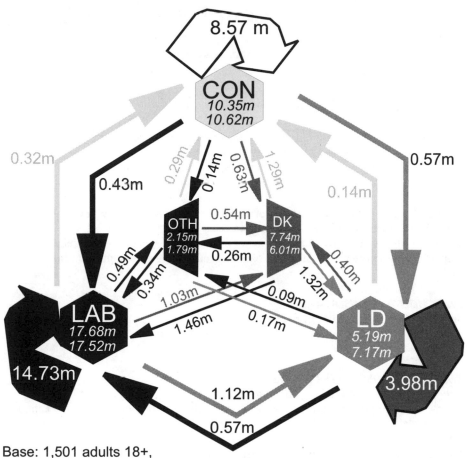

8.57 m

CON
10.35m
10.62m

0.32m   0.43m   0.29m   0.14m   0.63m   1.29m   0.14m   0.57m

OTH   0.54m   DK
2.15m   7.74m
1.79m   0.26m   6.01m

0.49m   0.34m   0.40m

1.03m   0.09m   1.32m

LAB   1.46m   0.17m   LD
17.68m   5.19m
17.52m   7.17m

14.73m   3.98m

1.12m

0.57m

Base: 1,501 adults 18+,
21-24 Mar, 11-14 and 30 Apr 1997   Source: MORI/Evening Standard

Figure 16: How 11½ million votes switched in six weeks

The hexagons show the number of votes (in millions) adhering to each party at
the start and end of the campaign, projecting the percentage figures from the
survey onto the total electorate. The arrows indicate the flow of votes over the
same period. (The figures include supporters not certain to vote, and are therefore
higher than the final actual votes).

had their doubts during the six weeks of the election but who on the
eve of polling day had returned to their original choice.

In the hours of polling day itself, there was almost certainly a further
late swing, though perhaps comparatively modest in its effects, consisting

both of last-minute tactical voting and of voters finally making up their minds. Our re-interviews of a sample of respondents from our final *Times* poll again allows us to let the voters who did switch at the last minute speak for themselves.

Table 52: Post-Election Recall

(MORI On-Line re-interviewed a representative quota sample of 1,192 British adults aged 18+ who had previously been interviewed in the final MORI/*Times* election poll on 29–30 April. Interviews were conducted by telephone on 7–8 May 1997. Data were weighted to the profile of the population.)

Q. **Which party, if any, did you vote for at the General Election last week? If you did not vote, or cannot remember, please say so.**
Q. (To all who say they voted for a different party from the one for which they had said they intended to vote on 29–30 April) **Why did you change your support to the . . . party?**

SWITCHERS TO CONSERVATIVE:
Switchers from Labour to Conservative
'I had a little time to sit and read through what they were saying'
'Better the devil we know'

Switchers from Lib Dem to Conservative
'I thought they were more likely to get in than the Lib Dems.'
'I am a Labour supporter however I voted Conservative as I do not like the local Labour candidate'

Switchers from Referendum Party to Conservative
'I wanted to vote for the Referendum Party but they only had a candidate in the local elections not the national so I voted Conservative as usual'
'I ticked the wrong box'

Switcher from Undecided to Conservative
'Really I think Tony Blair is good but there are too many old-style socialists in the Labour party and I don't know if he'll be able to make the changes he's promised without their support'

SWITCHERS TO LABOUR:
Switchers from Conservative to Labour:
'Give young people a chance'
'The Tories had a poor election campaign'
'Because of John Major – he let the party fall into disarray and did not take disciplinary action when it was called for'
'Just decided at the last minute – we needed a change'

'Because I thought that the Tories had been in power for long enough and it was time for a change'

'I work in social housing and the Conservative Party had changed its policy on social housing and Labour were offering a better alternative. Education and health, particularly the health service'

'I followed the majority'

'The Labour Party offered more policies to help education'

'Not happy about the Conservatives – spur of the moment decision'

Switchers from Lib Dems to Labour:

'I didn't think the Lib Dems had much chance of getting in'

'Wasn't interested then heard Tony Blair on ITV 500 and that swayed me'

'I was not really decided – in the end I voted Labour as I wanted rid of the Tories'

Switchers from Scottish/Welsh Nationalist to Labour

'The damage the Tory party has done to so many people – house repossessions and neglect for those in need and the general misery the Tories caused.'

'When I was previously interviewed I said I would vote SNP but was undecided – it was a spur of the moment decision.'

'I used to vote for Labour but I thought their policies were going out the window but I voted for them to get the Tories out.'

'I just followed my instincts'

Switchers from Green Party to Labour

'To remove Mr Gummer'

'I left my decision till the last minute – the coverage on the telly helped make up my mind'

Switchers from Referendum Party to Labour

'I can't really say – lots of little things but I can't put my finger on them, sorry'

'It was a last minute decision – time for a change'

'I was going to vote for Labour in the beginning but changed my mind to the Referendum party because I'm Anti-European – but I found they had a lack of policies so I changed back to Labour'

SWITCHERS TO THE LIBERAL DEMOCRATS
Switchers from Conservative to Liberal Democrats

'The policies generally, they seemed more trustworthy than the rest – the best of a bad job'

'I wanted a change'

'I voted Lib Dem for tactical reasons – the Tory candidate didn't stand a chance and I did not want Labour'

'I was upset with Mrs Bottomley'

'Time for a change – didn't want Labour to win. It's a strong Lib Dem area – it didn't really relate to the government it was more at a local level'

'I wasn't happy with what the Conservatives or Labour had to offer and I felt I had to vote for someone'

Switchers from Labour to Liberal Democrats
'Because they seemed the most likely party to beat the Tories in the constituency'

'The Labour candidate around here didn't stand a chance anyway – I changed my mind because of tactical voting'

'On principle they were a honest party, it was wrong to waste a vote'

'It was a tactical vote to get rid of the Tories'

'I thought Liberals had more of a chance in my local constituency'

'I always have voted Liberal Democrat but I had thought that I might vote Labour tactically in order to get rid of the Conservatives, however not even the local newspaper could advise me on this so I went back to where my heart is'

'The Tories seem to have lost touch with the ordinary people'

Switcher from Scottish/Welsh Nationalist to Lib Dem
'I preferred the Lib Dems policies. Labour and the Conservatives were very negative throughout the campaign. Blair is going to do so much but where is he going to get the money from?'

Switchers from Referendum Party to Lib Dem
'They are honest enough to say that they would increase spending by raising taxes which is rare in a politician.'

'I voted the way I did in the hope of unseating Michael Howard'

Switchers from Other to Lib Dem
'I did not want the Tory party back in because of raised taxes. I thought the Liberal Democrat party would take the area – it was a tactical vote plus Lib Dems are in line with my political views particularly on the issues of health and education.'

'I wanted somebody new – the Conservatives had plenty of opportunities to put things right and they never did so they deserved everything that they got. I quite like the Liberal Democrats' ideas about proportional representation.'

'It was a last minute decision.'

SWITCHERS TO MINOR PARTIES
Switcher from Conservative to Plaid Cymru
'Because I live with the Welsh people and I didn't want them to throw me off a cliff or shoot me.'

Switcher from Labour to SNP
'I believe in their policies. Tony Blair said in the national dailies that he was going to control Scotland from England and I don't think that that is feasible.'

Switcher from Lib Dem to SNP
'I felt we had more chance of getting the Tories out by voting SNP'

Switcher from Referendum Party to SNP
'No particular policy reason. I voted SNP because it was obvious the Conservatives were not going to win.'

Switcher from Conservative to the Referendum Party
'All that happened in the last 24–48 hours. I knew that the Tories didn't have a chance in hell and I didn't want Labour to win, so I just went for the people's party which is the Referendum Party.'

HOW AND WHY THE DON'T KNOWS MADE UP THEIR MINDS
Q. (To those who said they had voted but had been undecided how to vote on April 29–30) **When we interviewed you last week you said you were undecided how you would vote. What persuaded you to vote for the . . . party)?**

Those who voted Conservative
'I remembered what happened last time – I thought we weren't too badly off.'
'Apprehensive about Labour -I don't think Tony Blair will make a good leader. I think he'll have trouble with his deputies.'
'It was mainly about Europe. I didn't want to vote for a party that would take us into Europe as I think it would become a dictatorship if we did.'
'They'd stand up to Europe more than the others.'
'I didn't think much of any of them but I decided to stick to the party I knew.'
'I don't want a Labour landslide victory – worried that Labour might outlaw fishing.'
'I think that they have done all right up until now.'
'I've voted Tory for many years. I can remember the last Labour Government. They raised taxes and the nurses went on strike – if it was up to the people of South Wales we would be Labour for the rest of our lives and I don't want that.'

Those who voted Labour
'Things were getting so bad with the Conservatives that I decided to give the Labour party a try'
'It was time for a change'
'One of Blair's speeches on television at the last minute. His general view. . . . it was for everyone rather than the elite few'
'I voted Labour because, to be honest, I like Tony Blair – you know, he makes sense, doesn't he – in the end it was the best choice'
'I saw a interview of Tony Blair on TV and I liked some of the things he said and the country was heading the wrong way anyway with the current party. What he said swung my vote towards the Labour Party.'
'Well I just thought that they deserved a chance.'
'I would like to have voted Liberal but they had no chance in this constituency. I voted Labour to be sure of getting rid of the Conservatives.'
'Television and newspapers swayed me'
'I lost faith in the Conservative Party – I thought it was time for a change.'
'Fed up with the long Tory reign'
'I wanted to get the Conservatives out and at the time I spoke to you previously I was undecided between Lib Dems and Labour.'
'They were the best of a bad bunch'
'No other party sent me any literature except for the Labour Party so I voted for them.'

Those who voted Lib Dem
'Needed change. Fed up. Time to try something else. Something new.'
'I said to my wife if she got me to the election table I would vote so I had to vote for someone.'
'It was tactical voting because around here it is staunchly Conservative. There was no chance of Labour getting in – Lib Dems had a better chance so I voted for them.'
'I lost faith in Conservatives and I don't believe in Labour.'

Those who voted Referendum Party
'I liked Mr Goldsmith's ideas on not such strong ties with Europe.'
'I was still undecided when I went to vote but the issue of Europe clinched it.'

Those who voted Scottish/Welsh Nationalist
'I wouldn't vote Labour in my constituency and the Conservatives weren't going to win so I just voted Welsh'
'I was going to vote for either Lib Dem or Scottish Nationalist. I actually met both of the candidates and the Scottish Nationalist came across better.'

LAST MINUTE DECISIONS TO VOTE
Q. (To all who said they had voted but had said on April 29–30 that they would not vote) **When we interviewed you last week you said that you would not vote. What persuaded you to vote on May 1st?**

Those who voted Lib Dem
'There was no real reason – I just decided to on the day'
'I wanted to show that I was dissatisfied – I thought about spoiling my ballot paper'

Those who voted Conservative
'I didn't want to waste my vote.'
'It was my first vote.'

THE NON-VOTERS
Q. (To all who said they did not vote but had said they were certain to vote on April 28–29) **When we interviewed you last week you said that you were certain to vote. Why did you decide not to vote on May 1st?**

'Didn't have time because of the kids.'
'Away on that date'
'I was ill'
'Because I thought no matter who got in we're all going to suffer from now on.'
'Something came up and it was impossible to get there'
'I went away for the day and came back too late to vote'
'Queue was too big to wait'
'I was a Conservative voter who felt I could no longer trust them as a result of sleaze allegations'
'I did go down there and there were over 100 people in the queue and I am heavily

pregnant and didn't want to stand in the queue. Since my husband votes Labour and I
vote Tory we thought we would cancel each other out.'
'I went out on election day and did not make it back in time to vote.'
'I couldn't make my mind up at all'
'I had a deadline to meet and couldn't get away from work.'

Who won the campaign: conclusion

So who won the campaign? The Conservatives and Liberal Democrats made net gains in support, but Labour's campaign seems to have been the most effective and efficient. The electorate agreed. When asked 'Which of the political parties has run the most effective campaign so far?', by three to one the public thought that the Labour Party had, 36 per cent to 11 per cent for the Tories and 13 per cent for the Liberal Democrats.

So why then did the Liberal Democrats 'win the campaign', increasing their share of the vote by some 42 percent from their standing at the beginning, and by a third among *Express* readers, among *Guardian*, *Telegraph* and *Sunday Telegraph* and *Sunday Times* readers and *Mirror* readers by half, doubling their share of *Independent* and *Observer* readers and tripling their share, from 10 per cent in the first quarter of the year to nearly a third, 31 per cent, among readers of the *Independent on Sunday?* If Labour's campaign was so good, why did they lose 17 per cent of their supporters, some five million voters? Part of the reason is simple: many people at this election (especially across Southern England) realised that a vote for the Liberal Democrats was not a wasted vote, but potentially a double vote. They could simultaneously vote against the Government and to reduce Labour's huge majority by voting for the Liberal Democrats and others – and so they did. And most importantly, millions of disenchanted Tories knew from the polls that they did not have to vote against their (conservative) core values to get what they wanted – the Conservative government out of office and John Major replaced.

But in any case, it was always virtually certain that Labour would lose some support during the campaign: they entered it with a poll standing over 50%, a share of the vote which no party has approached in a modern three-party election in Britain. Liberal Democrat support tends to rise during campaigns, simply because they get more exposure than between elections and more of their potential supporters remember the possibility of voting for them. (In the run-up to the 1997 election, as in previous elections, we found that fewer than two-thirds of those who voted Liberal Democrat in 1992 recalled having done so; and the disproportionate impact of Liberal Democrat leaflets revealed by our survey of campaign effectiveness suggests that simply being reminded of the party's existence was indeed an important factor.) The Conservatives as an incumbent government would expect to win back some lost support simply because fighting an election campaign, which gives them an equal chance to concentrate on the opposition's weaknesses, is generally easier than governing the country to everybody's satisfaction.

To hold their support constant, Labour had a very uphill struggle. But Labour didn't need to hold all the support they had in mid-March, they only needed to hold enough to win, and they did so – to an extent that far surpassed most expectations. In that sense, Labour won the campaign as well as the election.

The result: who did what?

And so, on 1 May 1997 Britain went to the polls.

Who didn't vote?

The 1997 election had the lowest percentage turnout since the War. In 1992, the Conservatives won just over 14 million votes; in 1997, their support fell to nine-and-a-half million. Common sense suggests that much of the fall in turnout came from those who voted Tory in 1992 staying at home. Analysis of MORI's polls during the election campaign, drawing on 13,544 electors who told us both how they were going to

Table 53: 1997 British General Election – results

	SEATS (n)			SHARE OF VOTE (%)		
	1992	1997	Change	1992	1997	Change
Conservative	336	165	−171	42.8	31.4	−11.6
Labour	271	419	+148	35.2	44.4	+9.2
Lib Dems	20	46	+26	18.3	17.2	−1.1
SNP	3	6	+3	2.0	1.9	−0.1
PC	4	4	0	0.5	0.5	0.0
Others	17	19	+2	3.0	4.5	0.0
Majority	(21)	179		−7.8%	13.0%	+20.8

	VOTES (millions)		
	1992	1997	Change
Conservative	14.05	9.59	−4.46
Labour	11.57	13.52	+1.95
Lib Dems	6.03	5.24	−0.79
Nationalists	0.78	0.78	0.00
Referendum	−	0.81	+0.81
Others	0.41	0.55	+0.14
TOTAL (GB)	32.83	30.50	−2.33

Table 54: How the votes switched 1992–7 (estimate)

Millions of votes			*1992 vote:*				Too	
1997 vote:	Con	Lab	LDem	Nat	Other	Did not vote	young to vote	**TOTAL**
Conservative	7.7	0.2	0.2	*	0.1	1.0	0.4	9.6
Labour	1.4	8.6	0.8	0.1	0.2	1.8	0.7	13.6
Liberal Democrat	1.0	0.7	2.4	*	0.1	0.6	0.3	5.2
Nationalist	*	0.1	*	0.4	*	0.1	0.1	0.8
Green	*	0.1	*	*	0.2	0.1	*	0.4
Referendum Party	0.4	0.1	0.1	*	*	0.1	*	0.8
Others	0.1	0.1	*	*	*	0.1	*	0.4
Did not vote	2.5	1.1	2.2	*	*	5.6	1.1	12.5
No longer in electorate	*0.7*	*0.6*	*0.3*	*	*	*0.5*	-	*2.1*
TOTAL	**14.0**	**11.5**	**6.0**	**0.6**	**0.6**	**9.9**	**2.6**	

* *indicates fewer than 50,000 votes*

Source: MORI election aggregate
Base: 13,544 British adults, interviewed 21 March–29 April 1997

vote and how they had voted in 1992, enables us to construct an approximate model of where the missing voters went which partially confirms this. The figures can only be approximate, because they depend on the notoriously unreliable ability of the British voter to recall how they voted at a previous election. In 1997, as so frequently in the past, too few voters remembered having voted Liberal Democrat in 1992, and the calculations to correct for this mean that the table must be regarded as having a generous margin of error. With that caveat, it looks as if two-and-a-half million 1992 Tory supporters didn't vote at all, but also as many as a million and a half, roughly speaking, switched to Labour and a further million to the Liberal Democrats, whereas only 400,000 or so votes swung from those parties to the Tories.

This explanation has recently been challenged by Tim Hames (of *The Times*) and Nick Sparrow (head of ICM) in a Centre for Policy Studies pamphlet[1], on the basis of constituency results, drawing on Curtice and Steed's analysis,[2] but taking the conclusions a little further. They argue, on

---

[1] Hames, T. and Sparrow, N., *Left Home: The Myth of Tory Abstentions in the Election of 1997* (London: CPS, October 1998).

[2] Curtice, J. and Steed, M., 'The Results Analysed', in Butler, D. and Kavanagh, D., *The British General Election of 1997* (Basingstoke: Macmillan, 1997), p 299.

the basis that turnout fell most in safe Labour seats and that the swing was lower than average in those seats, that it must have been 1992 Labour voters who stayed at home. Unfortunately there is a gap in their logic. Either way, it is in the safe Labour seats where biggest falls in turnout could be expected, since those are the seats where the result was most certain and extra votes least needed. We agree with Hames and Sparrow's initial conclusion that 'the missing voters in 1997 were . . . disproportionately inclined to back Labour had they found their way to the polling station', but not with their unsubstantiated leap of logic that these voters had supported Labour in 1992. We think it was the disillusioned Tories, *who would otherwise have swung to Labour*, who didn't turn out to vote in Labour safe seats – like other disillusioned Tories they wanted Major defeated, but were happy to avoid going against the values of a lifetime by voting Labour if that end could be achieved without them. Thus the 1995 forecast that the 1997 general election would see the lowest turnout since the war.

The 'Gender Gap'

It is received wisdom that in British general elections women are more likely to vote Conservative than men. This was true in 1997, but only by a narrow margin – the 'gender gap' had narrowed a little since 1992. It is also received wisdom in some quarters that the gender gap arises purely from the fact that women live longer than men, and that therefore the average female voter is older than the average male voter (and since older voters tend to be more Conservative, the average woman is more Conservative than the average man). This explanation is a fallacy.

Further investigation yields two fascinating phenomena. First, it is quite untrue (as the simplistic age explanation for the gender gap would seem to assume) that men and women of any given age vote in the same way. There are very sharp differences between the voting behaviour of the sexes within each age group and, furthermore, the pattern of the voting differences is not uniform. In fact, young women are far *less* likely to be Conservative than their male counterparts; but above the age of 30 the position is reversed.

The second phenomenon worthy of note is that the gender gap is

Table 55: How Britain voted since Labour last won

All	Oct 1974 %	1979 %	1983 %	1987 %	1992 %	1997 %
Conservative	37	45	44	43	43	31
Labour	40	38	28	32	35	44
Lib/Alliance/LD	19	14	26	23	18	17
Con lead	−3	+7	+16	+11	+8	−13
Men						
Conservative	32	43	42	43	41	31
Labour	43	40	30	32	37	45
Lib/Alliance/LD	18	13	25	23	18	17
Con lead	−11	+3	+12	+11	+4	−14
Women						
Conservative	39	47	46	43	44	32
Labour	38	35	26	32	34	44
Lib/Alliance/LD	20	15	27	23	18	18
Con lead	+1	+12	+20	+11	+10	−12
18–24						
Conservative	24	42	42	37	35	27
Labour	42	41	33	39	38	49
Lib/Alliance/LD	27	12	23	22	19	16
Con lead	−18	+1	+9	−2	−3	−22
25–34						
Conservative	33	43	40	39	40	28
Labour	38	38	29	33	37	49
Lib/Alliance/LD	24	15	29	26	18	16
Con lead	−5	+5	+11	+6	+3	−21
35–54						
Conservative	34	46	44	45	43	30
Labour	42	35	27	29	34	45
Lib/Alliance/LD	20	16	27	24	19	19
Con lead	−8	+11	+17	+16	+9	−15
55+						
Conservative	42	47	47	46	46	36
Labour	40	38	27	31	34	40
Lib/Alliance/LD	14	13	24	21	17	17
Con lead	+2	+9	+20	+15	+12	−4
Middle class (ABC1)						
Conservative	56	59	55	54	54	39
Labour	19	24	16	18	22	34
Lib/Alliance/LD	21	15	28	26	21	20
Con lead	+37	+35	+39	+36	+32	+5
Skilled working class (C2)						
Conservative	26	41	40	40	39	27
Labour	49	41	32	36	40	50
Lib/Alliance/LD	20	15	26	22	17	16
Con lead	−23	0	+8	+4	−1	−23
Semi/unskilled working class (DE)						
Conservative	22	34	33	30	31	21
Labour	57	49	41	48	49	59
Lib/Alliance/LD	16	13	24	20	16	13
Con lead	−35	−15	−8	−18	−18	−38

Table 56: Profile of the Electorate

In the table below, the profile and voting behaviour of the electorate in 1997 is on the left, the change between the 1992 General Election and 1997 is shown on the right, including the swing for each sub-group.

Weighted base	n	%	Con	Voting Lab	LD	Oth	Con lead over Lab	%	Change since 1992 Con	Lab	LD	Lead	C-Lab swing
Weighted base	13,544	100	31%	44%	17%	7%	-13%	-	-12	+9	-1	-21	10.5
Gender		%						%					
Men	6,256	48	31%	45%	17%	7%	-14%	+1	-10	+8	-1	-18	9.0
Women	7,018	52	32%	44%	18%	6%	-12%	-1	-12	+10	0	-22	11.0
Age		%						%					
18–24	1,570	12	27%	49%	16%	8%	-22%	-2	-8	+11	-3	-19	9.5
25–34	2,805	21	28%	49%	16%	7%	-21%	0	-12	+12	-2	-24	12.0
35–44	2,358	17	28%	48%	17%	7%	-20%	0	-12	+12	-3	-24	12.0
45–54	2,253	17	31%	41%	20%	8%	-10%	+3	-16	+10	+2	-26	13.0
55–64	1,764	13	36%	39%	17%	8%	-3%	-1	-8	+4	-2	-12	6.0
65+	2,793	21	36%	41%	17%	6%	-5%	0	-12	+7	0	-19	9.5
Social class		%						%					
AB	3,026	22	41%	31%	22%	6%	+10%	+4	-15	+12	0	-27	13.5
C1	3,695	27	37%	37%	18%	8%	0%	+4	-15	+12	-2	-27	13.5
C2	3,035	22	27%	50%	16%	7%	-23%	-6	-12	+10	-1	-22	11.0
DE	3,788	28	21%	59%	13%	7%	-38%	-3	-10	+10	-3	-20	10.0
Region		%						%					
Scotland	1,217	9	18%	45%	13%	24%	-27%	0	-8	+7	0	-15	7.5
Northern	744	5	22%	61%	13%	4%	-39%	-1	-11	+11	0	-22	11.0
Yorks & Humbs	1,205	9	28%	52%	16%	4%	-24%	0	-10	+8	-1	-18	9.0
North West	1,502	11	27%	54%	14%	5%	-26%	0	-11	+9	-2	-20	10.0
Wales	690	5	20%	55%	12%	13%	-35%	0	-9	+5	0	-14	7.0
West Midlands	1,259	9	34%	48%	14%	4%	-14%	0	-11	+9	-1	-20	10.0
East Midlands	988	7	35%	48%	14%	3%	-13%	-1	-12	+11	-1	-23	11.0
East Anglia	514	4	39%	38%	18%	5%	+1%	0	-12	+10	-2	-22	11.0
South West	1,160	9	37%	26%	31%	6%	+11%	+2	-11	+7	0	-18	9.0
South East	2,599	19	41%	32%	21%	6%	+9%	-1	-13	+11	-2	-24	12.0
Greater London	1,665	12	31%	49%	15%	5%	-18%	-1	-14	+12	-1	-26	13.0
Work status		%						%					
Full time	6,097	45	31%	44%	18%	7%	-13%	+3	-13	+11	0	-24	12.0
Part time	1,403	10	32%	45%	16%	7%	-13%	-1	-12	+12	-4	-24	12.0
Not working	5,428	40	33%	42%	18%	7%	-13%	0	-11	+7	0	-18	9.0
Unemployed	616	5	15%	64%	12%	9%	-49%	-2	-10	+13	-5	-23	11.5
Housing tenure		%											
Owner	3,469	26	41%	32%	20%	7%	+9%	0	-12	+5	+1	-17	8.5
Mortgage	6,234	46	33%	43%	18%	6%	-10%	+4	-13	+12	-1	-25	12.5
Council/HA tenant	2,764	20	15%	64%	12%	9%	-49%	0	-9	+9	-3	-18	9.0
Ethnicity		%											
White	2,965	96	32%	43%	18%	7%	-11%		n/a	n/a	n/a		
Asian	250	2	22%	66%	9%	3%	-44%		n/a	n/a	n/a		
Black	216	2	12%	82%	5%	1%	-70%		n/a	n/a	n/a		
Trade union		%											
Member	2,412	18	18%	57%	18%	7%	-39%	-1	-13	+11	-1	-24	12.0
Non-member	11,011	81	34%	42%	17%	7%	-8%	0	-12	+9	-1	-21	10.5

Source: MORI

243

Table 57: Published polls of electoral sub-groups

Fieldwork dates	Agency	Client	Publ'n Date	Sample size	Con %	Lab %	LD %	Nat %	Oth %	Lead ±%	Swing 92–97
TEACHERS											
13–21 Mar	NOP	NASUWT	18 Apr	835	17	52	27	n/a	4	–25	n/a
UNIVERSITY/FE LECTURERS											
5–12 Mar	ICM*	THES	11 Apr	500	10	64	21	n/a	5	–54	7.0
FIRST-TIME VOTERS											
25–26 Mar	MORI	News of the World	30 Mar	980	22	62	9	3	4	–40	n/a
AGED 18–23											
24 Mar–5 Apr	MORI	Channel 4	24 Apr	539	23	56	11	4	6	–33	n/a
WOMEN											
26–27 Mar	MORI*	Mail on Sunday	30 Mar	800	30	52	14	1	4	–22	16.0
MAIL ON SUNDAY READERS											
19–21 Mar	MORI*	Mail on Sunday	23 Mar	933¶	48	36	10	*	6	+12	14.5
9–11 Apr	MORI*	Mail on Sunday	13 Apr	913¶	47	37	12	1	3	+10	15.5
16–18 Apr	MORI*	Mail on Sunday	20 Apr	905¶	46	36	12	1	3	+10	15.5
23–25 Apr	MORI*	Mail on Sunday	27 Apr	847¶	48	33	14	1	4	+15	13.0

Table 58: The Gender Gap 1974–97

	'Gender Gap': Con % lead over Lab among women minus Con lead over Lab among men
1974	+12
1979	+9
1983	+8
1987	0
1992	+6
1997	+2

Source: MORI election aggregates

much narrower now than it used to be – a feature not just of the 1997 election but of the last three. There has been a change in the structural behaviour of the British electorate, and it is mainly young women whose position in the structure has changed.

This is one of those structural changes that cannot really be diagnosed in the context of a single election but which in retrospect, from a vantage

Table 59: Gender Gap by Age

	1983	1987	1992	1997
All	+8	0	+6	+2
18–24	+5	–17	–18	–14
25–34	+14	–4	0	+3
35–54	+9	+11	+10	+9
55+	+5	0	+12	+2

Source: MORI aggregate surveys

point three elections on, seems obvious. We can now see that the 1987 election represented a decisive break-point in the relationship between men's and women's votes (whereas at the time, in 1987, it might equally have been simply a freak change arising from special conditions in that single election, or even conceivably a freak sampling error in the polling data). Over the three elections up to 1983, the average difference in the Conservative lead over Labour between men and women was 9.67 points (making almost a 5% difference in the national lead one way or the other, by comparison with what would have happened if men and women had voted the same, or put another way, the equivalent of a 2.5% national swing – which is worth quite a lot of seats). For the three elections from 1987, the average gap was only 2.67 points, equivalent to a national swing of less than 1%, representing only a handful of seats. (Though even this is not to be sniffed at – it was the extra votes from women that gave John Major his overall majority in 1992.)

There are a number of explanations that can be offered for this change. One obvious one, which would fit many past theses as to why the gap existed in the first place, is that its disappearance can be traced to the collapse of trade union power as a motive force driving Labour men or as a live election issue alienating Tory women. An examination of the age breakdown of the gender gap. However, tells a rather different story.

The collapse of the gender gap in 1987 was clearly age-based, and was primarily a startlingly disproportionate shift to Labour among women under 35. The youngest, 18–24, age group of women switched from being mildly more Tory to virulently more Labour; the next group up, 25–34 year olds, having been much more Tory than their male peers in 1983, were by contrast slightly more Labour than them in 1987. Among

245

Table 60: Voting by age and gender 1997

Age	Men					Women					
	Con	Lab	LD	Oth	C lead	Con	Lab	LD	Oth	C lead	G. Gap
	%	%	%	%	%	%	%	%	%	%	
18–24	30	45	16	9	−15	24	53	15	8	−29	−14
25–29	30	45	17	8	−15	26	51	16	7	−25	−10
30–34	27	50	16	7	−23	31	49	15	5	−18	+5
35–44	27	50	16	7	−23	29	46	19	6	−17	+6
45–49	27	44	20	9	−17	33	40	20	7	−7	+10
50–59	33	40	18	9	−7	35	38	21	6	−3	+4
60–64	35	42	15	8	−7	38	40	16	6	−2	+5
65–74	32	43	17	8	−11	34	41	19	6	−7	+4
75+	39	39	15	7	0	42	39	15	4	+3	+3

Source: MORI election aggregate 1997

Base: 13,544 British adults 18+

the older age groups, however, there was much less shift, little more than can be expected as the natural minor changes of circumstances and issues between any two elections. This table demolishes several possible theories. If the entrepreneurial jungle offered by Thatcherism had more appeal to young men than to young women, why was this not evident in 1983? Equally, it might have been imagined that the Falklands War would appeal particularly to the gung-ho or chauvinistic tendency in young men – again not so on these figures.

Which brings us to the question we have been asked several times since the election: why did the gender gap close in 1997? The genesis of the question is clearly in Labour's pre-election perception that the gender gap was a danger to them, and their consequent deliberate attempt to appeal to women and close the gap.

The age breakdown table makes it clear that the change was fairly trivial among all but the oldest age group, and also that this age group was simply returning to its behaviour in 1987 (as was the overall gender gap). It seems clear that in fact it was 1992 that was the aberrant case: the question of why the gender gap narrowed in 1997 really reduces to the question, why were women over 55 so reluctant to vote Labour in 1992?

Aftermath

The Outcome of the Election

The British electorate seem well satisfied with the outcome of the general election. MORI conducted 1,192 interviews with adults aged 18+ across Great Britain by telephone between 7 and 8 May 1997. Even some two in ten people who voted Conservative said they were satisfied with the outcome.

All the key polling indicators remained in Labour's favour following the election. Satisfaction with the Prime Minister reached 75% in September 1997, and satisfaction with the government was at 57%, in both cases the highest figures ever recorded in MORI's monthly polls. The positive polling indicators have long outlasted the familiar 'honeymoon' period. But can it last? What might the future hold?

Looking Forward

3 May 2001 is but 24 months away as of the date of writing, and in our view the most likely date of the next election, as it will be four years and would coincide with the local government elections. Twenty-four months have already elapsed since the last election, and thanks to the remarkable rapport Tony Blair has with the electorate, and the lack of any credible opposition, his poll ratings stay up (not yet lower than 58% satisfied), his support in the Party and the country remains remarkably robust (Labour's voting intention score not yet below 50%), and neither sharp drops in economic optimism nor colleagues tinged with sleaze of one sort or another seem to affect his standing.

Still, a week is a long time in politics, and this year, 1999, must be the

Table 61: Satisfaction with the Outcome of the Election

Q. **On balance, would you say you are satisfied or dissatisfied with the outcome of the election in your constituency?**

	All %	Con supporters %	Lab supporters %	Lib Dem supporters %
Satisfied	67	41	86	50
Dissatisfied	23	43	11	41
Neither/Don't know	10	16	3	9

Source: MORI
7–8 May 1997
Base: 1,192 British adults 18+ interviewed by telephone

Q. **And would you say are satisfied or dissatisfied with the national outcome of the election?**

	All %	Con supporters %	Lab supports %	Lib Dem supporters %
Satisfied	70	22	97	70
Dissatisfied	20	60	1	18
Neither/Don't know	10	18	2	12

Source: MORI
7–8 May 1997
Base: 1,192 British adults 18+ interviewed by telephone

year to deliver on its promises. At the time of the launch of the manifesto, Labour in Opposition made four principal pledges to the electorate: on the NHS, education, crime/law & order, and unemployment. As of yet, the electorate does not believe they have delivered. In a survey[1] in January 1999, only 33% thought that since it was elected the government 'has . . . improved the standard of education' (45% thought it had not), and just 26% that it 'has . . . improved law and order' (59% disagreed). In the NHS, waiting lists are proving intractable, and surveys to mark its fiftieth anniversary in 1998 found unease both among the public and healthcare professionals: the vast majority of the public think the NHS is underfunded, and almost half that it will not survive another fifty years[2];

---

[1] MORI survey for *The Times*: samples of 967 and 963 British adults aged 18+ were interviewed on 22–25 January 1999. The survey was published on 29 January 1999.

[2] MORI On-Line survey for the *Mail on Sunday*: 702 British adults aged 18+ were interviewed on 23–25 June 1998; the survey was published on 28 June 1998.

in response to the government's White Paper on NHS reform, three in five GPs said they thought that as a result the public's satisfaction with the NHS would get worse[3]. Overall in January 1999, only 40% thought the government had kept its promises while 47% thought it had not. So how much rope will the voters give to Blair? What is holding his poll ratings up?

Labour's greatest electoral asset remains, as it was in 1997, the Conservative Party. It has failed to convince the voters that it is a credible alternative to Labour, thereby ensuring that any dissatisfaction with the government's performance cannot be translated into a significant loss of votes. Almost two years after the election the Tories are still failing to match even their general election ratings on any aspect polled, let alone surpass them (though they crept up to a projected 33% vote share in the 1999 local elections). They remain seen as hopelessly divided over Europe, and there seems not the least possibility of a cure before the single currency issue has been resolved by referendum and finally drops off the political agenda. With William Hague firmly committing the party leadership to an anti-Euro line, Tory MEPs have already left the party to form a Pro-Euro Conservative Party. Whether this remains no more than a splinter or will presage a formal split in the party remains to be seen, and may depend on the attitudes of the senior ex-Cabinet Europhiles such as Heseltine and Clarke, but it will unquestionably siphon votes away from the party and further weaken its credibility as Her Majesty's Opposition.

Unless Blair against all expectations decides to call an early referendum on the Euro, the chances are that the Tories will be split for the next decade. Nor have they found a solution to their other woes. William Hague has entirely failed to make a positive impression as leader, or to rejuvenate the image of the party, and his poll ratings now show him almost as unpopular as Michael Foot after the Falklands War. Nevertheless, he is almost certainly secure at least until after the next general election at which, barring something entirely unforeseen, he will lead them to a second successive defeat. Following the saga of the leadership

---

[3] MORI survey for *Reader's Digest*: 200 British GPs were interviewed on 16–27 March 1998; the survey was published in the July 1998 issue.

challenges to Thatcher and the threat of a challenge to Major, the party rules have now been so stacked that there are only three ways to get rid of him: push him under the proverbial Number 9, he decides himself to resign for the good of the Party, or send round the 'men in grey suits' to persuade him to go. I said this to a former member of Major's Cabinet, adding, 'but there aren't any men in grey suits these days.' His reply: 'Yes, I know, I'm one of them.' The theoretical alternative – a no confidence vote by a majority of Tory MPs followed by an inevitably bloody leadership election in which Hague would be barred from standing – is, surely, too suicidal for even the Conservatives to seriously contemplate.

Labour is on less solid ground in Scotland and Wales, where there are other alternatives than the Tories, and the government may have dangerously underestimated the political implications of the constitutional revolution they have set in motion. The Scottish Parliament and Welsh Assembly elections were a sharp snub to Labour, denied an overall majority in both with dramatic nationalist advances since the General Election (especially Plaid Cymru's shock constituency victories in Islwyn and the Rhondda, which may owe something to resentment of the way the leadership election was handled). The Liberal Democrats now hold the balance of power in both assemblies, and Labour's local leaders will be forced to accept some compromises. In Scotland at least this may leave the implementation of Westminster policy a hostage to fortune – devolution applies not only to institutions but to the political parties that operate in them, and however loyal Donald Dewar and Alun Michael remain their parties may prove less amenable to control from Millbank than Labour's national election strategists might wish. The Scottish National Party and Plaid Cymru are in a powerful second place, and as official Oppositions will be able to act as a focus for resentment in the coming years. Furthermore, while the Scots may back away from insisting on outright independence (and some polls have suggested that even this may not be relied upon), the existence of the separatist option leaves Labour vulnerable north of the border in a way that is not the case in England. With so many members of the cabinet representing Scottish constituencies, and an obvious temptation for the Tories to foment any anti-Scottish backlash in England if the opportunity were to arise, this means that the longer-term consequences of devolution could potentially be damaging to the government – but probably not, at least, before the next-general-election-but-one.

There are other electoral hurdles to jump between now and 2001. Labour will lose seats at the European parliamentary elections, if only through Blair's munificence to the opposition parties in providing the electorate with a proportional voting system; but that impact will be dulled by the inevitable split in the Tories that the PR system makes practicable. Also critical will be the election of a Mayor of London: Labour seems unlikely to lose, but it is questionable whether they will do themselves more long-term damage by their scheming to prevent Ken Livingstone winning the nomination than he would be likely to do them once elected. (Will Labour learn the lesson of the reaction to their machinations against Rhodri Morgan in the Welsh leadership election?) If, by some combination of a general downturn in Labour's popularity and voter reaction against Livingstone's knifing, they contrived to lose the election, to Jeffrey Archer or anybody else, it would be the most humiliating setback Blair has yet suffered; but even a near-miss would be damaging. Furthermore, the assembly elected with the Mayor is unlikely to have an overall Labour majority. The Greater London Authority, like the Scottish Parliament, has the potential to become a focus of opposition and a very irritating thorn in Blair's side a couple of years down the line.

The local elections each year will presumably see the Tories continuing to regain seats – the 1999 local government elections and local by-elections show the Tories performing a little ahead of their national poll ratings at local level – but as they will only be regaining seats which they should never have lost in the first place, little credit will accrue to them for their hollow victories. But the importance of grass-roots morale should not be under-estimated, and the Tories' ability to rebuild their local campaigning machinery will be a significant factor in determining how long they must stay in the political wilderness; every council seat Labour can retain in naturally Tory wards may be worth its weight in gold.

Labour's standing in the opinion polls will also be tested by the Parliamentary by-elections that will be caused by deaths or possibly resignations. In the whole calendar year of 1998 there were, unprecedentedly, no by-elections; the laws of nature will catch up, and there will be a number, perhaps as many as 20, by-elections between now and May 2001, which will show if the hot-house atmosphere of the by-election will enable the Liberal Democrats to punch above their weight as they have tended to do in the past. Perhaps the Tories, too, can unite to win back some of the surprising lost seats in 1997; some winnable seats for them, surely, must come up[4].

So, assuming Labour win the election of 2001, with a reduced but still secure majority, what next? At the Liberal Democratic Conference in Glasgow in 1995 I made a fifth prediction, which I repeated in the Christmas issue of *British Public Opinion* newsletter[5] in December before the election, imagining Blair preparing to pick his Cabinet:

'I have been thinking. What do I want to be doing in four or five years' time? Do I want to be Vice Chancellor of a New Zealand University? No, I hear that's not up to much, even with a new swimming pool. Do I want to be Transport Commissioner in Brussels? No, I don't need the money. Besides, Cherie doesn't want to be an MEP. Do I want to be Warden of an Oxford College? Yes. . . . but maybe in about twenty years. What I really want to do in four or five years' time is to be Prime Minister'.

(Reaches for the telephone) 'Will you get me Mr Ashdown please?' (. . . drring. . . .) 'Good morning Paddy; thank you. Yes. No. No. I have been thinking. . . . Yes, I think we understand each other'.

'Defence? Done'. . . .

'No. No, you don't want him in the Cabinet any more than I do' . . .

'Paul Tyler? Agriculture? Yes, we can do that, but that's it. That's all I can give you Paddy'. . . .

'But you know the pledge in our Manifesto on Proportional Representation? If we can <u>really</u> understand each other'. . . .

---

[4] If they are ready to take the opportunity. It seemed, briefly, in 1999 that precisely such a by-election would occur, at Newark; but when Fiona Jones' disqualification for breaches of election expenses law was overturned on appeal and the by-election rendered unnecessary, one sensed that if anything the Tories' sigh of relief was louder than Labour's.

[5] Worcester, R., 'Letter to our Readers', *British Public Opinion*, volume XIX number 10 (December 1996), p. 1.

'Yes, I thought we could'. . . .

'If we can <u>really</u> understand each other, I'll call it today for six weeks from now'. . . .

'Paddy – we will be seeing a lot of each other'. (Replaces the telephone).
'I'll be Prime Minister for the next twenty years'.

Two years into the Blair's First Parliament, it seems closer than ever to coming to fruition. Tony Blair has aged a decade these past two years, and may not want to, or be able to, last the two decades projected by my forecast made now nearly four years ago. But barring that, or fate, there's nothing on the horizon to keep Blair from being in No. 10 until the two decades are up.

The game plan? Keep the Tories split over Europe until after the next election, which should guarantee a majority of at least fifty. Then the referendum on the single currency, backed by Blair, and a vote of about 55%/45% or greater. Then a year later, the referendum on electoral reform (which may have to be won in the face of a bad taste left by the closed-list system used for the Euro-parliament elections, the strange two-step voting for the London mayor, and any doubts propagated by the records of the PR-elected Scottish Parliament and Welsh Assembly).

The Liberal Democrats (no longer led, of course, by Paddy Ashdown) will be co-opted by the promise, and delivery, of a system of electoral reform. If the system proposed is the AV-plus mechanism recommended by the Jenkins Commission (which is not a system of proportional representation but rather first-past-the-post with rounded corners), he would have plenty to offer the Liberal Democrats, and would find it easier to sell to his own backbenchers the more likely it looked that their seats would otherwise fall to a renascent Tory party. While the Jenkins system holds out some hope of overall majorities for parties winning landslide vote victories, the chances that the Tories would be ready to take advantage of this by 2005 or 2006 look slim; victory in an electoral reform referendum in the next Parliament offers the chance of a Blair-led Labour-Lib Dem coalition in the Parliament after that, with Labour's dissidents kept in line by the combination of power and patronage.

The Tories ruled Britain for eighteen consecutive years, from 1979 to 1997. The general election of 1997 put an end to that, and has left

Labour and Tony Blair in a position of political dominance that neither Margaret Thatcher nor John Major ever achieved. Now it is Labour that looks like the 'natural party of government'. Of course things can change, but the sky is clear at the moment. There is nothing on the horizon to suggest it is impossible, or even unlikely, that Labour too can hold power for two decades.

Index